3/08

Jeanie,

Thanks so much for all you've done for the San Diego community! Keep up the good work and you will always occupy a special place in the Clarke family!

Woody

Justice and Science

Justice and Science

TRIALS AND TRIUMPHS
OF DNA EVIDENCE

GEORGE "WOODY" CLARKE

FOREWORD BY JANET RENO

Rutgers University Press
New Brunswick, New Jersey, and London

Library of Congress Cataloging-in-Publication Data

Clarke, George, 1951–
Justice and science : trials and triumphs of DNA evidence / George "Woody" Clarke.
p. cm.
Includes bibliographical references and index.
ISBN 978–0-8135–4192–1 (hardcover : alk. paper)
1. Clarke, George, 1951– 2. Public prosecutors—California—San Diego County—
Biography. 3. DNA fingerprinting—United States. 4. Forensic genetics—United States.
I. Title.
KF373.C564A3 2007
363.25´6—dc22

                                                                    2007008417

A British Cataloging-in-Publication record for this book is available from the
British Library.

Visit our Web site: http://rutgerspress.rutgers.edu

Manufactured in the United States of America

For my wife and daughter

CONTENTS

FOREWORD

JANET RENO

Protecting innocent suspects and identifying those who actually commit crimes against society are probably the two most important goals of any system of justice. For hundreds of years police, attorneys, and courts have used the tools at their disposal to attain these treasured goals.

Only in more recent time, however, has science presented the criminal justice system with the means to identify those responsible for some of the most serious crimes, including homicide and sexual assault. Borrowing from established fields like molecular biology and chemistry, scientists have provided law enforcement with the ability to pinpoint with laser-like accuracy the person or persons who may be responsible.

Deoxyribonucleic acid (DNA) is at the center of that technology. Although popular television and print media glorify the science that takes advantage of the differences in our DNA—and often stretch its already remarkable power—DNA typing has nonetheless revolutionized the process of identifying who left blood or other evidence at a crime scene. Whether fluid recovered from a victim of rape, hairs found clutched in the hand of a murder victim, or even chewing gum carelessly discarded by a burglar, DNA testing can routinely lead to the identification of the person who left that evidence.

More importantly, that same technology can quickly lead suspicion away from a person wrongly suspected of committing a crime. Its ability to exonerate those already convicted of crime—often after the service of lengthy prison terms—has already been widely chronicled. In 1996, while I was Attorney General of the United States, the National Institute of Justice released *Convicted by Juries, Exonerated by Science: Case Studies in the Use of DNA Evidence to Establish Innocence after Trial*. That publication detailed the cases of twenty-eight prison inmates who were determined by DNA testing to have been wrongfully convicted of serious crimes.

Because DNA profiles can be easily reduced to digital information, computer databases are used to search for the identity of those who have left evidence at crime scenes. Comparing profiles from evidence in unsolved cases to databanks of samples collected from those already convicted of crimes often leads investigators to offenders. Frequently, those scientific links can result in turning attention away from individuals wrongly suspected of being responsible for crimes.

Justice and Science: Trials and Triumphs of DNA Evidence is an up-close chronicle of the most serious and brutal crimes in San Diego, California. George "Woody" Clarke, a San Diego prosecutor who served on my National Commission on the Future of DNA Evidence, has been at the fore-front of DNA evidence in criminal cases for years. From the beginning of its use in this country in the late 1980s, Clarke helped pioneer the introduction of DNA test results in court. As each different DNA technology began to be used in court, he was tasked with convincing judges that those techniques should be admitted into evidence and heard by juries deciding the fate of charged defendants.

Unlike many television programs, motion pictures and other books, *Justice and Science* is a true account of how DNA evidence has changed investigations and the trial of defendants charged with crimes. More importantly, it is an opportunity to see intimately how American courts pursue the goal of justice for all through the amazing power of science.

ACKNOWLEDGMENTS

This book is an account of my involvement in DNA cases over a period of fourteen years while I was a prosecutor in a local district attorney's office. The inspiration to put that experience into writing comes from the extraordinary results DNA technology provided over that time period. The police officers, deputy sheriffs, investigators, evidence collectors, analysts, victims, witnesses, experts, attorneys, judges, and jurors who played key roles in each of the cases described in this book must be acknowledged. So should the defendants and suspects directly affected by DNA, including those whose guilt was proven by testing and those who were found to be innocent, whether before or after trials.

A small group of supporters who have made this work possible are truly appreciated. Nat Sobel, my agent, and Jim Wade and Pamela Fischer, both editors, have provided extraordinary instruction and help in making this project a reality. Chuck Rogers, a former colleague in the district attorney's office, constantly kept my enthusiasm for this manuscript alive. I am grateful also to the staff at Rutgers University Press, especially Marlie Wasserman, Christina Brianik, Anne Hegeman, Marilyn Campbell, and Liz Scarpelli.

Finally, my deepest thanks are expressed to those closest to me. To my mother, Evelyn, who provided me the opportunity to become a lawyer and judge. To my wife, Michele, for always being at my side when I needed help and inspiration. And, lastly, to my Lord and Savior, Jesus Christ, for the best bundle of DNA ever: our daughter.

Justice and Science

Science in the Courtroom

Sherlock Holmes, Sam Spade, and Jessica Fletcher spent careers tracking down suspects responsible for committing crimes. The fact they are fictional characters is of little significance. Their tools—like those used by real-life detectives and investigators—saw little change from the nineteenth century to modern times. Revolutionary changes to the world of detectives and investigators are rare. Interrogation, eyewitness identification, and other police techniques have been honed and improved. But few dramatic changes have taken place in the world of solving crime.

Fingerprints were universally hailed as one of the most significant new weapons placed at the disposal of law enforcement. But their utility is limited to the relatively few cases in which fingerprints are left at crime scenes and can be discovered. Tests to determine whether guns have been fired by a suspect, hypnosis, and even voiceprints have been used in investigations with mixed and controversial results. But when science joined with law enforcement and the legal system in 1986, the justice system began a transformation like no other it had ever experienced.

Any thought prior to that time that nucleotide sequences, restriction enzymes, and capillary electrophoresis would hold the key to solving murders and rapes would have been beyond fantasy. Yet each would later prove to be a critical element in determining whether a suspect, defendant, and even a convicted prison inmate could have been responsible for a serious crime. The reopening of old criminal cases—both those unsolved and those in which a defendant convicted years earlier claimed innocence—suddenly became possible. Examination of those cases would often provide dramatic and surprising results.

The development of techniques based on life and physical sciences was the easy part. The formal scientific method taught in schools and universities led to the discovery of deoxyribonucleic acid (DNA), its structure, and its function in the human body. Intense research bore fruit in the form of methods to detect DNA and to identify differences among people. (Scientific terms are defined in the Glossary at the end of this book.)

But a scientific transformation of the legal system doesn't occur easily. Trial judges, governed by precedent-setting decisions of higher courts, are naturally slow to react to changes in the real world. That reaction is magnified when a technology developed in the world of science arrives on the court's doorstep with a power never before seen in the justice system. Judges are told, for the first time, that a witness will take the stand and declare that a spot of blood, a human hair, or a saliva stain came from the defendant seated at the counsel table in the judge's own courtroom.

The worry? That science will take over the responsibility of a jury to decide what happened. Courts may be afraid that if a jury hears the testimony of an expert scientific witness that appears to point without mistake or doubt to a defendant as the person who left rape evidence on a victim, that jury will ignore the other evidence in the case and decide the defendant must be guilty. The contrary argument can be compelling: jurors are mature adults who can consider and weigh all the evidence presented in a case and decide guilt or innocence accordingly.

The power of DNA evidence—matched against a legal system built on the principle of precedent—led proponents of the science to victories, to defeats, and, perhaps most important, to change. This book chronicles that experience in San Diego, California, and in one county to the north, Los Angeles. It is an account of cases that showcased this new science, the problems associated with the interface of science and the courtroom, and the role of the ultimate fact-finder, a jury of twelve members of the community.

With little warning, I would be thrust as a young prosecutor into the eye of a scientific and legal hurricane that would ultimately define my career in the law. The cases that formed the path of that storm would prove to be fascinating, challenging, and often heartbreaking. And, ironically, they would begin with the unlikeliest of crime victims: a DNA scientist.

CHAPTER ONE

The Scientist Becomes a Victim

---·---

Dr. Helena Greenwood, a British citizen who had immigrated to the United States with her husband, Roger Franklin, was a molecular biologist engaged in research for a medical-diagnostics firm. Greenwood (she used her birth name in her work) and her husband eventually settled in the upscale town of Atherton in the San Francisco Bay Area of California.

On the night of April 7, 1984, her husband was out of town so Greenwood was alone in the house. Shortly after 10:20 she woke up to find a man in her bedroom. In the darkness Greenwood could see only the man's outline but did notice that his head and face were covered by something like a ski mask. The intruder had a flashlight and what appeared to be a handgun. She was filled with terror, which was intensified when the man ordered her to take off her nightgown. After she removed it and sat on her bed, naked and trembling, he demanded that she give him all her money. After she complied, the man was furious when he found that she had only a small amount of change in her purse. He pointed the gun at her and forced her to perform oral sex. Then, to her vast relief, the assailant abruptly left. Greenwood immediately telephoned the police. Officers came to her home and took her report of what had happened. She described the traumatic attack in detail. The Atherton Police Department began an investigation into the crime and determined that the intruder had removed a kitchen window screen to gain entry to Greenwood's home.

A critical piece of evidence was discovered outside near the kitchen window. Greenwood's favorite teapot, which she had brought from England and kept on the sill of the window, was found on the ground. Examination of the teapot yielded the type of evidence investigators were hoping for—a latent fingerprint. Invisible to the naked eye, latent fingerprints can be made visible by a number of different methods, including the use of powders, chemicals such as ninhydrin, and even fumes from superglue. The police quickly determined that the fingerprint had not been left by Greenwood or her husband. Unfortunately, a check run on the print against both local police records and those from the Federal Bureau of Investigation (FBI) did not turn up a match. There were no other leads.

The thought that her assailant was still out there led to a level of fear in Greenwood that became unbearable. She and her husband decided that the only solution was to relocate. Greenwood had, fortunately, been recently offered a new position in San Diego with a company named Gen-Probe. It was staking out a leading position in cutting-edge science: research, development, and marketing of products in a new biomedical area with enormous potential for growth—deoxyribonucleic acid (DNA) testing. Greenwood was recruited to lead the marketing department of Gen-Probe, and she and her husband decided to move to Del Mar, an oceanfront suburb of San Diego. Franklin could see his wife becoming more of her old self once they made the decision. They put their Atherton home up for sale.

Then came a break in the case. A few weeks after they had decided to move to San Diego, a man was arrested in a nearby town. His crime: standing in the garden of a home and exposing himself to a woman inside. The man's name was David Paul Frediani. The officer in charge of investigating the crimes committed against Greenwood learned of the arrest and obtained a set of Frediani's fingerprints. Comparison of one of those fingerprints with the latent print from the teapot revealed that they matched perfectly. Almost one year to the day after the assault on Greenwood, Frediani was arrested for the attack. He was charged in the San Mateo County municipal court with burglary and forced oral copulation, with allegations that he had used a gun in the commission of both crimes.

A defendant charged with a felony in California is entitled to a preliminary examination of the charges by a judge. The prosecutor normally presents a bare-bones version of the state's case against the defendant by calling witnesses to testify in court. The judge, after hearing that evidence, simply determines whether there is sufficient evidence—sometimes referred to as a "reasonable suspicion"—to believe that the defendant has committed the crime(s) with which he or she is charged. A later trial is then held in which a jury must be satisfied beyond a reasonable doubt in order for the defendant to be found guilty. Although California prosecutors are authorized to use the grand-jury system in felony cases, they normally favor the use of the preliminary hearing.

On May 7, 1985, the preliminary hearing of the charges was held in Redwood City, which was both the county seat and a neighboring town to Atherton. The prosecutor, Deputy District Attorney Martin Murray, was assigned to present the case against Frediani. Murray, a skilled and experienced prosecutor, was all too aware of how difficult it was, at that time, to get a guilty verdict in sexual-assault cases. The defense frequently asserted that the victim consented or was intoxicated or that the attack was simply made up by the victim for one reason or another. But some instinct told him that he stood a good chance of winning this one. Because Greenwood had never heard of, much less met, Frediani, none of these defense strategies was likely to be employed. Frediani would probably claim that he simply wasn't the person who assaulted Greenwood. His lawyer would attack the circumstantial evidence—in this case the fingerprint match—necessary to establish guilt. But Murray, like most prosecutors, believed he had an advantage—because of what normally would have seemed like a disadvantage. Judges and juries often have concerns about victims' identifying their attackers (particularly in cases with no corroborating witnesses) because reasonable doubt about the accuracy of eyewitness identifications has been a determining factor in thousands of court cases. In a number of publicized cases, eyewitness identifications were later shown to be totally wrong. But Murray knew this prosecution was unlikely to have that problem. Greenwood never even had a good look at her attacker's face.

Greenwood testified at the preliminary hearing in the case against Frediani. She described all the circumstances of the assault, down to the brutal details of what she was forced to do by her assailant. But she did not—and could not—identify Frediani as the individual responsible. Greenwood was able to testify only that Frediani had some physical resemblance to the man who attacked her. Murray called other witnesses for the prosecution. The police who investigated the assault were able to testify that Frediani's fingerprint was found on the teapot discovered outside the assailant's apparent point of entry. The judge decided the evidence was sufficient and ordered Frediani to stand trial on the burglary and forced-oral-copulation charges. The trial was set for September 1985.

Shortly before the preliminary hearing, Greenwood and Franklin moved into their new home in Del Mar. The house was expensive, but Greenwood's career had taken off. And, despite the strain of having to testify at the preliminary hearing, she had begun to put the attack behind her. Frediani, however, was not in jail awaiting his trial. Even before the preliminary hearing, he posted bail in the amount set by the court to ensure his attendance at the various court proceedings. Because he had made all his court appearances as scheduled, Frediani was permitted to remain free pending the outcome of his trial.

On August 22, 1985, a few weeks before Frediani's trial was scheduled to begin, Greenwood's secretary at Gen-Probe called Franklin at his office and expressed her concern that Greenwood was late for work. Because her vehicle was an older British sports car, her secretary was afraid it might have broken down while Greenwood was on her way to work. Franklin immediately drove home but could not get inside the front gate to their house. He stepped on a planting pot, looked over the wall, and saw the body of his wife. He immediately called 911 and frantically asked for help. Deputies of the San Diego Sheriff's Department went to Greenwood's Del Mar home. When they arrived, they found her lifeless and beaten body just inside the gate to the courtyard of the new home she and her husband had shared for only a few months. It was obvious that she had been in a violent struggle to save her life.

Homicide Detective David Decker of the San Diego Sheriff's Department was assigned to investigate Greenwood's slaying. Decker and other investigators carefully assessed the crime scene. Greenwood's purse, keys, some papers, and other items were scattered on and around her body. Greenwood's cash, jewelry, and car keys were found and noted. Her automobile was parked in front of the house. Evidence-collection specialists painstakingly recorded and seized potentially important physical evidence. The evidence included pieces of what looked like two broken fingernails, scrapings of material found under her nails, as well as clippings from both her fingernails and thumbnails. Such material could be the basis for serological—blood and other body fluids—analysis or other trace-evidence testing to link the victim with a suspect. In addition, a thorough autopsy of Greenwood's body was performed at the medical examiner's office. She had been strangled to death.

Beginning in the 1950s, scientists had developed methods for testing evidence commonly encountered at crime scenes or on victims of crime. It had been known since the early 1900s that people have different ABO blood types—the main ones being A, B, AB, and O—and techniques for analyzing those differences were developed in the 1930s. In addition, scientific research led to the use of tests in the 1970s that allowed scientists to look at biological samples for different types of human enzymes and other proteins. Genetic markers that reveal different protein types in individuals were used in crime laboratories to discover whether suspects or victims could be excluded or included as possible donors of crime-scene evidence.

The difficulties encountered in such testing became well known over time. Fairly large evidence samples were required to provide results. Blood, semen, or other fluid evidence is subject to rapid degradation, which makes it difficult or impossible to get definitive results from analysis. The reason: biological material is highly perishable, especially if exposed to heat, humidity, moisture, and other common conditions found in various environments. Bacteria cause particular problems with samples that do not immediately dry. Just as important, ABO and protein typing could not pinpoint the person who left the sample. Although four ABO types are found in humans, between 40 and 45 percent of most population groups have the ABO type O. Protein typing increased the possibility of telling people apart, but even then obtaining an identification remotely approaching those made with fingerprint matches was impossible. Frediani, his alleged attack on Greenwood, and his pending trial in Redwood City were all known to San Diego Sheriff's Department investigators. Frediani's motive for killing Greenwood was obvious to the investigating officers—he would simultaneously have eliminated a witness and retaliated for her reporting his crimes to the police. But the lack of evidence linking him to the murder of Greenwood was a major, and apparently insurmountable, problem.

However, the trial of Frediani for the sexual assault of Greenwood proceeded. Under California law, because Greenwood had testified at the preliminary hearing and Frediani's attorney had the opportunity to question her on cross-examination at that time, a transcript of her testimony at that hearing could be used. In fact, it could be read directly to the jury at Frediani's trial. That testimony, along with the evidence of Frediani's fingerprint on the teapot and other circumstantial evidence—including ABO evidence from semen found on Greenwood's pillowcase—was enough to convince the jury in Redwood City of Frediani's guilt. Frediani was convicted of the attack on Greenwood and sentenced to prison by the San Mateo Superior Court judge who presided over his trial. Frediani appealed his conviction and sentence. To the surprise of Deputy District Attorney Murray, arguments by Frediani's appellate attorney that legal mistakes made at the trial had deprived his client of a fair trial were upheld by the court of appeal. The errors identified by the court of appeal had nothing to do with the use of the transcript of Greenwood's earlier testimony at the preliminary hearing. A new trial was ordered by the appellate court. Murray again tried Frediani for the assault on Greenwood. He presented the same witnesses and the same evidence to the second jury. It returned the same verdicts of guilty. Frediani was sentenced to prison a second time, then appealed again. Remarkably, that conviction and sentence were also set aside, again for reasons unrelated to the use of Greenwood's preliminary-hearing transcript.

Before a third trial could take place, Frediani decided to plead nolo contendere, or no contest, to the burglary and sexual-assault charges. He was sentenced to state prison, but he had already served enough time in custody to be released without further incarceration. He walked away a free man for the first time in years. He found a job, worked his way up in a Bay Area communications company, and started to lead what most would call a normal life.

The key to justice for Greenwood would be provided by new developments in science, parts of which she was engaged in when she was slain. But the application and acceptance of the new technology that resulted from those developments would not come quickly or easily. It would take the law considerably longer than science to allow assertions of links between defendants and victims to be heard by others, notably jurors. The connection between Frediani and Greenwood's murder wouldn't be made for another fourteen years.

And I would spend many years of my life as a lawyer and prosecutor working on the problem of introducing compelling scientific evidence in trials, where the unpredictable and human process that unfolds can make using even the most powerful tools science has to offer a sometimes frustrating and usually complex task. Every trial lawyer quickly learns that even as a case nears its conclusion, there is no reliable way to predict its outcome.

CHAPTER TWO

A New Prosecutor

———

I certainly wasn't a likely candidate for becoming involved in pioneering the introduction of DNA evidence in trials. I had done everything I could to avoid taking science courses in high school and college. Law school was an easy choice for me. My oldest brother, Peter, was one of the most respected criminal defense attorneys in San Diego. We talked about some of his cases, even when I was barely a teenager. When I saw my brother in action in court and listened to him describe the practice of criminal law, I was hooked. After getting my bachelor's degree from the University of California at San Diego, I was accepted at the University of San Diego School of Law. With graduation in 1977 came looking for a job. Fortunately, I had worked as an intern law clerk with the judges of the San Diego Superior Court while still in law school, which helped me get hired by the court as a criminal research attorney to do the same work I had done as an intern—but now I got paid for it. I loved the rewarding nuts-and-bolts work: researching legal issues for judges, summarizing legal motions and applications for writs, and making recommendations to judges on how to rule in criminal cases.

After a couple of years helping judges I was eager to start practicing criminal law. So I applied for a position with Defenders Incorporated, the largest local group representing criminal defendants who needed, but could not afford, legal representation. I was elated when I got the job. But my brother Peter offered muted congratulations: "Tell them you appreciate the offer but you want to be a prosecutor first." Deputy district attorneys, as local prosecutors are called in California, usually try more cases than defense lawyers. It was the best way to acquire the experience required for defending clients accused of criminal offenses. So I took my brother's advice and applied for a position in the district attorney's office.

One application later, then two, I couldn't even get an interview. Unfortunately, there were applicants from the Harvards and Stanfords, so they had an edge. It took awhile, but I finally figured out that I had a leg up because of my work with judges hearing the district attorney's most serious cases. Fortunately, I had become close to one of those judges, who knew that I had acquired substantial expertise in the complex sentencing laws that took effect in California's courts just before I became a research attorney. That was enough to get me an invitation to become a deputy district attorney. I had to make a commitment to stay on the job for two years—more than enough time, I was convinced, to try some misdemeanor cases and learn how the system worked. Then I could leave and begin representing clients of my own.

I started out in 1982 working in the family-support division. It involved civil law, rather than criminal law, but it was a start. I went after fathers who were failing to provide child support. Six months later I was assigned to another division. But I had learned something that would prove crucial to me when I began to practice criminal law. To prove paternity, it wasn't enough in most cases for the mother to simply testify that the defendant was the father. Occasionally, the physical appearance of the child was enough corroboration when unique hair or skin color, for example, was shared by the child and the defendant. More commonly, blood testing was used to make comparisons. By the seventies the courts accepted scientific tests to compare blood types of a mother, a child, and a suspected father. Using ABO blood typing and the analysis of other protein markers in blood, one could statistically show the relationships of a mother, a child, and a defendant. For many years these tests were the best means of proof at our disposal—but they ultimately proved to be a narrow scientific window into a far more powerful way of determining biological relationships.

One trial that showcased the gray areas in this technique involved, ironically, a heated factual dispute as to whether the suspected father-defendant had even had sexual relations with the mother. In a divorce agreement the defendant acknowledged being the father of the child, but a forensic expert testified that the divorce papers had been forged. If they were valid, the defendant would have already conclusively admitted to being the father. But the defense expert claimed that the defendant's signature wasn't genuine and that the blood-test results offered into evidence by my experts were just plain wrong. One of my first witnesses was a blood-typing expert from the University of California at Los Angeles. Ultimately, the jury was convinced by that expert and the other evidence in the trial that the defendant was indeed the father. This was the first time that I fully understood that the decisions of jurors would increasingly come from evolving definitive science—as long as it was presented in a way they could understand. But to explain the evidence and to deal with expert witnesses I had to acquire a real understanding of the underlying fundamentals. Because I had avoided physics, chemistry, and biology in high school and college, I would be forced to learn a great deal about science. And, as it turned out, I had little time in which to make up for those gaps in my knowledge.

In April 1983 I was transferred to the division in the district attorney's office that handled most of the preliminary hearings in felony prosecutions. I was pleased with the new assignment, but I had no dream of where it was going to take me in my life and in the law. Six months of working on preliminary hearings led me to suffer from a feeling of "been there, done that," particularly because I was encountering many defendants for the second, and even third, time. I thought it was time for a change. So did my boss. In the fall of that same year I was assigned to a branch office in Chula Vista, several miles south of downtown San Diego. Now I focused on misdemeanor trials—DUI (driving under the influence of alcohol or drugs), petty theft, simple assault and battery, and other minor offenses. It wasn't exactly the legal Olympics. But I needed the experience badly. Then, in early 1984, a deputy district attorney in the appellate division needed back surgery and would be out of the office for a few months. Because of my experience dealing with these types of cases when I was a research attorney with the court, I was asked to fill in. I knew enough to get by about the various motions that were filed in court—motions to dismiss, motions to exclude evidence, motions to do almost anything imaginable in a criminal case; some were quite inventive. And now I was writing my own briefs in response to those motions instead of simply reading them and preparing recommendations for a judge on how to rule.

But trial work was what I yearned for. I got my wish—the deputy district attorney I was pinch-hitting for returned to work, and I was transferred to the branch office in the city of El Cajon. It was spring, but that season can be pretty warm out in eastern San Diego County. Employees of the D.A.'s office in El Cajon usually arrived early enough in the day to get parking in a covered structure and avoid burning their hands on the steering wheels of their cars at the end of long, hot sunny days. The cases that came my way were sometimes equally hot. Because I had six years under my belt as an attorney but not enough of the right trial experience, I got moved up to the front of the line in the trial unit. El Cajon was a fairly conservative area with what were usually law-and-order juries. However, few cases actually went to trial. The vast majority of defendants in El Cajon pleaded guilty rather than take their chances with juries. Still, I managed to try a handful of jury cases and felt I was back on track. The two years I had committed to the office passed, and although my trial numbers were lagging behind, I was thoroughly enjoying the experience. An extra year as a prosecutor, I thought, would only make me a better lawyer.

Then, in September 1984 fate gave me another break, though I wish it had not come in the way it did. Peter Lehman, the extremely popular chief of the appellate division downtown, developed serious coronary problems and required a long period of recuperation. Once again, my experience with legal motions put me into the breach, but I was less than thrilled. However, life took a dramatic turn on December 18, when Tom McArdle, who was subbing for Lehman as division chief, walked into my office. I'll never forget his words. "Woody, I want you to second-chair a murder case." My first question for McArdle was "What is a 'second chair'?" He laughed. You just respond to and write motions, he answered. Seems like no big deal, I thought to myself. The prosecutor assigned the first chair was Dan Williams. I knew a bit about Williams. I had put on the preliminary hearing in a case he later took to trial, one that involved a robbery committed by two codefendants. I even watched part of the trial. To me Williams was everything a trial lawyer should be. Jurors paid close attention when he asked questions. He knew how to speak to and handle witnesses. Judges treated Williams with the utmost respect. Obviously I could learn a great deal just carrying his briefcase and watching him perform in court.

However, the case was likely to move at a snail's pace because it involved more than one victim, and I had other goals in mind, although I was confident I could fill the bill. It was no secret in the office that I wanted to catch up with the other prosecutors who had been hired at the same time that I had. That meant trials day in and day out. Working on this one case was likely going to bring that experience to a halt. I told McArdle I'd rather not accept the assignment. McArdle asked me to do him a favor and think about it overnight. I agreed and then walked up the street to my brother Peter's office in his home, a few blocks north of the courthouse. I fed Peter the details. He asked what I had told McArdle. I recounted for him my answer. My brother smiled. I knew that particular smile all too well. The last time I was the object of it, Peter convinced me to turn down the offer from the public defender's office. I remember his exact words to this day. "Tell Tom McArdle tomorrow morning you'd be honored to work on the case." I went home, knowing that the next day I'd do exactly what Peter suggested.

I never believed in can't misses, but once again my brother was right. First thing the next morning, a Tuesday the week before Christmas, I made a right turn into McArdle's office. Before he could even say good morning, I told him I would take him up on his offer. I walked across the street to talk to Williams. The appellate division of the district attorney's office was located in a newer building across the street from the aging San Diego County Courthouse. The felony-trial division—in which Williams was a supervising trial lawyer—was on the top floor of the courthouse. I had just gotten off the elevator when I ran into him near his own office. "Woody," he laughed, "let's get to work."

Williams not only knew what he was doing in a courtroom but could also turn a lost moment into a victory. In one case in which I shadowed him, we entered the courtroom for a preliminary hearing before the defendant's attorney arrived. As Williams walked through the swinging gate that separated the actual courtroom from the area reserved for the public, the judge who would hear the case immediately asked him, "Mr. Williams, do you anticipate a *Diaz* motion?" I could see on his face that Williams had no idea what the judge meant. He immediately turned around and asked me in a whisper what a *Diaz* motion was. Attorneys and judges often cite a particular type of motion filed by a defendant—or a prosecutor—by referring to the defendant's name in the precedent-setting case that was then published in the fancy bound books that line every courtroom's walls. But I drew a blank on this one. I confessed to Williams that I had no idea. I immediately saw how quickly he could think on his feet. He turned to the judge and said in a firm voice, "It's certainly possible, your Honor." We later learned that Diaz was the name of a defendant in a decision that had just been handed down by the California Supreme Court; that decision gave a defendant a right to ask a court to close a preliminary hearing to the public and media if the details of the case might make it hard for that defendant to receive a fair trial.

In the case that I was helping Williams with, the evidence included blood recovered by police. The technology that was available to crime labs at that time was limited to testing ABO blood groups and a few protein types also known to exist in blood. This type of testing was the best science had to offer in the early 1980s. DNA testing would not be allowed in a court of the United States until 1988 in a rape trial in Florida. And it was an interesting case that debuted DNA testing in the United States. A man named Tommie Lee Andrews was charged with the knifepoint rape of a woman inside her home in the Orlando area. Andrews had been convicted of another sexual assault and sentenced to prison, and prosecutors believed he was responsible for a number of attacks on other women. In one, semen evidence left was subjected to DNA testing. The result: the evidence matched DNA taken from Andrews himself. The chances that someone else could have left the semen were estimated at one in billions. Andrews claimed an alibi for the time of the assault, but the jury convicted him based on the DNA evidence. Andrews was then sentenced to a term of over one hundred years in state prison.

As DNA evidence began to be used in courts in the United States, attorneys representing defendants linked to crimes by DNA sometimes fought the use of that evidence in court. Even before that time, in the early 1980s, attorneys would frequently file written motions asking trial courts to exclude the results of ABO blood grouping and protein testing. Their claim: the technology used by crime labs for typing ABO and proteins had not yet been legally approved in California. No decision of a higher California court, they contended, had found such testing admissible in court. They were right—no legal opinion by a court of appeal or the Supreme Court of California had decided that ABO and protein testing was appropriate for a jury to hear about and consider at that time. When defendants objected, it would have to be proved in court that the technologies were, in fact, reliable before a jury could properly hear the evidence.

In California, in order to present to a jury the results from a new scientific technique, the attorney for the side that wants to use the evidence is required to first prove to the judge that the science meets what is known as the *Kelly-Frye* rule. Based on a federal court of appeal decision that reached all the way back to 1923, the rule required that the party—whether the prosecution or defense—first prove to the trial judge that the technology used was "generally accepted" by the scientific community. Then—and only then—could the results of that testing be heard by a jury deciding the guilt or innocence of a charged defendant.

In the few cases that included challenges to ABO and protein testing (often called serological testing) the prosecutors assigned the cases looked for help. In the murder case I was working on with Williams, he confessed to me that he didn't understand any of the science that was involved. Would I, he asked, take care of the hearing that was needed in this case? The hearing on whether Williams would be able to use the serological results ended up lasting nearly a full year. Many experts were called and provided lengthy testimony in front of the judge. Ultimately, the judge allowed the evidence to be heard by the jury. But that case, although I didn't know it at the time, would shape my future in the law. A few of the experts who had testified in that hearing on bloodstain-testing evidence—even before the Tommie Lee Andrews case—had told me that an evidentiary tool even more powerful and definitive than serology testing would soon become available. Its name was so long I had difficulty pronouncing it: deoxyribonucleic acid. One expert laughed and said to me: "Woody, just remember the letters D-N-A."

At that point I could have no conception of how powerful DNA evidence would later prove to be. Nor could I have imagined how difficult it would be for DNA to get its day in court. Today anyone who watches television shows like *CSI* must think that the forensic power of DNA evidence has been applied in both criminal and civil cases for a long time. After all, the discovery of its structure had taken place all the way back in the 1950s. Why, then, did it take so long for this technology to become admissible, and what happened along the way? There were many reasons, starting with the complex business of learning to work with DNA in the laboratory, and many early obstacles had to be overcome before DNA acquired the starring role it has today in solving crimes, clearing the innocent, and linking those responsible for offenses. As I would learn from personal experience, when human and other factors come into play no evidence can be taken for granted.

CHAPTER THREE

The Transition to DNA Evidence

I followed up on the tip that the blood experts had given me. To begin, I had to understand the basics of a revolution in genetics and molecular biology. By reading scientific journals and reaching out to the blood-test experts I knew, I learned why James Watson, Francis Crick, and Maurice Wilkins had been awarded the Nobel Prize for their discovery of the molecular structure of deoxyribonucleic acid, or DNA, which came to be referred to by many as the "genetic blueprint of life." (Only in the years that followed would the crucial work of another scientist, Rosalind Franklin, be acknowledged.) Two papers Watson and Crick published in 1953 in the British journal *Nature* presented their findings about the double-helix structure of the material on which all life is based, the instruction manual for every living cell.

As I read and learned about the initial evidentiary uses of DNA, I became increasingly excited. I knew this revolution in biology would have a profound effect on the entire legal system, from criminal trials to paternity suits. I also knew that the same hurdle that I faced in the earlier serology-testing cases, the *Kelly-Frye* rule, would be the first of many we would encounter getting DNA evidence accepted by the courts. Why? Because DNA would be even more complicated to explain than serological testing. Yet my sketchy science background, paradoxically, would serve me well. I had to absorb all this knowledge by explaining it to myself, in terms that would not only help me understand but help me explain it to others. Arguing in court previously against highly skilled defense lawyers bolstered my confidence that I could explore this complex science and learn how to use its stunning evidentiary power in trials.

Since the mid-1930s, the FBI Crime Laboratory has stood as the hallmark of forensic testing in the United States. The term *forensic testing* is worth defining: generally, it can be described as the application of science to legal matters, especially the investigation of crime. An expert I called to the witness stand in one hearing on blood evidence was a scientist with the FBI, Dr. Bruce Budowle. Budowle's experience, research, and publications in the field of bloodstain testing were significant and would later prove pivotal as the Bureau developed techniques in the late 1980s to test DNA. The work of the FBI and other laboratories resulted in a fundamental change in the way biological material could be analyzed.

In 1988, I was invited by the director of the FBI, William Sessions, to be one of several speakers at an international symposium planned for the fall at the Bureau's academy in Virginia. The seminar was designed to bring together scientists from around the world to discuss this new, cutting-edge technology. I telephoned Budowle in Virginia. The first question I asked him was why me. Bruce deadpanned, "Who else?" His point was, I suppose, well taken. I was one of a tiny group of prosecutors who had been riding the scientific and legal roller coaster of getting serological test results used in court.

I saw his point. If this new DNA technology was going to be used to test samples in criminal investigations, it was going to have to be used in court and at trials. That meant hearings on admissibility. Given the predictions about the extraordinary power of DNA testing, results from serological methods were going to pale in comparison. As the meeting date drew near, I put together a presentation based on my experiences with previous cases. I was convinced that the many lessons I had learned from using ABO and protein testing in court were likely to apply to the introduction and acceptance of DNA evidence. My goal: to tell scientists from around the United States and the world about the interface of science and the courtroom and to give them some tips about what could be expected to happen with DNA in the courts. Best of all, preparing the presentation would push my own learning curve about DNA.

The lectures by scientists from the FBI, Scotland Yard in London, and other laboratories around the world were fascinating. Analyzing DNA was made possible by a tool called *restriction-fragment-length-polymorphism* testing. Referred to as RFLP, this tool could be used to detect the differences in individuals' DNA. It was the result of the work of two scientists from the United States and Great Britain—Dr. Ray White from the Howard Hughes

Medical Institute in Salt Lake City, Utah, and Dr. Alec Jeffreys from the University of Leicester. White spoke at the meeting about discoveries that had been made in his lab a few years earlier.

Jeffreys had already used the RFLP technology in a criminal case in Great Britain in which he compared evidence collected from the bodies of two teenaged girls found murdered in 1983 and 1986. Police in Leicestershire had a suspect in the two killings. They knew about Jeffreys's work with DNA because he had previously assisted British authorities in an immigration case. Investigators asked Jeffreys if he could use his technique to compare DNA evidence believed to have been left behind by their assailant on the bodies of the two raped and murdered girls to a DNA sample obtained from the suspect, a local man named Richard Buckland. Jeffreys agreed. His results staggered the investigators. Although the testing revealed that the same man raped both girls, the RFLP analysis showed that Buckland was not that man. The first use of DNA testing in a criminal investigation showed the suspect was innocent—an early example of how DNA could be used to definitively establish innocence.

Left with no viable suspects, the police turned to the community and asked men to voluntarily give samples of their blood to compare to the evidence collected from the two victims. Each sample was tested, although the majority of men who volunteered to give a sample could be excluded by existing serological techniques like those used in our San Diego cases in the early 1980s. Some samples, however, had to be analyzed using the RFLP process. But not one of the men from whom those samples were collected could have left the DNA evidence recovered from the two girls. Finally, the police got a lucky break. A man was overheard bragging in a local pub that a baker named Colin Pitchfork had paid him to give blood and tell the police that he was Pitchfork. Investigators immediately sought out Pitchfork to see whether he could be the killer. After obtaining a sample of Pitchfork's blood, Jeffreys made the comparison. The RFLP test was conclusive: Pitchfork's DNA profile exactly matched the samples taken from the girls. Pitchfork was arrested, convicted of the murders, and sentenced to prison for life.

Other speakers at the FBI meeting talked about how evidence samples need to be collected and preserved for later testing. A few spoke to the group about how statistics are used to describe the degree of significance of DNA matches. I felt a little more comfortable with math than with biology. I was familiar with statistics from my previous hearings, but terms like "Hardy-Weinberg Equilibrium" and "Bayes's Theorem" were enough to send me more than once to the water fountain outside the auditorium. More intriguing was an even greater cutting-edge DNA technology that was described at the symposium. As if RFLP typing wouldn't be enough of a challenge to understand in the years to come, I had to learn a new term: the *polymerase chain reaction*. Known by its acronym, PCR, the technique allows an analyst to genetically duplicate very small amounts of DNA over and over until millions, or even billions, of copies are created. (This information wasn't exactly a staple of the curriculum when I went to law school.)

I developed many new friends at that meeting, but one who stood out was Dr. Brian Parkin. Parkin was a highly respected forensic scientist from the Metropolitan Police Forensic Science Lab in London, a unit of Scotland Yard. On an afternoon off at the seminar, we drove to downtown Washington in order to play tourists. Visiting Ford's Theater, we walked down to the basement, which houses a few exhibits devoted to the assassination of Abraham Lincoln. Inside a glass case was the cloak Lincoln wore when he was shot by John Wilkes Booth. In pure British fashion, Parkin pointed to the lapel of the coat and asked whether I could see a brownish stain. I could—it was dark brown and was fairly easy to see against the blue fabric. Parkin asked whether I recalled the presentations on PCR the day before. Of course I did, and I had at least a general idea of what PCR was capable of doing. In a few years, Parkin explained, some of that bloodstain on the cloak could be used to create a new Lincoln. "What?" I yelled. Some of the other tourists looked my way. Parkin was a pro. He took particular delight in telling me he was just kidding.

But the point was a good one. Although the RFLP test we had heard about at the symposium earlier in the week was powerful in telling people apart, it had shortcomings. Among those was the fact that it required a bloodstain about the size of a quarter to get a reliable result. Unfortunately, police frequently don't have an abundance of physical evidence in criminal cases. Small bloodstains and other body fluids are just as, if not more, common in investigations as large ones. PCR would find a place in DNA testing once it was fully developed in the laboratory. Later that afternoon the two of us drove back to Quantico. The next day was my turn to give a presentation to the group. Science was going to take a back seat to the law. At least that's what I thought.

Before I had flown east for the meeting, I carefully prepared slides to use as visual aids during my lecture. Unfortunately, when projected onto the auditorium screen they were dark and unreadable. Despite the fiasco, the audience of scientists was enthusiastic. (I'm convinced that each of them must have had a bad experience or two with slides.) The group seemed to be fascinated with the cases I had worked on and how U.S. law determined whether different types of scientific evidence could be used in trials. I hoped that I had made it clear to the listeners that DNA testing in future trials would be vigorously challenged in courts around the world. The questions they asked me after the presentation made it clear to me that they felt the same way.

I came home from the meeting excited about the new challenge that lay ahead. Instead of telling jurors that bloodstains, hairs, and other evidence might possibly have come from someone, DNA was going to significantly enhance the probability that evidence derived from scientific tests would persuade jurors. Although everyone at the meeting was careful to point out that RFLP testing couldn't identify someone in the way a fingerprint does, I knew better. Sure, the results would be that a suspect could not be excluded as the donor of a piece of evidence. But by comparing the types found in both the evidence and a sample of the suspect's own blood, and then consulting databases that contain genetic types of large numbers of people from around the world, statistics can take over. If a match is made, the chances that someone other than that person left the evidence are typically one in millions, billions, or even trillions. This technology was going to revolutionize how cases were solved and proved. Little did I know how it would change my own life and career. I would get some on-the-job training in science and technology that would propel me into playing a role in revolutionary changes in criminal law and procedure.

*A*fter my experience with cases that involved serology testing, it was time for me to move on. I was moved to the felony-trial division of the district attorney's office to work closely with the other prosecutors in the office, and I began to try my own felony cases.

One of the laboratories that early on provided DNA RFLP testing, Cellmark Diagnostics, was located in Germantown, Maryland. Its parent laboratory was in Abingdon, Great Britain; it offered RFLP testing in the United Kingdom as a result of an agreement with Jeffreys. Cellmark was asked to perform RFLP testing by the San Diego Police Department in the handful of investigations in 1989 and 1990 that were believed appropriate. Those cases were largely rape cases in which the identity of the attacker was questioned. Prior to that time, law enforcement, prosecutors, and juries had to rely on serological testing, with its obvious limitations. But DNA promised much more. At first the science seemed terribly complex to me, but I soon found that it was possible to break this complicated subject down into basic, manageable units I could comprehend. And I knew that many other lawyers would soon be able to understand how this powerful evidentiary tool could be used in court.

DNA, as mentioned previously, is frequently referred to as the genetic "blueprint" of life and is the material located in chromosomes found within the nuclei of most cells. It consists of long, tightly coiled strands containing approximately 3.3 billion pieces of information called *base pairs*. The bases that make up the pairs are one of four variations, individually named adenine, cytosine, guanine, and thymine (abbreviated A, C, G, and T). The sequence of DNA, or order of the base pairs, is the same in every cell except for those that govern reproduction—female eggs and male sperm. Each reproductive cell contains only one-half of a person's DNA. That fact permits the creation of a full complement of DNA as a result of the fertilization process and the creation of an embryo and then a fetus.

Approximately 99.9 percent of the order of these 3.3 billion bases is identical for all humans and essentially serves as the instruction manual for the body's growth, structure, and functions. As a result, each person has two eyes and hair of a particular color, a stomach that produces the acid needed for digestion, and every other fragment of blood, bone, and tissue that makes up the human body. All living things on earth—humans, animals, and plants—have DNA. However, about one-tenth of 1 percent of the sequence of the base pairs of human DNA can vary from person to person. Although the percentage difference is small, that means roughly three million of these A, C, G, and T bases are combined in different sequences in different people. The one exception is identical twins, who share the exact same DNA sequences. The fact that humans vary at these DNA locations allows scientists to distinguish among people. By testing samples at those particular locations—or loci—scientists can determine whether a particular person could, or could not, be the donor of a specific piece of biological evidence.

Cells that have a nucleus, and therefore DNA, are found throughout the body. Blood, bloodstains, sperm, hair roots, bone, teeth, organs, and other tissue all contain DNA that can be tested by scientists. Body fluids in liquid or dried form, such as saliva and vaginal secretions, can also be tested. These fluids usually contain DNA in what are referred to as epithelial cells, which come from the lining of the mouth, vaginal vault, or other mucous membranes of the body.

In criminal cases the types of evidence from which DNA can be removed and tested are many and varied. Examples include blood and semen stains on clothing, weapons, bedding, and other surfaces; swabs taken from victims of sexual assault; hairs with attached root follicles; even envelope flaps and postage stamps that have been moistened with saliva. The RFLP testing method described by White and Jeffreys wasn't restricted to criminal cases. In fact it began to be routinely used in medical diagnostics, genetics, molecular biology, and other scientific fields unrelated to investigations of crimes.

This technique requires the division of DNA into fragments of various sizes. Because some of these fragments of DNA are relatively large and consist of thousands of base pairs, the DNA must be in good condition and appropriately preserved. Because DNA is a biological substance, it is perishable and degrades with time. The result of degradation is a gradual breaking up of the DNA fragments. At a certain point in the degradation process it becomes impossible for DNA results to be obtained.

The RFLP technique itself involves several steps. After the removal of DNA from an item of evidence, an evaluation is made to determine how much DNA is present and its quality. If enough good-quality DNA is present, the analysis can proceed. The second step is referred to as *restriction*. Enzymes—proteins that act as catalysts, or enablers, for biochemical processes on which life depends—are used to divide DNA into discrete portions where DNA varies from person to person. This step, which uses "molecular scissors," allows scientists to look at smaller, variable sections of our DNA instead of the unmanageable three billion-plus pieces of information. These particular sections of our DNA contain variations in which small sequences of the same As, Cs, Gs, and Ts are repeated a different number of times. For example, the sequence at a particular genetic location may be CATAGGCA. One person may repeat that sequence 1,250 times; another person may repeat the sequence 4,755 times; a third may repeat it 2,670 times.

The third step is referred to by the rather intimidating term *electrophoresis*. The process, however, is simple. When the restricted—or cut—DNA sample is placed in a gelatin-like substance and electricity is applied, the samples move from one end of the gelatin toward the other. The larger the DNA sample—in other words, the greater the number of repeats of the target DNA sequence—the harder time the sample has moving across the gel because the gel is constructed in a honeycomb formation that acts as a sieve. Because this process is like trying to move granular material of differing sizes through a filter screen, the smaller the piece of DNA, the farther it can travel. Thus, smaller DNA fragments that have fewer repeats of the sequence travel farther than the larger fragments. In the fourth step, a technique known as *Southern blotting* is employed to transfer the DNA from the gel to a membrane. Because the fragments of DNA have had a radioactive "label" attached to them, an analyst can then expose the membrane to X-ray film. The resulting exposure reveals a pattern, or band, at the location on the film where the segment of DNA came to rest during the electrophoresis process. The end result: an X-ray film, known as an *autoradiograph,* which shows where the person's DNA fragment has traveled to on the gel. Because each person receives one length of repeated DNA from each parent, most people have two fragment lengths, or bands, on each film.

In the fifth step, an analyst takes the samples of evidence and known samples from defendants, victims, or other persons and compares the locations of bands to determine whether those persons can be excluded or included as possible donors of the evidence. Not unlike the bar codes, or Universal Product Codes, found on almost all products purchased in stores and read by devices at cashier stands, DNA banding patterns from samples either match or do not match. If the patterns from an evidence item do not match those derived from a sample taken from a known person, that person is excluded as a possible source of that evidence. If the patterns are consistent or matching, the person is included and may have been the donor of that sample. The final step, taken with matching results, is to estimate how rare or common the DNA characteristics are. By referring to databases of DNA results from human populations worldwide, scientists are able to calculate random match probabilities for matching DNA samples. Those probabilities are estimates of how often the DNA profile shared by the evidence and the person would be found in different major population groups throughout the world.

Because of the power of the RFLP technique, statistical estimates of the rarity of matching DNA profiles are frequently extremely persuasive. Many cases, including those in the late 1980s, revealed rarity estimates such as one in billions or even trillions. Although DNA analysts were careful not to equate matching DNA profiles to identifications testified to by fingerprint experts, the result in the view of jurors and the legal system was frequently the same. Testimony that the chances are one in 500 million, for example, that someone other than the defendant has left a sample of evidence is extraordinarily powerful. But what about the reliability and accuracy of this new tool? No one thought attorneys representing defendants charged with serious crimes would blindly accept the results of DNA testing in court. But no one anticipated how truly ferocious the response would be.

CHAPTER FOUR

The Fight for Acceptance

———·———

*T*he first cases in San Diego in which DNA evidence was offered proved to be difficult tests of the legal system. Many other forms of scientifically obtained evidence, ranging from finger- prints to drug-test results, had become accepted in courts not only in the United States but also around the world. Each new scientific technique had to overcome initial resistance until established over time. But certain techniques have faced protracted legal barriers. These include polygraph examinations— or lie-detector tests—hypnosis, and the analysis of voiceprints to try to iden- tify voices. The use of each of these tests has met repeated opposition in the courts. Laws in many states prohibit the use of polygraph-exam results and statements made by witnesses while under hypnosis.

The admissibility of scientific testing technologies that are capable of providing powerful information in the investigation of crimes depends on evidence laws and the decisions of appellate and supreme courts of the fifty states and of the federal system. The *Kelly-Frye* rule, mentioned previously, which was the determining legal standard in the hearings on serological evi- dence in California, had an interesting origin. James Alphonzo Frye, a vet- eran of World War I, returned to his home in the District of Columbia after the Great War. Shortly after his return, he was arrested and charged with the murder of his physician. In preparing his defense for trial, Frye's lawyer had him undergo an early lie-detector examination referred to at the time as the systolic-blood-pressure deception test. The results: according to his attorney, Frye was telling the truth when he denied involvement in the killing of his doctor.

As his case came to trial, the prosecutor objected to the jury's hearing any evidence about the test because, the prosecuting attorney insisted, the test had no scientific reliability and should not be allowed. On these grounds, the judge ruled that the evidence was not admissible. Frye was convicted and sentenced to prison. In his appeal to the U.S. Court of Appeals, Frye argued that he deserved a new trial because the trial judge should not have prevented the jury from hearing his exonerating lie-detector results. But the appellate court held that the trial judge had been correct in prohibiting the testimony, thereby fashioning a new rule of law. The court declared that from that point on, before results of a new or novel scientific test could be used in a trial, the side trying to use the evidence had to first show that the test was "generally accepted" in the scientific community. In Frye's case, the court concluded that the defense had not shown that the systolic-blood -pressure deception test enjoyed general scientific acceptance. The simple rule set out in the 1923 opinion of the U.S. Court of Appeals in *Frye v. United States* became the dominant standard in both federal and state courts. Most supreme courts across the United States adopted the reasoning of the *Frye* court, and it became the generally established criterion for the admissibility of new types of scientific evidence. The California Supreme Court adopted the *Frye* rule for trials in California in a ruling in a 1976 case, *People v. Kelly,* and the standard came to be known in California courts as the *Kelly-Frye* rule.

In the case of DNA, the effect of allowing such biological evidence in courts would be dramatic. After all, this new technology clearly was going to revolutionize the identification of some of the most violent offenders in communities around the world. Unlike fingerprints, biological evidence is far more frequently found at crime scenes and can be routinely used in the investigation of the most serious crimes. But attorneys representing criminal defendants fought tooth and nail over whether juries should be able to hear DNA testing results. The reason was clear. Because the evidence was more powerful and conclusive than any they had been forced to confront before, the defense of their clients frequently depended on it. Different standards for the admissibility of scientific evidence were used in some of the other forty-nine states, although the *Frye* rule was the most common in the late 1980s. But the import was the same. Lawyers representing defendants accused of serious crimes feared that if a jury heard that a critical piece of DNA evidence came from the accused or could otherwise be connected to that defendant, the defense faced an uphill battle.

And for good reason. Science frequently carries great weight with jurors. DNA seemed invincible to many because, unlike other tests used by detectives or crime labs, such as voiceprints and lie detectors, DNA testing appeared to be an objective and detached science. If anyone disagreed with the results, a retest could usually be done. So the common way to attack DNA results early on was to try to keep juries from even hearing the evidence. The *Frye* rule was invoked in most cases when DNA played an important role. That meant judges, in case after case and before a trial could even begin, were required to hear testimony from expert witnesses about whether DNA testing was reliable. During those evidentiary proceedings, experts frequently described the underlying science of RFLP testing, the techniques used to type samples, and how estimates were made of the statistical rarity of matching profiles. The testimony that was required for a judge to decide whether a jury should hear DNA testing results was frequently lengthy, tedious, and sometimes confusing. But judges usually ruled that the jury could hear the DNA test results because those judges were satisfied by expert testimony at the hearings that set out in detail the basic biology of DNA, the RFLP technique, and how the statistical estimates were made. But defense lawyers continued to fight against admissibility and contended that the technology had not been sufficiently evaluated by the scientific community at large. Possible problems, they often complained, included contamination of the samples, the inability to obtain complete results, and the "exaggerated" probabilities of "one in billions" and even rarer estimates.

The whole experience was reminiscent of the previous battles over ABO and proteins. That litigation, however, would prove extremely valuable to me in what would later come to be referred to by many as the DNA wars. Several of the same experts who testified in the serology evidentiary hearings applied their scientific backgrounds and experience to forensic DNA testing. Both supporters and detractors of the new RFLP technology began to appear in courtrooms across the United States and Europe. The stakes were high: unlike prior bloodstain technology, which simply pointed in the direction of a suspect, DNA test results focused with much greater precision on defendants who were often accused of the most serious crimes, particularly murders and sexual assaults.

The San Diego experience was similar to that in other large counties in California and the rest of the country. Even after bitterly contested hearings, nearly every trial judge in the United States who was asked to rule on the admissibility of RFLP testing permitted its use at trial. Judges heard from expert witnesses that the RFLP technique was used daily in a variety of scientific settings. When questioning experts at these hearings, I always highlighted some of those uses. My personal favorites were, I believed, familiar to people in San Diego. The first was the use of RFLP technology to diagnose genetic illnesses and disorders. In numerous hospitals and clinical laboratories in our own county patients were routinely tested for muscular dystrophy, cystic fibrosis, Tay-Sachs, and scores of similar diseases.

The second nonforensic use I focused experts on was in a field even better known than the medical one in our county—saving endangered animals. In a laboratory at the world-famous San Diego Zoo, the Center for Reproduction of Endangered Species, samples from protected animals worldwide were regularly tested using the RFLP technique. The purpose: to track migration and breeding patterns and then develop programs to prevent further endangerment and even extinction.

I also invariably asked my expert witnesses about a third nonforensic use of RFLP technology—the identification of the remains of U.S. soldiers killed in battle. Unlike any other country in the world, the United States attempts to identify the remains of every soldier killed in combat. San Diego is home to a large active and retired military community. Testimony from experts detailing the use of the RFLP technology to identify those remains—typically when fingerprint and dental exams were impossible—seemed particularly helpful.

The experts who testified in opposition to RFLP testing generally acknowledged the other, nonforensic uses of the technique. They contended, however, that clean, freshly drawn samples from patients in hospitals and doctors' offices were those used in the testing. Samples taken at crime scenes, they contended, were different. Exposure to sunlight, rain, dirt, and other real-world contaminants made testing unreliable. On cross-examination I would usually ask those experts about the remains of U.S. military personnel recovered from degrading, humid environments like that in Vietnam, or samples of animal hairs of endangered gorillas left behind in their nests in the forests of Africa. Experts would sometimes concede that those samples had to be used and scientists were still successful in obtaining accurate results.

Opponents also frequently pointed to the absence of national standards governing DNA. It is true that there were no national governing bodies regulating and applying uniform standards to forensic DNA testing. Unlike human blood banks, diagnostic laboratories, and other medical organizations, crime laboratories were not usually required to follow any national regulations in performing testing, although the FBI was in the process of developing suggested guidelines for use in crime labs. Courts, however, usually found that problem not to require keeping the evidence from a jury's consideration. DNA was like other techniques used in crime laboratories, they often concluded. Judges would note that crime laboratories, whether fingerprinting, testing drugs, or comparing hairs and fibers, were not normally subject to any standards. The work of crime labs throughout the country, some courts pointed out, was routinely accepted in court, even though doubts were cast on the validity of test results provided by analysts in those labs who did not have to perform their work according to any mandatory standards. Admissibility was also found even though crime laboratories were not usually accredited or certified by national agencies. Courts often noted the existence of rigorous standards for testing that were implemented by the individual laboratories themselves.

Questions raised about probability estimates did cause some judges concern. Opponents noted the increasingly small probabilities presented to describe the rarity of matching DNA profiles and often expressed fear that the absurdity of numbers like one in trillions, based on population databases that might consist of only a couple of hundred people, might well persuade juries to render a guilty verdict immediately and not weigh the rest of the evidence in a case. Most judges were used to presiding over trials in which ABO or enzymes had been tested and the results reported in court. DNA was clearly different. Instead of a bloodstain from a crime scene matching the blood type of the defendant and one in ten people having the same type, now estimates of the rarity of matching samples were in the billions and even trillions; the probability that a sample came from someone else was usually remote. However, the argument about the disproportionate weight a jury might give to DNA evidence usually didn't prevail. Neither did complaints by some of the detractors that there was a possibility that even the way labs calculated those statistics was flawed. Courts were satisfied that the methods used to calculate the statistical estimates were appropriate because they were used in a variety of settings and were even similar to those already used in ABO and protein testing. Juries, they concluded, had a right to hear this scientific testimony and were capable of evaluating the significance of the evidence in individual cases. Cross-examination, the presentation of their own evidence, and closing argument provided sufficient protection for defendants. So prosecutors, who felt that obstacles to DNA testing's admissibility had been removed, more freely used the technology than they had in the past. Few, however, foresaw the course that would be traveled in the way courts viewed DNA evidence.

The evidentiary successes of DNA testing were immediate. Proving stranger rapes became much easier than it had been in the past. Instead of relying on often unconvincing—or even mistaken—eyewitness identification, courts and juries now had access to the results of an apparently objective science. The impact of DNA on cases of sexual assault wasn't surprising. Unlike many other violent crimes, sex crimes commonly involve exchanges of biological evidence. And that transfer is not limited to traditional rapes. Perpetrators of sexual assault can leave evidence in the form of semen, saliva, and even hairs, all of which can be sources for DNA testing. Even clever offenders could be identified by biological evidence. A used condom thrown in a garbage can outside an apartment building, for example, can be the source of scientific evidence. Testing of the material inside the condom can pinpoint the rapist; DNA on the outside will likely match that of the victim. A scientific connection can then be made. A cigarette left in a victim's house, a half-eaten apple, a glass used to drink water, even discarded chewing gum, can all be used to associate a suspect with a crime. Each might contain the unique DNA code of its donor.

But the battle over the admissibility of RFLP evidence took an unexpected turn in the fall of 1992. The National Academy of Sciences, a prestigious scientific organization based in Washington, D.C., decided to take a look at forensic DNA testing in the United States. Through its research arm, the National Research Council, the academy put together a committee of scientists and members of the legal profession to closely examine the field and report on its findings. Over a two-year period, the committee reviewed publications and heard descriptions of the state of forensic DNA testing in the country. After that scrutiny, the committee issued a report in October 1992 entitled *DNA Technology in Forensic Science.*

The publication sent shock waves through courts in a significant number of states. The report fully endorsed the scientific reliability and accuracy of RFLP testing. However, the committee felt that the methods used by laboratories to calculate the statistical estimates of how rare matching DNA types are might be flawed and might overstate the rarity of matching DNA profiles. If true, defendants would be unfairly prejudiced in front of a jury. If the match was one in a million, for example, many individuals even in the United States might have the same profile. If one in trillions, it was unlikely anyone else in the world would match the sample. To be cautious, the group devised an artificial, ad hoc mathematical formula to act as a substitute for the methods used by laboratories. The committee recommended that laboratories use the formula until sufficient scientific research was performed to uphold the methods already in use in crime laboratories. The response from the forensic community was immediate. The techniques used to calculate the rarity of matching DNA profiles were already conservative, they claimed. The recommended artificial formula, dubbed the *ceiling principle,* was overly conservative, inaccurate, and unscientific, DNA proponents complained.

The reaction of courts, however, was mixed. In Massachusetts, New Hampshire, Arizona, Washington, California, and Connecticut, appellate courts decided that it was not proper to let juries hear RFLP testing results as determined by labs that had used the earlier statistical techniques. Citing perceived scientific controversy about the accuracy of those statistical estimates, most of those courts recommended that labs follow the formula suggested in the National Research Council's report. Courts in other states disagreed, deciding that the report's findings were simply recommendations. If a laboratory provided statistics calculated using the earlier mathematical methods, questions on cross-examination by a defendant's attorney about the National Research Council report would be permitted. However, a jury would still be allowed to hear the evidence.

The result seriously affected prosecutions in those states that decided the report's recommendations accurately reflected existing scientific opinion. Some cases were overturned on appeal on the grounds that the statistical approaches used in preparing and presenting the evidence were not those approved by the committee. More important, trial courts in those states—and courts in other states that were concerned about the report's conclusions— often required use of the ceiling principle. Usually, the result was a dilution of the statistical significance of matching DNA profiles in those cases. For example, if a calculated estimate of the rarity of a match in a case was one in twenty million people, use of the ceiling method might change that to one in 500,000 or an even greater likelihood. The resulting statistic was still meaningful; the power was simply reduced. A skilled attorney sometimes exploited that increase in probability. One common approach in DNA cases is to ask an expert how many people in a given area could be expected to have the same DNA types shared by the evidence and the defendant. If the statistic is one in twenty million, only two people in the State of California, for example, would on average match the profile. If the probability is one in 500,000, five or six would match in San Diego County alone, and the argument that someone else could have left the evidence carries more weight.

Several events over the next handful of years changed the landscape and the way courts decided the admissibility of DNA evidence. A number of studies were completed of population groups around the world to determine whether the possible problems raised in the report were real or imaginary. The results of that research reassured courts and crime laboratories. The possible sharing of DNA types cited as a concern in the National Academy's report appeared to be unjustified. Also, the extent and potential validity of both scientific and legal criticism of its 1992 report were recognized by the Academy.

As a result, a new committee was put together by the National Research Council to specifically examine the subject of population groups and the way estimates of matching DNA profiles were provided. This time, the committee was staffed with population geneticists and statisticians—in other words, scientists with extensive knowledge of the controversial issues that were raised in the first report. In the new committee's final report, issued in 1996, *The Evaluation of Forensic DNA Evidence,* the concern about isolated populations was minimized. The studies undertaken after the 1992 report showed that the steps labs had normally taken to ensure that their probability estimates were conservative—that is, did not overstate how rare matching DNA was—were appropriate ones. In reality, many experts noted, the statistics ultimately reported probably understated the actual rarity of matching profiles. Thus, the 1996 report concluded the ceiling approach was no longer necessary. In fact, the report was critical of the previous report's nonscientific recommendation that analysts follow its ad hoc recommendation. The new committee noted that the recommendation had been made without any hard scientific or statistical support. The new report did include additional recommendations for cases in which the donor of the evidence might be someone who was a member of a relatively small ethnic or isolated population group.

Confidence in DNA in courts across the country was again high. Courts were reassured to the extent that statistics appear to have never again been rejected by an appellate or supreme court after that time. The way was paved for daily evidentiary use of this powerful scientific tool. But what was it like in the trenches? The expertise I developed in litigating DNA evidence was called on in over a hundred cases in San Diego courts. As with anything else in life, if you've done something unusual at least once, you're the expert.

The hearings were sometimes extensive but usually involved the same issues. Defendants accused of serious crimes often demanded pretrial hearings in which they would ask a judge to decide whether DNA testing results should be allowed at the eventual trial. Our legal system depends on precedent—law as interpreted by higher courts—and trial judges are required to follow precedent. Because case law from the California Supreme Court and courts of appeal was sparse and sometimes conflicting on DNA, trial judges were required to hold these hearings.

In many cases the hearings consisted simply of providing transcripts of the testimony of expert witnesses in other cases and then arguing to the court about whether the evidence should be allowed. Other cases required calling witnesses to the stand and often lengthy questioning by the attorneys on both sides. Even judges would join in the questioning to find answers to questions they had about the science of DNA and the techniques used in testing. The more serious the charges, the more resources attorneys on both sides devoted to presenting their cases. Hearings sometimes lasted days, even weeks. Experts I questioned in court would testify to the scientific validity of RFLP testing, its nonforensic uses, steps taken in the lab to help ensure quality work, and the scientific acceptance of the statistics that were calculated. By this time, virtually everyone, including defense lawyers and their expert witnesses, conceded the scientific reliability of DNA testing. Their complaints, therefore, usually involved the way results were interpreted, the possibility of laboratory errors, and the numbers. Other experts might thus address the appropriateness of the lab's testing protocol, the training of analysts who performed the testing, and whether the results were interpreted correctly.

The defense frequently called its own expert witnesses. They included college professors, researchers, medical doctors, private DNA analysts, and scientists familiar with population genetics and statistics. Cross-examining those experts proved challenging and time consuming but appeared to be helpful to judges deciding on admissibility. The defense witnesses who were most critical of DNA testing results were sometimes the easiest to cross-examine. In the case of a few of these experts, the bulk of their income came from testifying for defendants in criminal cases. Often the expert's scientific qualifications were in areas only remotely related to human DNA testing. Others simply didn't understand some of the circumstances unique to forensic DNA testing. A medical-diagnosis expert, for example, might be unfamiliar with the techniques used to remove—or extract—DNA from a human hair root or a semen stain on clothing. Once confronted with the laboratory protocol or scientific publications validating a procedure, the expert frequently conceded the reliability of the method.

Judges were, obviously, an important part of the process. Few, if any, were schooled in molecular biology, genetics, or any of the fields touched by DNA testing. Yet, those same judges were called on to decide whether the testing methods and their results could be heard by juries who would be selected to decide the guilt or innocence of defendants in criminal trials. Legally, California judges are required to decide only whether the technology is generally accepted in the scientific community. Yet understanding and deciding many of the issues in these pretrial hearings demanded at least a working knowledge of the theory and procedures.

Cases that led to pronounced battles over DNA included some of the most serious attacks on victims in the San Diego community in the early 1990s. In one, a man was charged with the murders of several women. RFLP evidence linked the defendant to sexual contact with one of the victims. Deputy District Attorney Dan Lamborn, then a young but extremely talented prosecutor, faced a hearing that would pit many of the same scientists I had usually gathered for my own hearings against defense expert witnesses who disagreed with the scientific acceptance of RFLP testing. Lamborn, with guidance I provided him, ultimately convinced the trial judge that the DNA evidence could be presented in front of the jury.

In another homicide case, DNA testing was used to compare a semen stain recovered from a victim's clothing to a sample obtained from the suspect. The samples matched. I put witnesses on the stand in a hearing on the admissibility of that RFLP evidence for Deputy District Attorney Jeff Dusek, the office's premier homicide prosecutor. The hearing focused on whether the jury should be allowed to hear the statistics that described the DNA match to the defendant. The trial judge pointedly asked Dusek and me whether the prosecution wanted to use the population numbers that had been determined by the laboratory rather than the numbers recommended by the National Research Council just months earlier in its first report. I told the judge that we were ready to go forward with the full numbers, unaffected by the report's recommendation to use the ceiling method. After listening to the evidence in our pretrial hearing, the judge agreed that the statistics calculated by our laboratory should be heard by the jury that would decide the defendant's fate.

In the end, San Diego judges admitted DNA evidence in every contested case. The underlying theory and technology of RFLP testing were scientifically established and generally accepted, each of those courts concluded. The procedures in place in laboratories were found to be appropriate. Any dispute about the accuracy of the probability estimates that were provided for matching DNA profiles would ultimately be resolved by juries, our courts decided. The only remaining question: How would that DNA evidence be evaluated by jurors?

CHAPTER FIVE

A Stranger Rapist and a Murderer

EARLY SUCCESS WITH DNA EVIDENCE

————•————

*A*s the use of DNA evidence became common, some trials were avoided. Defendants connected to sex crimes by the scientific tool of DNA testing frequently decided to simply plead guilty. But the other side of the coin was equally important. Instead of relying heavily on eyewitness identification, prosecutors in sex cases involving victims and defendants who were strangers to one another now frequently had the benefit of scientific evidence linking the defendant to the crime. In some cases, that meant fewer offers to defendants to plead guilty to lesser charges. And because the California legislature had dramatically increased the penalties for forcible sex crimes in 1981, prosecutors were less inclined to agree to reduced charges. Defendants, faced with little benefit in pleading guilty, demanded trials. One result was that DNA testimony became a staple in felony trials, particularly rapes and homicides. Even out-of-town expert DNA witnesses were on a first-name basis with attorneys, judges, and court staff. The landscape had again changed.

After I returned to the felony-trial division in late 1989, my time was divided between my own caseload and assisting other prosecutors with DNA hearings in their cases. The division of time couldn't be avoided. Deputies in my own office were often desperate for help. When their own trials were about to begin and there was an objection to the use of their DNA evidence, those prosecutors knew my help was a phone call away. Most simply had no time to prepare for the often complex and technical admissibility hearings that were demanded by the defendants they were about to try.

And the requests weren't limited to San Diego cases. Prosecutors in other California counties would call, often in despair. Some asked whether I would do their hearing for them. Others just needed technical assistance and legal guidance. I didn't hesitate to help. But I drew the line at appearing in courtrooms in other counties. One by-product of these frequent requests was my creation of a DNA outline of cases decided by appeals courts across the country. Now I had the luxury of simply sending that outline to other prosecutors—first by U.S. mail, later by electronic means, including an invention called e-mail.

One San Diego case caught my attention unexpectedly. Another deputy district attorney was in the middle of trying a stranger-rape case. The prosecutor's supervisor, Deputy District Attorney Mike Carpenter, took me aside. He needed my help. The prosecutor trying the case was having trouble and didn't feel he could put on the DNA evidence. That evidence was critical. The case was a particularly serious one. A young woman had been attacked in her home by a stranger just before sunrise one morning. Using a knife, the man forced the victim to undergo a series of degrading and brutal sexual acts. I asked Carpenter what he wanted me to do. A veteran prosecutor who had tried every type of serious crime over the years, Carpenter explained that he wanted me to go into court and put on all the DNA evidence in front of the jury. That's a first, I thought to myself. I was going to be sent in to try to put out a fire in the middle of a trial instead of at the beginning. Within minutes I contacted the prosecutor and assured him I would help. I was briefed on what had happened in the trial so far. The victim apparently had not testified well, was emotionally flat during her testimony in front of the jury, and had difficulty remembering some key events. At least I had a couple of days to prepare for the DNA testimony in the trial, which would include results from semen found on vaginal swabs and clothing that had been collected from the victim. I was also lucky. The scientist who would be coming to court to testify in the case was a good friend and an outstanding expert witness. One of the greatest rewards of being involved in DNA typing and its use in criminal cases was getting to know the people from all over the country whom I had the opportunity to work with.

During the first several years of using DNA as an investigative and court tool, the testing was not available in local crime labs. That meant that either a private laboratory would be retained to perform the testing or the FBI in Washington, D.C., would be turned to for help. Unfortunately, the FBI was so overloaded with testing requests that it took several months or even a year for results to be available. To speed the process, the San Diego Police

Department and the San Diego Sheriff's Department would often use Cell-mark, the private lab in Maryland mentioned previously, for DNA testing. Cellmark was usually able to test samples quickly and efficiently.

As a bonus the Cellmark scientists who came to court to testify were remarkable. One, Lisa Forman, was always at the top of her game. Lisa had a fascinating background. She received her bachelor's degree at the Berkeley campus of the University of California and then pursued her graduate studies at New York University. Forman concentrated her research on genetic variations in endangered animals through the National Zoological Park, part of the famed Smithsonian Institution in Washington, D.C. That research took her to the jungles of South America. Her goal: to get DNA samples from tree monkeys and analyze their genetic profiles. Unfortunately, she wasn't able to find the monkeys in sufficient number, so she switched her focus to the rather unusual kinkajou, another jungle animal. Forman's education and experience eventually led her to Cellmark. With her expertise in population genetics and DNA, she was fascinated by the prospect of using DNA in the criminal-justice system. Cellmark was a perfect fit for her. The lab in the United States was the second facility opened by Cellmark after its first was established in England as a result of the work of Alec Jeffreys. Forman's role as a Ph.D. scientist at Cellmark was to oversee DNA testing in casework, to develop the databases used for the statistics provided in cases, and to testify in court. She was remarkable in each role.

The first time I met her, in 1989, I sensed how effective she would be as a witness in front of juries. She told me a story I remember to this day. Describing a recent, hotly contested trial, Forman said the defense attorney was obviously going to test on cross-examination not only her results but also her credentials. In describing those credentials during initial questioning by the prosecutor, she was asked about her doctoral degree. The defense lawyer began his cross-examination in a somewhat testy tone, asking, "Dr. Forman—does anybody really call you 'Doctor'?" Without missing a beat, Lisa calmly replied, "Well, my mother likes to." The attorney sat down and asked no other questions.

I introduced myself to the jury in the case in which I was now co-counsel and called Forman to the witness stand. Her testimony about DNA and the lab's results were, I thought, persuasive. The defendant, Kerwin Hall, sat stoically at the defense table and stared into space during the testimony. Hall was described earlier in testimony by the victim as the man she saw when she walked out of her bedroom in the apartment she shared with three other women in the Mission Beach area of San Diego. Wearing only boxer shorts, Hall placed a knife to her throat and forced her to commit a series of sexual acts. After the victim began to cry, Hall forced her to take part in additional sex, then made her get dressed and follow him to a neighboring garage. At that location she was raped again. Hall then let the victim go. She used a telephone at a nearby taco shop to call police.

The initial investigation uncovered no suspects. Two months later, however, the victim and her friend were driving over a bridge a short distance from the apartment. The victim saw Hall walking on the sidewalk, and she immediately phoned police. Hall was arrested and denied to officers that he had ever been involved in any sexual assault. Forman described the results of DNA testing that was performed by Cellmark on the vaginal swabs taken from the victim immediately after the assault, as well as the semen stains taken from her clothing. RFLP testing that was conducted on the swabs was compared with a sample taken from Hall after his arrest. The results: Hall matched the DNA profile from the evidence. How rare was that profile? It would be expected to be found in only about one out of 910 million people. I asked Forman whether that figure was about three times the population of the United States. She agreed that it was. Hall testified in his own defense. Hall had two choices in his defense. The first: to claim that he had been misidentified by the victim and the DNA results were wrong. The other: to concede the accuracy of those DNA tests and to claim the victim had made up her story about being raped. He chose the latter. He recounted how he had met the victim at a party at her apartment three days before the alleged attack. He testified that he saw the victim at a local nightclub that same night; they had danced and then returned to her apartment and had consensual sexual relations. Two days later, according to Hall, they met again at the club, went to her apartment, and had sex again. No assault ever occurred, according to his testimony.

The jury deliberated for days but was unable to reach a unanimous verdict. They were divided 6–6 on the most serious charges. The other prosecutor was assigned to a different branch of the district attorney's office, and I was asked to retry the case. I felt the DNA evidence had Hall in a bind—he had to admit that the results of DNA testing in his case were 100 percent accurate. Especially because he and his victim were of different races, Hall could have claimed at the first trial that he had been misidentified. That theory would have been consistent with the victim's testimony that her assailant was a stranger. But his testimony at that first trial now meant that identification would not be an issue at the retrial. If Hall had claimed no involvement whatsoever with the victim, I would have had to show the jury at the second trial that she had been sexually assaulted by a true stranger, namely Hall. But that was no longer necessary. Now the only issue was proving to a second jury that the victim's allegations were real and not the result of a lovers' quarrel.

The victim was more comfortable and emotionally convincing when she testified at the retrial. Hall took the stand in his defense and repeated the story he had testified to at the first trial. I confronted him with his denial of even knowing the victim when he was originally arrested by police. He steadfastly maintained his innocence. However, during my cross-examination I noticed that Hall obviously fancied himself a ladies' man. I decided to pursue that line of questioning. Describing the victim as "coming on" to him at the nightclub, Hall was clearly confident about his appeal to women. I asked Hall why women were so attracted to him, knowing there was probably no good answer. Hall couldn't come up with one, other than to say that women found something about him irresistible. The point was made. Hall was narcissistic and living in a dream world in which he was the center. Forman's science firmly linked him to the crime; but the jurors' perception of what sort of man he really was probably helped them in their eventual decision that Hall was guilty of all the charges against him. After an emotional hearing at his sentencing that included the victim tearfully addressing the court, Hall was sentenced to prison for eighty years. Even though he was twenty-one and had no criminal record, Hall obviously had disgusted the judge with what he had done to the victim. His appeals were later denied, and he was required to serve at least forty years in prison before his release.

Science had provided the foundation for this case, but another part of the trial process, one sometimes overlooked, is how a witness testifies. Demeanor and nonverbal communication can sometimes speak volumes about a witness. Science alone isn't always decisive. In trials like Hall's, the human element also played a starring role. But what would happen if the science was insufficient to offer such a foundation in a trial?

The term *polymerase chain reaction* always sounded to me like a step in making an atomic bomb detonate. Just how in the world could a scientist copy DNA from a piece of evidence like the spot on Abraham Lincoln's cloak and make millions of versions of the same, identical DNA? The answer was an idea first conjured up by a research scientist in the San Francisco Bay Area in 1985. Dr. Kary Mullis, a South Carolina native and biochemist, worked for the Cetus Corporation, a biotechnology company located near Oakland. He once described his conception of the polymerase chain reaction (PCR) in a

San Diego death-penalty trial. Unlike more traditional scientific discoveries, it didn't take place in a lab. Mullis was driving to a weekend home he owned in the Mendocino area of Northern California. During the drive north, Mullis thought about the possibility of simply duplicating DNA in a test tube in the same way DNA is copied as part of the natural reproduction of human cells. He quickly dismissed the idea as absurd. Someone else would have thought of something that simple previously, he thought to himself. In fact, science is full of instances in which a researcher independently arrives at some new insight or discovery—only to later find that it had indeed already been discovered by someone else. In this case, it had not.

Mullis returned to Cetus and worked on the details. The end product: copying small portions of human DNA in an artificial environment. The process itself is magnificent in its simplicity. Here's how it works. By targeting small sections of human DNA at specific locations—called *genes*—relatively short portions of DNA strands can be set aside for copying, also known as amplification. Cutting up DNA at specific genes was already a common step in RFLP testing. The PCR technique simply involves placing those segments from many cells in a test tube and adding other ingredients: individual As, Cs, Gs, and Ts; "primers" to start the copying process; and an enzyme harvested from geysers such as Old Faithful in Yellowstone National Park. Heating and cooling a test tube containing these ingredients a defined number of times causes the sections of DNA to copy themselves. In the course of thirty or more heating and cooling cycles, what started out as simply fifty to one hundred cells' worth of DNA becomes millions or even billions of copies of the same DNA segments. The enzyme, named *Thermus aquaticus*—or Taq, for short—is critical. Because the PCR process must operate at high temperatures, the enzyme that allows the copying to take place must remain active and stable in that environment. The use of Taq, which comes from high-temperature geysers, makes sense.

Mullis and his colleagues at Cetus critically examined the PCR technology and determined that it could successfully and reliably copy many different human DNA segments. The discovery led to a revolution in molecular biology. No longer would the time-consuming and laborious RFLP technique be needed to diagnose genetic diseases, determine blood types for transfusions, or perform many other of the host of DNA tests.

The applicability of PCR to criminal cases was immediately obvious but slow to catch on. At first, only one specific DNA location was determined to have enough variation between individual humans to merit use. That gene, called *DQ-Alpha*, was used in a number of cases beginning in the late 1980s.

A bloodstain, hair, or other piece of biological evidence would first be subjected to the PCR copying, or amplification, process. After making millions of copies of the DNA at the DQ-Alpha location, a test was then used to determine the DNA types of that sample. The only problem was that even if an evidence item was found to have the same DQ-Alpha types as a suspect or victim, a test from just this one location couldn't be used to tell people apart. Matching profiles might be as common as one in five or, at best, perhaps one in one hundred people. The potential of the test, however, was enormous. It was simply a matter of time before scientists determined that people differed in their DNA at other locations as well and could use that fact to the test's advantage. The ability of the technique to someday separate people and even identify the donor of a sample to the exclusion of anyone else in the world was apparent.

Of greatest importance, PCR DNA technology had enormous advantages over the RFLP test in criminal cases. In disease diagnosis, if an analyst doesn't have enough of a sample to test, the patient can simply be asked to provide additional blood in order to successfully type the sample. But in criminal cases analysts can't simply return to the source for more samples. What's left at a crime scene or on a victim—often just a single hair root, tiny bloodstains, or even minute semen stains—is usually all there is. Samples of that size would never be enough to provide RFLP testing results because the technique usually requires at least fifty thousand cells to produce reliable and accurate DNA results. That equates to blood or semen stains at least the size of a dime. Thanks to Mullis's invention, the PCR technique can obtain accurate results from fifty cells or even fewer. Bloodstains barely perceptible to the eye can frequently be successfully typed. A single hair root—rather than a handful of hairs—can lead to the determination of a DNA profile.

PCR's other advantages over RFLP testing were equally compelling. Instead of the weeks or months required for RFLP typing, PCR-based techniques can be used and completed in days or even hours. Equally important, RFLP testing methods normally require DNA in good condition. Older or poorly preserved samples—"degraded" DNA—caused difficulties. PCR copying can be successfully carried out on samples in poor condition. Even crime-scene samples exposed to rain, sunshine, dirt, and other contaminating conditions can usually yield PCR testing results.

As the first cases with PCR results came to court in San Diego in 1991, it was truly déjà vu all over again. Even though the early power of PCR techniques for telling people apart was limited, the results still helped prove the guilt of many defendants charged with the most serious crimes and exonerated numerous innocent suspects. And because the PCR process included some different techniques than did the methods used in RFLP testing, admissibility hearings once again became common. The whole process was critically examined by scientists and concerns were aired both in the scientific literature and in courts across the United States. The ability of PCR to successfully copy very small samples immediately led to concerns about contamination of DNA from other sources. A sneeze by a detective or crime-scene technician, reuse of a pair of tweezers, or an analyst's going from the room where the PCR copying process occurred to another room where evidence was laid out could all lead to inaccurate results. But the court hearings led to uniform results. Despite all the problems that could be encountered in actual casework, the scientific community was remarkably supportive of the technology.

One admissibility hearing, the 1991 San Diego death-penalty prosecution of Jessie Ray Moffett, stood out. Results in the case—using the DQ-Alpha gene—helped prove the defendant's guilt of one of the murders with which he was charged. Because a PCR hearing had been held in a similar capital prosecution in Northern California only a few months before, I was able to obtain a copy of the transcripts of the scientific testimony in that case. But, to my amazement, after hearing extensive testimony from expert witnesses who described the scientific acceptance of the PCR technique, the judge in that case prohibited the jury from hearing the testing results. His reasons for doing so were alarming to both scientists and lawyers. He accepted the testimony of the experts that the PCR technique was indeed used to diagnose diseases and even make decisions on whether to abort fetuses. However, that judge concluded, the need to be accurate in testing in those fields was not as great as the need to be accurate in criminal cases.

Because I was confident about the scope and compelling nature of that evidence, I asked the judge hearing the case against Moffett to read those transcripts. I also called to the witness stand the DNA expert who performed the testing in the Moffett case to supplement the testimony in the Northern California hearing. That man, by no coincidence, was Dr. Ed Blake. Blake, a noted forensic serologist, had become a pioneer in the use of PCR testing in criminal cases. Because his laboratory was located in the same building as Mullis and the Cetus Corporation, Blake was a natural resource for Cetus to turn to in order to determine whether PCR technology could be used in criminal investigations. Blake collaborated with Cetus to make sure the DQ-Alpha marker could be appropriately used on forensic samples, and he was frequently turned to for PCR testing when evidence samples were too small or too degraded to produce RFLP typing results. Blake was a familiar face from previous hearings on the admissibility of ABO and protein testing. He was highly sought-after even before DNA testing became available because of his experience in serological typing. Once the PCR process was available, prosecutors and defense attorneys alike enlisted Blake for testing and advice.

Blake was also one of the most compelling witnesses any attorney could wish for. He minced no words and was not afraid to give his opinion on almost any topic. As long as he believed that a particular DNA result was accurate and reliable, he would support those results without reservation or hesitation. Blake testified in our hearing and gave his own opinion about the previous decision reached by the Northern California judge about PCR. Most of his venting about that case was in my office or his hotel room. Fortunately, the judge assigned to hear our case was as angry about the earlier court decision as we were.

In a decision that was directly to the point, Judge William Mudd decided that the PCR results in our case would be allowed in front of the jury. Disagreeing with the Northern California judge's decision, Mudd specifically pointed out that the life-and-death decisions made in other scientific fields amply demonstrated scientific acceptance of the PCR technology. Moffett was later convicted of multiple murders and eventually sentenced to death. But before his appeal was heard by the California Supreme Court, he died of natural causes on death row at San Quentin. Although Moffett's appeal of Mudd's decision would ultimately never be decided because of his death, courts of appeal and supreme courts in California and across the United States consistently concluded that PCR technology was admissible in criminal cases.

Why was it easier to gain acceptance by the courts of PCR than of RFLP testing? RFLP results, from the outset, were extremely powerful in telling people apart. Jurors who heard testimony that only one person in billions or trillions would be expected to have the same types as were shared by a defendant and a piece of evidence were probably convinced beyond any doubt that the defendant on trial left that sample. But, as we have seen, PCR cases couldn't hold a candle to RFLP in telling people apart. Matching DQ-Alpha profiles might be found in as many as one in five people. As a result, higher courts simply weren't as concerned with jurors' blindly convicting defendants based on PCR results. What those courts couldn't know was that the power of PCR testing would increase exponentially. By adding additional genetic locations where human DNA differed to the DQ-Alpha marker, scientists were able to dramatically increase the ability of the test to tell people apart. In fact, by 1994, many laboratories were testing samples at five or even more genetic markers in addition to DQ-Alpha. When evidence was matched to a suspect or a victim, the results might reveal that only one in two hundred thousand people would be expected to have those same DNA types. Even rarer profiles were encountered. A single hair root or a blood, semen, or saliva stain the size of the head of a pin was now capable of linking someone to a crime. Could DNA technology possibly be improved and be used to solve even more cases? Time and incredible scientific research would prove that it could.

CHAPTER SIX

A Double-Edged Sword

DNA FOR AND AGAINST THE PROSECUTION

———•——

DNA became the defining part of my career. Lectures became a way of life. Whether at the local Kiwanis, Lions, or Rotary club, university and law school classes, or meetings of state and national organizations, I tried to educate the public about DNA and its impact on the criminal-justice system. Fortunately, my audiovisual techniques improved from the days of the dark and unreadable slides I projected at the FBI Academy. Some of the visuals I used were professional-quality depictions of DNA testing. Others summarized court cases and rulings on the use of DNA evidence. I had entered the multimedia world of the 1990s. I became a spokesperson for the use of DNA in the legal system as well. I was enlisted as a regular lecturer for prosecuting and defense attorney organizations like the National College of District Attorneys, statewide prosecuting attorney groups in different regions of the country, and state bar associations. I even gave presentations to groups of judges who wanted information on DNA and the legal system. Scientific organizations also were hungry for information about the experience of admitting DNA evidence in court. Annual meetings brought together scientists and the growing number of prosecutors and defense attorneys with a stake in DNA testing and its use in criminal investigations and cases.

Soon I found myself venturing to countries outside the United States. My longest journey came in early 1994, when I made a presentation at a meeting in the United Arab Emirates in the Middle East. I had to look at a map to find out that the Emirates were centered in the city of Dubai, close to the Persian Gulf. The city was remarkably clean, beautiful, and new, as was the large and impressive lab at the Dubai Police Department. Although DNA testing had only recently been started in the lab, the types of evidence that had already been tested in actual cases were extensive. The scientific meeting itself was designed to educate forensic analysts and research scientists from the entire Middle East. Simultaneous translation of the first-day speakers, which included me, was provided in Arabic. Among those attending was Dr. Henry Lee, the famed forensic scientist from the Connecticut State Police in New Haven. Born in Taiwan, Lee was a legend in the forensic community. He had worked on cases that included the deaths of John F. Kennedy, Sam Sheppard, and Vincent Foster.

Dubai was the most exotic place I visited during my years of evangelizing for DNA testing, but the conference held there was just another sign that forensic DNA testing was becoming internationally accepted. Yet back in the 1980s plenty of fine-tuning was needed. Perhaps the most exciting development in the science of DNA since Watson and Crick first defined its structure, the Human Genome Project, was still years in the future. Prosecutors like me still had plenty of surprises and problems ahead of us—particularly when some expert witnesses turned out, I believed, to be something less than expert.

One case that led to a duel between scientific witnesses was the murder of a sixteen-year-old schoolgirl, Melissa Orchulli, in 1988. The defendant, Willie Ray Roberts, had previously been convicted of assault with a deadly weapon in Los Angeles. After he was released from custody, he moved to San Diego and attacked a woman with a butcher knife. The victim loved Roberts nonetheless and married him even after he was arrested and convicted and had served three years in prison for the attack on her.

Roberts worked for a construction company close to his home. On mornings before work, he got into the habit of spending time at a convenience store between 6:30 and 7:30 trying to impress teenage and preteen girls on their way to school. He often walked along with them uninvited, offering them clothing and money and even handing out his telephone number and asking them to call him. He would compliment them, ask for hugs, and occasionally grab one if the opportunity presented itself. When a girl hesitated, Roberts would insist that he simply wanted to be her friend.

Orchulli was one of the girls Roberts talked to, and he had, on one occasion, convinced her to hug him. In April 1988, Orchulli complained to a school friend that a man kept following her and talking to her when she walked to school. When summer school began, Orchulli asked her stepfather to drive her to school so that she wouldn't have to walk through the area. Unfortunately, on the day of her death, she had decided to walk to school and left her home at 6:45 A.M. At 6:50, video cameras at the convenience store showed Roberts walk up to the store with his bike, talk to the store clerk, then leave. Ten minutes later Orchulli approached the store. For some reason, Orchulli apparently did not discourage Roberts on this particular morning. An eyewitness saw Roberts walk over to Orchulli, kiss her on the cheek, and talk to her. The two began walking down the street in the direction of a vacant house two doors away. Another witness saw Orchulli standing by a brick wall some ten yards from the front door of the vacant home. A third witness saw the front door to the house open and a man hold the screen door open and beckon a young girl to go inside.

Twenty minutes after Roberts and Orchulli were observed walking together, Roberts was seen washing his hands and drinking from a garden hose at a home two blocks away from the vacant residence. Roberts was wearing work clothes and work boots. Within minutes, Roberts returned to the convenience store and was in the area of the store's gas pumps. He then telephoned his supervisor and told him he would have to miss work that day because he had to see his parole officer later that morning. Investigation eventually revealed that Roberts had no appointment with his parole officer and did not speak to him that day.

At around 8:00 A.M., a transient went inside the vacant house to try to steal coils from the home's kitchen refrigerator. From the living room the transient could see the body of a teenaged girl. Her skirt was pulled up and her underwear was off and attached to only one ankle. Schoolbooks she had with her were tossed aside and covered with blood. A piece of notebook paper lying next to her body had writing on it: the initials J.R. and a phone number. The first four digits could be made out and were later matched to Roberts's home phone number. An autopsy of the body showed that Orchulli had been strangled to death. Bruises to her neck were consistent with a chokehold having been used on her. She was badly beaten in the face with resulting bleeding and a fracture of her skull. The opinion of the pathologist was that she had been struck repeatedly with a blunt instrument.

That same day, Roberts gave his bicycle to a neighbor. The next morning an employee of the construction company found Roberts hiding in the cab of one of the company's trucks. He told the other employee that he was wanted by his parole officer. For two days Roberts failed to report for work and was fired. One week later he was arrested for Orchulli's murder. He denied having any contact with Orchulli on the day of her killing and told police a drug addict had stolen his bicycle. He contended he had worked that day. He adamantly denied talking to or bothering any young girls in the area.

Roberts was subsequently charged with the murder. Special circumstances were also alleged, making Roberts eligible for the death penalty. Those allegations included that Roberts had murdered Orchulli during the commission of the crimes of both rape and burglary. The evidence against Roberts was entirely circumstantial. Although he could be placed together with Orchulli near the store, no witness could identify either Roberts or Orchulli either in the house or at the front door. The notebook paper linking Roberts was critical but still failed to put him inside the vacant house. Other evidence would be essential to prove Roberts was indeed the killer.

The missing pieces were assembled through the painstaking investigative work of San Diego Police Department detectives. Other young girls were interviewed by police and described encounters with Roberts that were similar to Orchulli's. Two weeks before Orchulli's death, Maria Garcia, an eighteen-year-old, had been in the area of the convenience store at 7:30 in the morning and saw Roberts across the street walking with several school-aged girls. Roberts crossed the street toward Garcia and approached her. Garcia spoke only limited English and largely ignored Roberts when he talked to her. Roberts followed Garcia as she turned and walked down a different street. Roberts then pointed to a vacant house and told Garcia he lived there and wanted to show it to her. He convinced Garcia to walk up the home's driveway a short distance. When Garcia turned and began to walk away, Roberts grabbed her by the neck in a chokehold and forced her up the driveway toward the house. Garcia lost consciousness. She remembered nothing from that point until she awoke in a hospital bed several hours later. Garcia didn't initially report the assault to police because she feared it might affect her immigration status.

Even more important, Kerry Morton, a twelve-year-old, was walking to school at 6:00 A.M. the morning of Orchulli's slaying. She was approached by Roberts, who was riding a white Beach Cruiser bicycle. Morton had never met or even seen Roberts before. Roberts talked to Morton and asked her if she wanted to go to his house. Morton refused and the two went in different directions. Morton ran into Roberts thirty minutes later at the store. Roberts again talked to her, asking Morton if she needed money or any other help. As she walked away, Roberts followed her, pointing to the vacant house two doors away from the convenience store. Roberts told her that he lived at the house and wanted to show it to her. He told Morton to wait until he opened the door. He went toward the back of the house and Morton waited at the same brick wall that Orchulli would be seen standing next to only minutes later. Roberts then opened the front door and told Morton to come inside.

Morton refused to go in. Roberts walked out of the house over to where she was standing at the brick wall. Roberts told Morton to write down his telephone number so that she could telephone him later.

Physical evidence was taken from the body of Orchulli at her autopsy and methodically examined by the San Diego police crime laboratory. The condition of Orchulli's clothing implied that she had been sexually assaulted. Swabs taken from her vaginal area showed that a small amount of semen was present, but analysts observed only a very limited number of sperm on the swabs. In addition, a lone pubic hair—which was determined with the aid of a microscope to be visually inconsistent with having come from Orchulli—was found. Because the vaginal swab had almost no sperm, it was clear that RFLP DNA testing would be futile. PCR would be the only technique that could be used to even attempt to obtain results. As for the pubic hair, the prospects of gaining any information from it were remote. The root of the hair appeared to be in poor condition.

The case moved slowly. Denise McGuire, the deputy district attorney assigned to prosecute Roberts, began the process of assembling her evidence in 1989. The witnesses who would describe the movements of Roberts and Orchulli were essential. The notepaper with what turned out to be Roberts's nickname, J.R., and partial telephone number found beside Orchulli's body, as well as the other evidence of Roberts's similar acts with Garcia and Morton, would be compelling. The biological evidence, however, appeared unlikely to be of much assistance. The chances of getting any DNA results proving who left the semen or pubic hair on Orchulli were minuscule. To all appearances, instead of providing helpful information to a jury, that evidence was going to prove to be a dead end.

But the attorneys representing Roberts had different ideas. Christopher Plourd was assigned the lead role of defending Roberts. He was assisted by another skilled San Diego attorney, Patricia Robinson. Plourd and Robinson were dogged in their defense of Roberts. Sensing the importance of the pubic hair, they focused their efforts on obtaining at least a portion of the root of that hair for their own testing. If DNA results showed that the hair could not have come from their client, their chances of avoiding a guilty verdict would improve.

Defendants in criminal cases have a right to get access to physical evidence seized during an investigation by law enforcement. If the seizure includes items containing biological evidence, the defense normally may obtain a portion of that evidence—if there is enough to permit multiple tests—in order to conduct their own testing. The results of testing done at the request of defense attorneys in California and most states are usually not revealed to prosecutors unless the results are to be used by the defense at the later trial. In the Roberts case the prospects that Plourd and Robinson could get some of the biological evidence for their own testing weren't good. So little of the root was attached to the hair, for example, that it was unlikely that a judge would give the defense any of the evidence. To do so would increase the probability that no one—including both the district attorney's office and Roberts's attorneys—would be able to get any results from testing.

But McGuire, a seasoned prosecutor, felt differently. In a motion she brought herself, she asked the court to split the biological evidence so that both sides would have a portion to conduct any testing they desired. It was a bold move designed to avoid any later claim, in the event Roberts was convicted, that the defense was denied an opportunity to test the evidence. After a court hearing, and with the agreement of Roberts's attorneys, the judge decided to grant McGuire's request to split the evidence. Plourd and Robinson would get a chance at their half of the evidence, which would include both the pubic hair and the vaginal swabs.

Whatever DNA existed in the pubic hair root was removed in Ed Blake's lab (the same lab used in the Moffett case discussed in Chapter 5). Ironically, it was Blake who vehemently objected to the splitting of the sample. His concern was that dividing the root DNA would eliminate the possibility of getting any results at all. But, because of the judge's ruling, half the sample was provided for testing by the prosecution; the other half was preserved for forwarding to a private investigator hired by attorneys Plourd and Robinson. A portion of the vaginal swabs taken from the body of Orchulli was similarly provided to the defense. Apart from the unusual splitting of the pubic hair DNA, nothing was out of the ordinary.

But further developments were hampering McGuire's preparations. The judge assigned the case for trial was Norbert Ehrenfreund, one of San Diego's foremost judges. During a hearing on a motion filed prior to the beginning of the trial, Ehrenfreund ruled that the previous assaults committed by Roberts on the Los Angeles victim and Roberts's wife would not be admissible during the trial. Because those attacks had little in common with the killing of Orchulli, the judge decided, they would unfairly prejudice a jury against Roberts if testimony about them were allowed.

However, Ehrenfreund did conclude that evidence of the incidents involving Garcia and Morton would be heard by the jury. Unfortunately, because of the delay between the arrest of Roberts in 1988 and the beginning of jury selection on February 1, 1991, the testimony of those witnesses was compromised. Over time their memories of the events had become less sharp. Garcia could not identify Roberts in court. Morton had forgotten a number of important details of her encounter with the defendant.

But lapses of memory and changes in testimony are common. The case would stand or fall on the other evidence linking Roberts to the killing of Orchulli. Blake performed PCR testing on the vaginal swabs and one-half of the pubic hair root. Not surprisingly, Blake was unable to get any interpretable results from the extremely low number of sperm on the vaginal swab, and he got no results whatsoever from the hair. Not even the extremely sensitive PCR process could provide any information about the DNA content of either sample.

The case was finally ready for trial in Judge Ehrenfreund's court. But before a jury had even been selected, the defense team dropped a bombshell. During a recess, Plourd informed both Ehrenfreund and McGuire that the defense had exonerating DNA results from testing by their own experts of their half of the pubic hair root and one of the vaginal swabs. Someone other than Roberts left the pubic hair and the semen, Plourd asserted. McGuire knew she had a problem. I was providing assistance to McGuire on issues involving the DNA evidence in her case. But I hadn't been working closely—or even daily—with her. Because we all believed that DNA was going to play no role, I had turned my attention to other cases. But McGuire was now in a tough spot. If the jury believed this new DNA evidence showing that the pubic hair and semen had not come from Roberts, then the jurors probably would find him not guilty of the murder of Orchulli. If they were indeed accurate, those results might prove that Roberts wasn't even Orchulli's killer. The key was to determine the accuracy of those results. That would prove a daunting task. I simply had to drop everything else and concentrate on the case against Roberts.

To start I had to obtain all the available information about the testing done by the experts hired by Roberts's attorneys. It was a reversal of roles. Now the prosecutor would have to evaluate the lab's reports, raw data, testing protocol, photographs of the evidence, and any other information that might shed light on the results we had only heard about in court. If all this information were properly disclosed, I was convinced we would get to the bottom of the defense's DNA testing. Plourd provided me with an initial report from the lab, an outfit in Dallas, Texas, named Genescreen. I wasn't familiar with the laboratory. Some quick checking revealed that it was run by Dr. Robert Giles. The only California criminal case I could determine his lab had been involved in was in San Francisco. I spoke on the telephone with the local San Francisco Police Department crime-lab analyst who had worked on that case. She said that Genescreen's work had had little impact on their case. She expressed her concern to me that the scientists there seemed to have little forensic experience and expertise. No one else in my circle of scientific and legal friends had even heard of the laboratory.

When I finally got preliminary information on the tests of the hair and swab that allegedly exonerated Roberts, I found they involved a DNA genetic marker I had never heard of. Named DQ-Beta, it was obviously related to the well-known forensic marker DQ-Alpha, which Blake and the Cetus Corporation had pioneered. But its use in criminal cases was unknown to any of my contacts.

The bare report's conclusions were clear: DNA from the pubic hair root and the vaginal swab provided to Genescreen contained the same DQ-Beta types of 3.1 and 3.2. Testing of Orchulli's known sample revealed she was a type 1.2, 3.2. Roberts was determined to have the types 1.1, 1.1. That meant that if the test results were accurate, neither Roberts nor Orchulli had left the DNA found on the hair and swab.

This result was suspicious because it excluded Orchulli, and it didn't jibe with the other findings. Blake was the second analyst to examine the vaginal swabs. The first examination of the swabs took place in Brian Wraxall's laboratory, the Serological Research Institute. Before forming the SERI lab, as it was frequently referred to, Wraxall had performed serology testing at the famed Scotland Yard laboratory in London. Wraxall immigrated to the United States in 1978 as part of a U.S. government-sponsored program to develop blood testing techniques for use in U.S. crime laboratories. In Wraxall's lab, only a tiny number of sperm could be seen on the vaginal swabs under a microscope. Blake examined the same swabs and saw only a single sperm head. The PCR technology of DNA testing was simply incapable of producing results from such a small quantity of DNA. Blake had tested the female cells from the vaginal swabs and had gotten DQ-Alpha results consistent with Orchulli. That was as expected—Orchulli's DNA on swabs taken from her. No typing was even attempted on the sperm because of the severe shortage of sperm cells for testing. Blake also had attempted to use the PCR amplification method on the half of the DNA that had been removed from the pubic hair root. He got no amplification whatsoever. That result only confirmed our expectations. The root had been in relatively poor condition. And, at that, it had been divided in two. Yet Genescreen reported unambiguous results in its report from both pieces of evidence.

Slowly, copies of the raw data from Genescreen's testing were forwarded to me. It was clear that their testing was going to have to be reviewed in detail by DNA scientists. McGuire and I scheduled a meeting with Blake in his laboratory in the East Bay area. We flew to Oakland and drove the short distance to Blake's lab in Emeryville. Blake had the foresight to recruit a few others for the meeting. Joining us were three scientists from Cetus who were responsible for the development of the DQ-Alpha typing system used by Blake and other scientists. Dr. Henry Erlich was world-renowned for his research in the application of the PCR method to both disease diagnosis and forensic testing. Dr. Rebecca Reynolds and Dr. Russell Higuchi also had played key roles in the development and validation of the techniques that used PCR for DQ-Alpha typing.

McGuire and I shared the data we had received from Genescreen with the four scientists. Although initially surprised that anyone would type a criminal case evidence sample at the DQ-Beta genetic marker (normally used in medical, not forensic, procedures), the Cetus scientists had no reason to reject any results on that basis alone. Rather, they were all troubled by the same fact that had bothered me from the beginning—how could Gene-screen's testing produce results while Blake's testing showed that there simply wasn't enough DNA to get any information? Slowly, we pieced together how Genescreen had approached the task. With the pubic hair root DNA, they had tried the PCR process on many different occasions. Only one of those attempts produced enough DNA to get results at the DQ-Beta location. We looked at the data from the various unsuccessful attempts at PCR copying. Although working from photocopies, we studied the typing results that led the laboratory to conclude that neither Orchulli nor Roberts could have left the DNA in the hair root.

We were concerned that every possible type seemed to have produced a reaction of some sort in the testing done by Genescreen. The types reported by Genescreen from the root were certainly stronger than the others, but why was each type "lighting up" to a significant degree? In DQ-Alpha or DQ-Beta testing, results are most commonly read by observing visible, dark reactions in circled areas of a test strip to which the DNA is applied. Our team of experts was concerned that the results were anything but clean and definitive. The vaginal swab results were equally problematical. Again, there appeared to be reactions at each possible type. No reason could be discerned for the across-the-board typing reactions. But we needed more data before we could mount an attack on the evidence that the defense would present to the jury. Erlich was just as concerned as we were. He seemed convinced that the results reported by Genescreen were seriously wrong. He assigned Reynolds to assist us in trying to uncover the reason for the disparity between the findings of Blake and those of Genescreen. We welcomed the help. We would need every bit of that assistance to show why those results were inaccurate, if in fact they were. If they were correct, the last thing we wanted was to convict an innocent man of a capital murder.

The most immediate problem was what to tell Judge Ehrenfreund. A jury had not yet been selected, but the process had begun. We needed to let the judge know that we wanted to have a hearing on the admissibility of Genescreen's DNA results. I would break the news to Ehrenfreund. It was decided that I would simply let the judge know our concerns with the manner in which Genescreen had carried out its testing. Under no circumstances were we challenging the science of PCR testing and its general acceptance in the scientific community. After having been a vocal and highly visible proponent of its use in criminal cases for nearly two years, my turning around and attacking the testing technology used in just one case (and a case I was now helping to prosecute) might raise questions about my integrity and objectivity. Besides, the science wasn't the cause of any problem that may have been encountered in the analysis done in Texas. Reynolds and I were convinced that the testing simply hadn't been performed correctly. Roberts's attorneys didn't oppose our request, and Ehrenfreund agreed to allow a hearing. He scheduled it for the next week. The prospective jurors would simply be given a few days off before the selection process would continue. I forwarded additional materials I received from Genescreen to Reynolds at Cetus as quickly as possible. Rather than photocopies, we requested and received high-quality X-rays of the typing results. The across-the-board reactions at all types became even easier to see. Genescreen had problems with their testing that were leading to a significant amount of contamination, artificial reactions, or both.

We also found it impossible to understand the results from the vaginal swab. Because the swab was taken from Orchulli, it was natural to expect, on the basis of common sense and of hundreds of cases, that her DNA would be found. That expectation—made even more natural by the extraordinarily low levels of sperm—was confirmed by Blake's results. Yet Genescreen's results showed no DNA consistent with the victim. Instead, their results excluded Orchulli. How could they have gotten results that eliminated Orchulli when it was obvious that her own DNA was present in quantities that appeared to dwarf those from anyone else?

The hearing started in Ehrenfreund's courtroom, and I got my chance to start questioning Genescreen's scientists. The two scientists who were involved in the analysis and interpretation of the results from the hair root and swab were Giles and Judy Floyd. Both came to San Diego and testified over the course of three days in January 1991. Reynolds sat with us at our counsel table and was of immense assistance. I asked detailed questions about the lab and the qualifications and experience of each of them, particularly in criminal cases. It turned out that Genescreen was primarily a paternity laboratory; it typically compared DNA taken from liquid blood samples from mothers, children, and alleged fathers. Only recently had the company entered the field of testing specimens in criminal cases. No other labs, Giles agreed, used the DQ-Beta genetic marker in forensic testing. He also acknowledged that they had encountered problems during their testing in the Roberts case, including seeing reactions of some sort at all possible types. Giles conceded that neither he, nor Floyd, had even examined the vaginal swab under a microscope to determine whether any sperm were on it. Giles testified that he himself had never extracted DNA from a piece of evidence or even amplified a sample using PCR in a criminal case. He agreed that the absence of results consistent with Orchulli from her own vaginal swab was troubling.

McGuire was pleased. We were getting important information from the laboratory's director that would probably give the jury cause to be concerned about the reliability of the lab's results. Floyd then testified. She had handled the samples, performed the PCR amplifications, and read the eventual results. Floyd was a Texan who didn't seem to want to give an inch. Although no master of the art of cross-examination, I felt comfortable in the world of scientists and DNA. I wasn't quite prepared for an expert witness who would concede little or nothing. Floyd may have become defensive and intransigent when I questioned her at the outset about the fact that she had no advanced degrees in any science. It may have stiffened her resolve even more when I pointed out to Judge Ehrenfreund that she was a member of no forensic scientific organizations and had testified as an expert witness on only a handful of occasions. But no one said death-penalty litigation was friendly. Although Giles had frequently conceded the problems his laboratory had come across in its testing in the Roberts case, Floyd was adamant about the accuracy of her results. Her concessions were few and far between. I admired her moxie.

At the end of the three days I thanked Ehrenfreund for allowing the hearing. The People, I stated for the record, would not oppose Roberts's attorneys calling the Genescreen witnesses to testify during the defense case in front of the jury. We were satisfied that the testimony was properly admissible. Although Reynolds, McGuire, and I all believed that the results were inaccurate, Roberts was legally entitled to present the evidence. It would be up to me to show the jury why those results should play no role in their determination of Roberts's guilt or innocence.

A jury was selected, and McGuire presented witnesses for several weeks, trying to methodically prove her case against Roberts. The events witnesses described included: Roberts's activities on the day of Orchulli's killing; the incidents with Garcia and Morton; the autopsy results; and the evidence found at the crime scene. In all, the evidence seemed to provide good circumstantial proof linking Roberts to the murder.

I told McGuire I would be glad to question Blake on the stand about his examination of the biological evidence. I think McGuire was relieved because our presentation of the prosecution's case was obviously going to delve rather deeply into sometimes highly technical issues in anticipation of the later testimony from Giles and Floyd during the defense portion of the case. I knew Blake well enough to know that his testimony would be anything but dull. Blake, as it turned out, was incensed by what he believed was unscientific testing that had been performed by Genescreen.

When Blake took the witness stand, I took time, as always, to point out to the jury his education, background, experience, and central role in the evaluation and development of PCR for use in criminal cases. Piece by piece, I went through his examination of the evidence in the Roberts case in order to give the jury early on reasonable grounds to later conclude that this was not a case in which DNA could provide reliable answers. Blake described how his examination and that of SERI had revealed little or no sperm on the vaginal swabs. He talked about the pubic hair and how unlikely it was that there was enough DNA in the root to get results. He detailed how his own DNA testing and the lack of probative results were consistent with the nature of the evidence items.

Blake had done what I thought was an excellent job of describing why DNA was providing no answers in the case. Plourd cross-examined Blake. Plourd knew Blake personally and didn't want to give him any opportunity to launch into a tirade about the testing by Genescreen that the defense would later present to the jury. But Plourd asked a question in an apparently innocuous area that called for Blake to give an opinion. I could see on Blake's face that he had had enough. "Do you really want me to give you my opinion?" Blake asked. Wisely, Plourd declined Blake's offer and sat down with no more questions. Emboldened, I stood up for redirect questioning and immediately asked Blake, "And what is that opinion?" I don't know whether Plourd had let his guard down or didn't think the answer was that important. Blake wasted no time giving it. "My opinion is that the taxpayers of San Diego have had to spend an incredible amount of money on DNA testing in this case that tells us absolutely nothing." I had to turn away from the jury to hide a smile. It was pure Blake. But as far as McGuire and I were concerned, there couldn't have been a better introduction to the defense's presentation of the DNA evidence. McGuire rested her case, and Robinson and Plourd began calling their witnesses. I felt ready for cross-examination of both Giles and Floyd. I had questions already prepared from the transcripts of their testimony during the admissibility hearing, and I had as well other areas to explore and question them about thanks to Reynolds.

Giles was scheduled to take the witness stand in a few days when Roberts's attorneys dropped another bomb. They had just received additional results from Genescreen, Plourd told Judge Ehrenfreund. McGuire and I were again dumbfounded. From RFLP testing of the vaginal swab, Plourd said, Genescreen had gotten results that excluded their client. RFLP results? That would require tens of thousands of sperm heads. We were talking about, at most, a tiny number on the swab. It seemed like a bad dream. Make that a nightmare. We were immediately given the raw data of the new testing. McGuire and I talked about objecting to the jury hearing the new results based on the lateness of our being provided the information, but decided not to. If the judge agreed with us, an enormous issue would be created on appeal. We gritted our teeth and dove into the details.

At least we were quickly given all the raw data. The RFLP X-rays provided us were easily the blurriest and most difficult to interpret that I had ever seen. Not unlike the DQ-Beta results that showed reactions at all types, the RFLP data, I thought, looked as though they had been drawn by my daughter when she was three years old. Reynolds was speechless, but for another reason—there were absolutely no RFLP results for the victim's known sample. With no RFLP pattern from the victim for comparison, Orchulli could not be excluded as the donor of the very DNA that was alleged by Genescreen to have come from someone other than Roberts. But Genescreen had an answer to that obvious question: the particular "probe" they used in the testing detected only male DNA, not female DNA, they said. Therefore, any pattern revealed by the test was necessarily from a man, not a woman.

Or so the argument went. I told McGuire not to be concerned. The RFLP exclusion of Roberts based on DNA on the vaginal swab wasn't likely to be persuasive to a jury. For example, why hadn't Genescreen done everything it could to get another known sample from Orchulli to compare with their RFLP results? Blood collected from the crime scene, samples that were taken from her body, even samples from her relatives could have been obtained. Genescreen's lack of diligence in this regard spoke volumes, I assured her. In addition, the results were so blurry, smudged, and difficult to read that I was convinced the testimony could work to our benefit. With problems of cross-reactions in the PCR results, unreadable patterns in the RFLP testing would only bolster our argument. I'm not sure McGuire believed me, but she didn't have much choice.

Giles took the witness stand and described his lab's results to the jury. On cross-examination, just as he had during the hearing, Giles conceded the difficulties his laboratory had encountered in the testing they had done. McGuire's confidence level rose. Floyd was called next. She was cordial during Plourd's questioning, but determined. My turn came, and her body language noticeably changed. I sensed that she had learned a thing or two from our first go-around. After we went over her qualifications—which the jury was hearing for the first time—Floyd performed much more effectively than she had during the hearing. I would have to narrow my questioning. I made Floyd point to the X-rays of both her PCR testing and the RFLP results that had only recently been provided to us. The poor quality of the raw data appeared to be having an impact on the jury. Floyd seemed defensive in her answers to my questions about the problems that were apparent in her testing.

Then I made a sudden decision to cut short my questioning. One of the most effective tools a trial lawyer can use is to ask a witness a question to which there is no good answer. I had saved one for Floyd. I went back to the steps she had taken to examine the vaginal swabs. Floyd conceded that she had not personally looked at the swabs under a microscope to determine whether any sperm were visible and that she was not even qualified to identify sperm. Instead, she had had someone else look for them. I then asked her whether she was familiar with the fact that Blake had seen very few sperm on the swabs. She said that she was. I then asked whether she was aware that Blake had been unable to detect any DNA on the swab other than that from the victim. She agreed the she was. It was time for the no-answer question. "Do you think you're as qualified as Dr. Blake in DNA testing?" "Yes I am," she replied firmly. I didn't have any other questions, I told the jury and Ehrenfreund. There wasn't much comparison in their stature and qualifications in the DNA world, I thought to myself. I hoped the jury would see it the same way.

But McGuire and I hadn't wanted to put all our money on my cross-examination of the Genescreen scientists. We had discussed having Reynolds ready to testify after the defense had finished calling witnesses to rebut the testimony of Giles and Floyd. But we thought that Reynolds might be seen by the jury as too invested in the DQ-Alpha testing system because of her work at the Cetus Corporation and might be viewed as a natural opponent of the method used by Genescreen. Instead, we turned to the medical-diagnostics world. And what better place than a hospital that treated children's diseases.

Children's Hospital in San Diego was famous for its expertise and skill in the treatment of children. Less well known was its Molecular Genetics Laboratory. Inside a facility that took up less space than a few school class-rooms, scientists were using DNA testing on a daily basis to diagnose diseases commonly suffered by children. The man who ran the laboratory was Dr. Brad Popovich. I spent a good deal of time with Popovich and was able to gain his interest in our case. Although he had no personal experience in criminal testing, Popovich had extraordinary experience in the use of both RFLP and PCR testing, both in disease-diagnosis and paternity cases. He had also been a regular attendee at scientific meetings that often included segments on forensic testing. When we discussed developments in the Roberts case, he agreed to help.

Popovich reviewed all the data we had been provided by Genescreen. When he had completed his own analysis of the information, Popovich gave us his opinion. The results Genescreen had reported, he believed, were not scientifically sound. The problems that Reynolds had identified for us were those that troubled him the most. During the prosecution's rebuttal, Popovich took the witness stand. He set out in detail during my questioning why he believed the results that allegedly excluded Roberts from having been the donor of the pubic hair and semen on the vaginal swabs were wrong. His testimony, we thought, was powerful.

The evidence was complete, and both sides argued their cases to the jury. Unfortunately, Roberts's jury was unable to reach a verdict. Some of the jurors told McGuire after a mistrial had been declared by Judge Ehrenfreund that they had rejected the DNA results from Genescreen, but were nonetheless deadlocked on whether there had been proof beyond a reasonable doubt that Roberts was the man who killed Orchulli.

The case was set for a retrial. New experts took a fresh look at fingerprints and a bloody palm print that had been found in the vacant house. The palm print had come from the wall above where Orchulli's head was lying. Although described as unreadable during the first trial, it was examined by additional experts and identified as having been left by Roberts. Prior to the retrial and with the death penalty still looming as possible punishment, Roberts pleaded guilty to murder in the first degree. He was sentenced to a term of thirty years to life in the California Department of Corrections.

Maybe Blake was right. Tens of thousands of dollars had been spent in one case on DNA testing that eventually led nowhere. But the importance of DNA testing was beginning to be understood by jurors who decided the fate of defendants. And that could only help them in making the decision about guilt or innocence in cases yet to come.

DNA testing had already proved to be the most powerful tool ever developed to determine who had committed the most serious of crimes. Its importance in identifying those offenders, however, was clearly exceeded by its ability to exonerate those wrongfully suspected—or even convicted—of criminal acts.

Frederick "Ricky" Daye was arrested in 1984 and was soon charged with a series of crimes committed against an adult woman in January of that same year. The woman had been leaving a drugstore in the city of San Diego on her way to her car in a parking lot. Before she reached her auto, a man suddenly opened her car door and forced her into the passenger seat. That man then let a second man into the backseat of the car. When they were able to find only a few dollars in the victim's purse, the men took a number of items of jewelry and then drove her to another location. Rather than let her go there, the men removed the woman's clothes, and both of them raped her in her car. Eventually, they dumped her by the side of the road in a residential area of the city some distance from the parking lot. The victim reported the crimes to police. She was interviewed and provided police with descriptions of both of her attackers. One of the men, she said, had a distinctive silver, or gold-capped, front upper tooth. The detective who was assigned the case began an investigation to try to identify the suspects.

An important feature of the case was that a bystander outside the drugstore witnessed the men forcing the woman into her car; the bystander knew the first person to be arrested for the crimes, a man named David Pringle. The case was brought to the district attorney's office by detectives of the San Diego Police Department. The case was reviewed by prosecutors in the Major Violators Unit. The division specialized in robberies and other serious crimes, particularly those committed by repeat offenders. Pringle was charged with the crimes committed against the victim, including robbery, kidnapping, and the sexual attack. At his trial, Pringle denied having anything to do with the crimes. Nevertheless, he was convicted of kidnapping to commit robbery and rape and was sentenced to prison for life.

Eight days after the attack, Daye was detained by police when they stopped a vehicle he was driving for a mechanical violation. Daye had an open container of alcohol and also had no identification with him. He then gave police a false name. One of the officers was aware of the ongoing rape investigation and thought that Daye resembled the victim's description of one of her attackers. The police drove Daye to the station and had photos taken of him. The police told Daye that because he had given them a false name, the photos would assist them in identifying him in the future. He was cited for the open container and the false-information violation and was then released. Daye appeared to fit the description of the woman's second assailant, even down to the metal-capped front tooth. As a result, the detective who was assigned the case was notified of Daye's brief detention, and he put together a photo lineup in which Daye's photograph was placed alongside photos of men who were similar in appearance. When the lineup was shown to the victim, she immediately picked out Daye as the man who had raped her.

Daye was arrested two days later. He denied having anything to do with the assault. Daye said he was at a completely different location at the time of the crimes. The case against Daye seemed strong. At the time of his initial detention, Daye had given the patrol officer a wrong name and other false information. He matched the description given by the victim. Both the victim and the other eyewitness selected him from a photo lineup.

And the evidence mounted. A semen stain was located on the jeans the victim was wearing at the time of the attack. An analyst at the San Diego Police Department crime lab tested the stain in 1984 using ABO blood group typing. That testing showed that the semen had been left by a man who had blood type B. Roughly 15 percent of the male population has that type; so did Daye. Ironically, the evidence in Pringle's trial established that Pringle was also a type B.

The case against Daye went to trial. Pringle was called to the witness stand to testify against Daye, but he successfully used his Fifth Amendment privilege against self-incrimination to avoid answering any questions. Daye's attorney was able to convince the trial judge to disallow—or "suppress"— the photo-lineup identifications by the victim and the eyewitness. The judge agreed that the photos taken of Daye during the brief traffic stop were the result of an unlawful detention. The judge did decide, however, that the victim and eyewitness would be permitted to testify in court that Daye was the man who had kidnapped the victim.

The jury heard the testimony of the victim and eyewitness and their identifications of Daye; they were shown Daye's upper right silver tooth. They learned of his lies to police at his first detention. Scientific testimony in the form of serological testing placed Daye in the group of men who could have left the semen on the victim's pants. Daye decided not to testify in his own defense. If he had, the fact that he had been convicted previously of robbery in another state would have been heard by the jury. Daye's alibi witnesses—including his fiancée and friends—were unconvincing, and their stories unraveled during cross-examination by the prosecutor.

The jury convicted Daye of the kidnapping, robbery, and rape charges. His sentence: life in prison plus an additional term of over fourteen years. Daye was devastated. He maintained his innocence of the charges from the time of his arrest up to and including his sentencing by the judge. Two years after he began serving his prison sentence, his appeal was heard and denied by the court of appeal. The attorney appointed to represent Daye for his appeal was unable to convince the California Supreme Court to hear the case. Appeals based on a claim of innocence are rarely successful unless new evidence becomes available that raises a serious question about the guilt of the person who was convicted. Daye was limited to raising claims that procedural mistakes had denied him a fair trial. Those claims failed.

In 1990, after Daye had served six hard years in prison, a glimmer of hope appeared. After Pringle learned that Daye had been convicted of crimes for the same attack that Pringle had been sentenced for, Pringle signed an affidavit swearing that Daye had had nothing to do with the attack and that another man had helped him in the assault. Pringle named the other attacker. Daye went back to court and was appointed another attorney to represent him based on the new information from Pringle. For two years nothing happened. To Daye's disappointment, the attorney did almost nothing in his case.

But Daye had also been in contact with a nonprofit group of appellate attorneys in San Diego known as Appellate Defenders. In particular, he had dealt with Carmela Simoncini, a highly skilled appeals lawyer. Simoncini was familiar with Daye's case. She also was aware that one of the problems with older cases in which the appeals are complete is that physical evidence in the case may already have been destroyed by the police agency that collected that evidence. Simoncini learned that the agency that had investigated the case, the San Diego Police Department, planned to do just that. The court appointed Simoncini to take over Daye's case from the previous attorney. The department agreed to preserve the remaining physical evidence in the case.

Simoncini pressed forward. She requested a hearing in the San Diego Superior Court to get access to the physical evidence for purposes of DNA testing. Eight years after Daye was sentenced to prison for life he wanted to use this new tool to demonstrate his innocence. Eventually, the court of appeal ordered that two thousand dollars be provided by the County of San

Diego to investigate Daye's claim of innocence. The court of appeal also ordered that the physical evidence be released for DNA testing. That testing was performed by Cellmark, and a report describing the results was issued in April 1994. The laboratory had used PCR DQ-Alpha testing. The results conclusively proved that the semen stain on the victim's jeans could not have come from either Daye or Pringle. I reviewed the results and could immediately tell they excluded both Daye and Pringle as contributors of the semen. As a result, the district attorney's office agreed that charges against Daye should be dismissed. His conviction was reversed, and Daye was released from prison.

Daye had served ten years in the California state prison system for a set of crimes he had not committed. DNA had conclusively demonstrated his innocence, despite the fact that previous scientific testing had indicated that Daye could have left that evidence. Equally important, two eyewitnesses had been shown to be wrong in their identifications of the person who had committed extremely serious crimes. Eyewitness identification corroborated by scientific evidence had led to many prosecutors' greatest fear: convicting someone of a crime that he or she did not commit.

Two postscripts to the exoneration of Daye stand out. First, in 2000, six years after his release from prison, the California legislature and governor enacted legislation authorizing the payment of compensation to defendants convicted of and imprisoned for crimes they did not commit. The law calls for the payment of one hundred dollars for each day an inmate was wrongfully imprisoned. After its enactment, a lawyer in the California attorney general's office telephoned me and asked me whether the State of California should provide compensation to Daye. The law did not require compensation to inmates exonerated before the date it became effective, January 1, 2001. I told the deputy attorney general that I believed that Daye deserved far more than any government agency could provide. The deputy agreed and decided to pay Daye despite not having any statutory obligation to do so.

Second, what about the other man that Pringle named? The same PCR test that exonerated Daye included that man as someone who could have left the evidence. A photograph of him obtained by police revealed that he had a metal cap on the same tooth as Daye did. His photograph was shown to the victim after Daye was released from prison. She adamantly denied that he was the man who had attacked her along with Pringle and continued to insist that Daye was, in fact, the other assailant. As a result of the victim's insistence that it was Daye who had assaulted her, the district attorney's office decided not to file charges against the man.

Daye was saved by DNA after losing ten years of his life in state prison. But this new tool, PCR, could now be applied on a larger scale to solve more and more cases and, more important, to absolve innocent men and women who were suspected of committing crimes. As we will see in the next chapter, one man would learn that lesson in a way that no one could have anticipated. Keeping a family from crumbling would rely on those very initials, PCR.

CHAPTER SEVEN

A Child and a Critical Nightshirt

―・―

Child-molestation cases are often the most difficult, challenging, and draining ones for investigators, lawyers, and judges. They can evoke primitive and emotional responses from jurors and court watchers alike. But abuse of children is a fact of life and is often met head-on in courts across the United States. Courtrooms in San Diego are no exception. Other than in a handful of cases, I had managed to avoid the often-complex area of child molestation. One case, however, became a memorial to the difficulties and unique problems that can be encountered with child victims, their interviews, and the social-services systems that deal with the abuse of children.

Alicia, a vibrant eight-year-old, lived with her father, mother, and six-year-old brother, Joshua, in U.S. Navy housing in the Serra Mesa area of San Diego. Her father, James, was in the navy and stationed on a nearby ship. On an early Tuesday morning, May 9, 1989, young Alicia told her mother, Denise, that it hurt when she went to the bathroom. Denise saw blood coming from Alicia and phoned James at work. Because Denise didn't drive, James came home and took both Alicia and her mother to a navy clinic. Denise and James were concerned about their daughter's condition, but Alicia had a history of infections of her urinary tract and was frequently treated for them.

The three waited in the reception room while Alicia watched television and read books with her parents. At about 8:30 that morning the family was seen by a doctor. The parents told the physician about Alicia's problems going to the bathroom and said that they had observed blood on the back of her nightshirt and on her bedsheets. The doctor examined Alicia and was stunned to discover that she had suffered serious injuries. Those injuries included a tear between her rectum and vaginal area, along with a gaping opening in her anus that also revealed multiple lacerations. The doctor believed the injuries were the result of molestation. Alicia denied to the doctor that anyone had done anything to her that led to her injuries.

Alicia's parents were questioned by the treating physician, but they denied any knowledge of how Alicia could have been hurt. James and Denise were told by the doctor that he would have to inform the county's Child Protective Services (CPS) of his findings. Alicia, he explained, would need to be seen at the Center for Child Protection, a facility attached to Children's Hospital. Personnel at the center specialized in the examination and treatment of victims of child abuse. James and Denise acknowledged what was going to happen and agreed to cooperate.

San Diego police and CPS were both called and arrived later at the navy clinic. Alicia, after talking to a representative of CPS, was transported by police to the Center for Child Protection, where she underwent a comprehensive examination that included looking for other evidence of sexual abuse. The findings mirrored those at the clinic. Fresh blood was observed from a tear in her perineum, the area bounded by the vagina and anus. The rectum itself was unusually large and two fresh cuts were observed inside. The doctor who conducted the examination believed the injuries were the result of forced penetration of Alicia's genital and anal openings. The same doctor believed that the object used to penetrate Alicia was approximately the size of an erect male penis. The physician did not, however, observe any evidence of semen on Alicia. Fortunately, that same day a surgeon was able to successfully repair the injuries that Alicia had suffered.

The doctor who initially examined Alicia at the Center for Child Protection told Alicia that someone must have hurt her. Alicia answered that a man had come in her bedroom window, taken her out of the house, and then hurt her. A CPS worker came to the navy clinic and interviewed Alicia and her parents that same day. Alicia told the representative that she did not remember anything out of the ordinary happening the night before, between going to bed and getting up the next morning. Alicia denied that her father or anyone else had ever touched her inappropriately. Confused, the worker asked Alicia why she had not told him about the intruder that she had described to the doctor. Alicia answered that she had forgotten.

James and Denise told the CPS worker that they had no idea how the injuries had occurred. All they could speculate was that Alicia might have hurt herself while playing on a swing the day before. They did notice that the window to the bedroom that Joshua slept in was open that morning, but they had seen no sign of an intruder. They also told the representative that Alicia had awakened a couple of times that night to use the bathroom, but that she had not complained to either of them of any pain or other problem.

San Diego police began an investigation into the cause of the horrible injuries that Alicia had suffered. A detective with the Child Abuse Unit talked to Alicia the afternoon of the same day, May 9. Alicia told the detective that a man had come into the house through her brother Joshua's window and had then carried her out. The man told her that he was her uncle, but she knew that he was not. Alicia described the man as white, in his twenties, and a little taller than her mother. The man, she told the investigator, had short brown hair, some freckles, and a pimple on the lower right side of his lip. The clothing he was wearing included a short-sleeved white shirt with red stripes and brown pants. Alicia described how the man had taken her outside through the window and then put her in a car that was green like her grandfather's. The man drove around the corner near Alicia's house and stopped by a grassy area near a fence. When the detective asked Alicia what the man did, she answered, "He stuck his private part in my butt and here," pointing to her vaginal area. She said that when she started to cry, the man threatened her. She was then driven back to her home and the man placed her back in her bed. Alicia said that she went into her mother's room, got her cat, and then went back to her own bed.

The same investigator then interviewed Denise. The mother recounted that she and her husband had gone to bed about 8:00 the night before. Another child-abuse detective interviewed James while Alicia was being examined at the Center for Child Protection. James described how he had gone into Alicia's bedroom to check on her at about 10:30 P.M. He noticed that Alicia had the kitten in her bed, so he took the cat with him as he left her room. He told the detective that that was the last time he saw Alicia before he awoke the next morning. The detectives discussed their interviews and were troubled. James's statement that he had last seen Alicia at around 10:30 P.M. appeared to contradict both his and Denise's earlier statement to CPS that they had seen Alicia get up twice at approximately midnight to go to the bathroom. The investigators were also bothered by a statement James made to the detective during his interview: "If I did do it, I don't remember if I did it or not."

James and the detectives drove to the home in Serra Mesa. Fingerprints were lifted from the window that had been opened, and a shoe print found underneath that window was photographed. The shoe print was only a partial one, and the fingerprints were smeared. One of the partial fingerprints turned out to be consistent with that of a child. The investigators took the clothing worn by Alicia, her bedsheets, and a pillowcase. Each had on it what appeared to the investigators to be blood.

The next day, James sat for a polygraph examination with police. The results were inconclusive. James told the examiner during the questioning that if he was involved in his daughter's assault, he had completely blanked it out of his mind and didn't recall the incident in any way. Denise was interviewed again. In her interview that day, she told a detective that it was at about 6:45 A.M. that Alicia complained that she didn't feel well and that it hurt to go to the bathroom. Denise told the investigator that it was not unusual for Alicia to have urinary infections and that it had appeared she had developed another one. The investigators directed their attention toward James as a potential suspect because of his statement about possibly "blanking" the incident out of his mind. Alicia was reinterviewed days later by a social worker at the center. She told the social worker that she didn't like talking about what had happened to her because it had been so scary. When asked by the worker whom she would feel safe with at home, Alicia answered that it would be her mother and brother. But Alicia again told the social worker that a stranger had come in the window and taken her out of her brother's bedroom. The worker concluded from her statements and demeanor that Alicia was afraid to describe exactly how she had been hurt.

A second polygraph examination was administered at the request of the attorney who would later represent James in juvenile-court hearings to determine whether Alicia should be made a dependent child of the court rather than be permitted to remain in the custody of her parents. The examiner concluded that James was telling the truth when he denied any involvement in Alicia's injuries.

The San Diego Police Department crime lab was given the task of examining the evidence collected during the investigation. After sampling more than sixty areas of staining on Alicia's clothing and the bedding, the lab reported in late July that no semen was found. Blood was detected on a rectal swab taken from Alicia, along with the crotch and rear area of her panties, her nightshirt, the fitted sheet, the bedspread, and a piece of paper that was also collected by police.

But the consequences of the attack on Alicia weren't limited to law enforcement's efforts to determine who was responsible. As a result of what had happened to her, custody of Alicia was temporarily taken away from her parents. If Alicia was to be placed with anyone other than her parents, a petition had to be filed by the county Department of Social Services (DSS) within forty-eight hours of Alicia's originally being removed from her parents. The decision was then made by the attorney representing DSS—which by law was my own office, the district attorney's—that a petition would be filed seeking an order of the court that temporary custody of Alicia be with someone other than her parents. From just before her surgery on May 9, Denise was denied any opportunity to see Alicia. James was forbidden by DSS to even talk to Alicia. At a later time, limited, supervised visits with Alicia by Denise and Joshua were permitted. Alicia was placed in a foster home, then a second home, and later with a third set of foster parents. James was allowed to see Alicia for the first time since the May 9 incident on July 17. On August 16, a month after James was allowed to see his daughter, Alicia's then-foster mother returned Alicia to the Center for Child Protection for a follow-up visit with her original treating physician. The foster mother told the doctor that Alicia was afraid at bedtime, wanted to check all windows to make sure they were locked at night, and wanted the foster family's young child to sleep with her. The foster mother also told the physician that Alicia knew who had attacked her but had not said to her who that person was.

Legal proceedings and hearings in the juvenile court continued for months to determine who should have custody of Alicia. Separate attorneys were appointed to represent Alicia, James, and Denise. The formal petition filed in the juvenile court claimed that Alicia needed to be taken away from James and Denise as a result of her being molested while in their care. The petition also alleged as a basis for her removal from the home that Alicia was unable or unwilling to name her attacker. From that point, James was appointed an attorney to represent him. He would later hire an attorney with money he borrowed from his parents. The case moved through the juvenile "dependency" process, albeit at a slow pace. For months, the case for removing Alicia was grounded on the allegation that the attack had occurred while Alicia was in the care of her parents and that that care was negligent, rather than on the direct claim that her father had committed the attack.

Fights in and out of court took place about whether the attorney representing James was receiving all the reports, documents, and other information—referred to as "discovery" in the legal system—that he was entitled to. Part of the problem was the number of agencies involved: the San Diego Police Department, the Center for Child Protection, Children's Hospital, DSS, even separate divisions of the district attorney's office. One of the areas James's attorney wanted discovery of were reports of what he believed were similar molestations that had occurred in the same area where Alicia had lived with her family. Such reports could be used to try to determine whether someone else could have attacked Alicia. But the road to getting that information was full of potholes.

Some of the detectives who were investigating the attack on Alicia were also involved in the quest for the person or persons who were responsible for other assaults in the Serra Mesa area. And not just in the same general area. Four young girls who had been attacked resided not only within the same navy housing project as Alicia but also within approximately one block of Alicia and her parents. The time of the attacks was just as important. They began in late April, just a few weeks before Alicia was injured. In some of the other assaults the perpetrator apparently entered the homes of the victims through a window. One of the victims—a four-year-old girl—was removed through her bedroom window, kidnapped, and then sexually assaulted. This attack occurred on May 13, five days after Alicia was attacked. That victim also described being taken away in a car.

San Diego police eventually focused on a suspect in the other molestations based on information that was gradually provided to investigators. However, the possible connection to Alicia apparently eluded police. The suspect, Albert Carder, had come to San Diego from San Luis Obispo, California, and lived in an apartment in another part of the city. But he spent time with a friend he knew from the navy who lived in the same housing project as Alicia and the other victims. Carder stayed with the family off and on for about a year before allegations surfaced that he had been molesting the family's daughter for some time. In fact, the night before Alicia was attacked, Carder had tried to enter the same family's home and kidnap the same victim; she later told police that Carder had been molesting her for months. But the sharing of information was difficult, in part because the other molestation cases were being investigated by the San Diego Police Department Sex Crimes Division. Alicia's case was assigned to the Child Abuse Unit, probably because of the early belief that Alicia's father was responsible for his daughter's injuries. Ironically, on May 23, two weeks after the incident with Alicia, someone attempted to break into the bedroom of Alicia's brother, Joshua. An alarm placed at the window by James after the attack on Alicia probably thwarted the entry. Police responded. Hours later, the alarm was tripped again. Police again came to the home. Fingerprints were collected each time; however, the prints could not be located when police looked for them later. In June, only a month after the molestation of Alicia, Carder was arrested for three of the attacks that had occurred in the neighborhood. He was charged with and convicted of those assaults and sentenced to prison.

A year later, DNA testing would link Carder to the kidnapping and assault of the four-year-old neighbor of Alicia. The match came from a comparison of a known sample taken from Carder to a semen stain found by criminalists on the child's T-shirt.

James had hired Michael McGlinn, a skillful defense attorney, to represent him in his criminal case. McGlinn knew that the existence of any other attacks on young girls, especially in the same neighborhood, could be extremely important to James's defense. But McGlinn was severely hampered in his efforts to investigate the other attacks. He had been told by James and Denise of other assaults in the neighborhood but had been given no copies of the police reports of those incidents. McGlinn hired a private investigator, Michael Newman, to try to get additional information. Newman spoke to others who lived in the neighborhood and obtained details. His reports to McGlinn were ultimately provided to the district attorney's office.

Alicia was undergoing counseling and therapy in the months that followed her assault. Finally, in June 1990, a DSS worker spoke to one of the child-abuse detectives and told him that Alicia had finally revealed the identity of her attacker. The worker told the investigator that Alicia had named her father as the person who had molested her one year earlier. Alicia was returned to the Center for Child Protection for an interview with a social worker. In that interview Alicia named her father as the person who had hurt her. Alicia also stated that her father had used what she described as his "private parts" to hurt her. Alicia then told the social worker that her father had told her to tell the story about the man who had come through the window to hurt her. Alicia told the worker that she felt nervous talking about what had happened to her and that she felt bad about her father. She said that nothing came out of her father's penis during the molestation, which was then believed by police to be consistent with the absence of any findings of semen by the crime laboratory.

In September 1990, sixteen months after the injuries were inflicted on Alicia, the case was finally submitted by the San Diego Police Department to the district attorney's office for a decision about whether to prosecute James. The deputy district attorney who was assigned the case for review discussed the evidence at length with one of the child-abuse investigators who had been involved in the case from its beginning. Three months later, in December, James was arrested, and formal charges were filed against him for the assault on his daughter. The complaint alleged two counts of committing a lewd and lascivious act on Alicia and also charged that in the commission of each crime James had inflicted great bodily injury on her. The charges included allegations that there had been substantial sexual contact in each instance and that James had violated a position of special trust in the commission of the crimes. The allegations, if proved or admitted in a guilty plea, would make it highly likely that James would be sentenced to state prison.

A preliminary hearing of the charges against James was held in late February 1991. The original physician from the Center for Child Protection testified to the medical findings from the physical examination of Alicia on May 9, 1989. The physician also detailed Alicia's statements, including her account of someone coming through the window, taking her outside, and then hurting her. Alicia, now ten years old, also testified at the hearing. She said that her father had hurt her in her "private" and her "butt." She used the term *molested* in describing what had happened to her, a word she said she learned from one of her therapists. Alicia testified that the therapist had told her what the word meant. Alicia told the judge who presided over the preliminary hearing that on the night of May 8, after she went to bed, she heard someone walking down the hallway outside the bedroom. The footsteps scared her. Alicia testified that her father came into the room. Although there were no lights on inside the room, there was light from the outside. Her father took off his shirt and pants, touched her with his hands and his private part, and then put his private part into her own. She told the judge that she had made up the whole story about the man who came in the window and took her away. She said she had told the story about the other man because she was scared and thought that her father would be mad with her if she told the truth about what had happened. Alicia also acknowledged that she told people, even after she left the Center for Child Protection and was not living with her parents, that she had been hurt by the man who came in the window and took her away.

The judge who heard the preliminary-hearing testimony decided that the evidence was enough to hold James to answer the charges in superior court. The formal charging document that would trigger a trial, an information, was filed on March 7, 1991. A trial date was set. But the deputy district attorney who was assigned to the case, David Rubin, was concerned. He knew that proving the case against James would be difficult, particularly because the physical evidence that was seized in the investigation of the crimes had revealed little. The fact that Alicia had told conflicting stories about who had attacked her, without other circumstantial evidence pointing to the father, was crucial. The case was also troubling to Rubin for another reason. McGlinn had been successful in the dependency case in persuading the juvenile-court judge to order the release to him of records of therapy sessions that Alicia had taken part in since her attack. After reviewing those records, McGlinn was convinced that they showed that Alicia had been brainwashed into identifying her father as the man who had assaulted her.

As soon as the preliminary hearing was over, Rubin spoke with criminalist Annette Peer at the police crime lab. Would it be possible, Rubin asked, for toxicology tests to be done on the bloodstains from the sheet and Alicia's clothes to try to determine whether Alicia might have been drugged before or during the course of her molestation. If so, that might explain why Alicia hadn't immediately complained either at the time of the attack or the next morning about what had happened to her. Peer did some checking. It turned out that to perform the tests, the evidence would have to be examined by the FBI at its Washington, D.C., laboratory. Rubin requested that the items be forwarded for the testing.

Before the evidence was shipped, Peer decided to take another look at it because the laboratory had updated its instruments and obtained an alternate light source, a device used to screen items for the presence of semen. Peer wanted to take another look at the clothing and sheet, just in case she had missed any semen stains when the evidence had been examined two years earlier with the department's now-outdated equipment. The result was a shocker. Peer located what she confirmed to be a semen stain on the front center area of young Alicia's nightshirt. Even before the discovery by Peer, attorney McGlinn wanted an opportunity to have the physical evidence examined by his own experts. It was clear to McGlinn that the possibility existed that that evidence might have some clue that would establish James's innocence. Before he could gain access to the evidence for that purpose, the existence of the semen stain came to light.

McGlinn and Rubin—who had now enlisted my help—both wanted Ed Blake to look at the semen stain in his Northern California lab. The evidence collected from Alicia was sent to Blake for examination and analysis. Although Blake observed no sperm heads under a microscope from his own samples taken from the semen stain on the nightshirt—and could see only one lone sperm head when he examined a slide prepared by Peer from her earlier discovery of the stain—he was able to identify the stain as semen by chemical methods. Because of the absence of an enzyme called amylase, Blake also determined that the stain was not mixed with saliva. He concluded that the semen was from an individual who either did not produce sperm or who had an extremely low sperm count. A sample of James's semen was obtained and forwarded to Blake. From his examination of that known sample, Blake was able to conclude that James was not aspermic (a person who does not produce sperm), and furthermore his sperm count was that of a normal male. Based on those results alone, Blake concluded that it was unlikely that James was the donor of the stain found on Alicia's nightshirt.

Blake continued with additional testing. He was unable to detect any ABO blood-grouping types in the semen stain. Blake turned to DNA analysis using the PCR technique and the DQ-Alpha genetic marker to try to determine who could, or couldn't, be the person who left the stain on Alicia's nightshirt. The testing revealed DQ-Alpha types 1.1 and 4 in the stain on the shirt. Alicia was determined by Blake to be a 2, 3. She was obviously not the donor of the semen stain to begin with, but her types were different. Thus, the 1.1 and 4 types were likely to be those of the semen donor. In addition, only about 9 percent of the population carry the types 1.1, 4. Blake got the same results from a stain he found on Alicia's panties. The first conclusion that Blake could reach was the result of pure genetics. Because Alicia's types were 2, 3, her biological father must have had either the 2 or the 3 type (or allele) or both to contribute to Alicia at conception. Whoever left the semen could not be Alicia's father.

Blake telephoned me with his preliminary results. A report followed in short order. I reviewed Blake's report and the attached photographs and data. The results were clear. His interpretations, not surprisingly, were completely supported by his test results. I discussed them with Rubin. The next step was obvious. Samples of blood from both James and Carder would need to be forwarded to Blake, as well as a sample taken from Denise. McGlinn agreed with our decision. When he tested the known sample from James, Blake confirmed his preliminary results. James was determined to be types 1.2, 3. Denise proved to be types 2, 2. Alicia could therefore have inherited the 2 allele from Denise and the 3 allele from James. Her types were perfectly consistent with her being the daughter of James and Denise. More important, James was thereby excluded as the person who left the semen stain on Alicia's nightshirt and panties. Carder's sample provided the results that filled the picture: his types were determined to be 1.1, 4—exactly the types found in both semen stains.

Rubin, after he told James's attorney McGlinn of the discovery of the semen stain on the nightshirt, kept everyone apprised of the progress of the further testing. He agreed with McGlinn that James's trial should be delayed until Blake obtained his results from testing of the clothing, as well as the samples from James, Denise, and Carder. Rubin also kept the parties in the juvenile-court proceedings informed of the ongoing analysis.

But the case in juvenile court was continuing. For over two years who would eventually be granted permanent custody of Alicia was in doubt.

McGlinn, who was substituted in as James's attorney in the juvenile-court hearings, fought to delay the hearing scheduled to determine whether James's and Denise's right to custody of Alicia should be forever terminated. That hearing was set for October 1991, even though the preliminary results from Blake were already known. The attorneys trying to permanently remove Alicia from her parents argued that even though James was likely not the donor of the semen stain, the attempt to terminate parental rights was based on neglect rather than on James's being the person who attacked Alicia. The hearing was continued again to November.

Blake prepared a brief, summary report of his findings on November 14, 1991. That report was immediately transmitted to prosecutor Rubin. We discussed the findings and informed the district attorney of them. The decision was then made to dismiss all criminal charges against James. Rubin hastily prepared a motion to dismiss the case that day and filed it the next morning in the San Diego Superior Court. A hearing was held the same day in front of Judge Fredric L. Link. Link granted the district attorney's motion to dismiss the criminal charges against James. Link also granted a request by McGlinn for a specific finding by the court that James was factually innocent of the charges that he had attacked and assaulted his daughter.

James was exonerated by DNA testing, and the court agreed. Alicia was ultimately returned to her parents. But the story didn't end there. RFLP DNA typing requested by the district attorney's office was later conducted by Cellmark on the same semen stain originally discovered by Peer at the San Diego Police Department. That testing, like Blake's PCR analysis, showed that Carder could be the person who left the stain. The chance that someone other than Carder was that person: less than one in three million. Carder was later formally charged by Deputy District Attorney Robert Eichler with the May 1989 attack on Alicia. Carder was already serving a state prison sentence for the assaults on the other girls who lived in the same neighborhood as Alicia. In 1995 Carder pleaded guilty to the molestation and was sentenced to state prison for twenty-five years, that sentence to begin only after he finished the prison term he was already serving.

The lives of Alicia, her mother and father, and her brother were forever altered by the events that began the morning of May 9, 1989. Law enforcement, the criminal-justice process, and the juvenile-court system seemed to the family to create a roadblock at every step in their attempt to show that someone else was responsible for the vicious attack on young Alicia. Alicia came within days of being permanently taken away from her family. But justice eventually prevailed, albeit years later. Many came to the aid of James and his family in the midst of their tragedy. But two individuals in the criminal proceedings stand out. Deputy District Attorney Rubin doggedly pursued testing of the physical evidence, even though it appeared that it could not provide any information. Even more important, McGlinn never gave up in his quest to show that James was innocent of the acts that law enforcement, the social-services system, and even the district attorney's office had already concluded he was responsible for. DNA proved to be the tool that led to an innocent man's being exonerated and a young child's being reunited with her family.

DNA would play a role on behalf of the innocent in a significant number of cases yet to come. But it would not always prevail in convincing a jury to return a guilty verdict, even when the evidence was overwhelming. Although the power of DNA testing was becoming well known to attorneys, judges, and jurors, so were counterarguments that cast doubt on the conclusiveness of DNA evidence. For instance, it was argued that DNA testing could not pinpoint when a particular sample of DNA material was left or deposited at a crime scene or on a victim. Other objections included allegations that DNA test results, even if believed, did not prove that the defendant committed the crime; that contamination or mistakes made during the testing process made DNA evidence unreliable; and even that the evidence was planted by law enforcement. Only in Southern California would a case arise in which all four objections were used.

CHAPTER EIGHT

DNA and a
Football Hero Collide

O n Friday, June 17, 1994, I was sitting in our new house in the Mission Hills area of San Diego watching a National Basketball Association play-off game on television, when a curious news flash came across the screen. Suddenly, the network cut away from the game to a white sport-utility vehicle traveling down a Los Angeles freeway. What made the scene so odd was the fact that there was no other traffic on the interstate. In LA that happens only in the movies. This episode, of course, was the beginning of the investigation and trial of Orenthal James "O. J." Simpson.

We had all heard about the gruesome killings a few days earlier of Simpson's former wife, Nicole Brown Simpson, and Ron Goldman, a waiter and aspiring actor. O. J. Simpson, who had left his nearby Rockingham home shortly after the killings, we were told, had flown to Chicago for a marketing promotion. Simpson was contacted by LA Police Department (LAPD) investigators about the murders and immediately flew home. Shortly after his arrival, he was detained, questioned by police, and then released. I remember thinking that week that Simpson had an outstanding attorney representing him, Howard Weitzmann. Weitzmann had obtained an acquittal of drug charges leveled years earlier against the innovative car designer John DeLorean, another of his clients. But Weitzmann was quickly replaced by another well-known LA lawyer, Robert Shapiro. Ultimately, on the Friday of the basketball game, LA District Attorney Gil Garcetti announced that two counts of murder had been filed against Simpson. The charges included special circumstances that would make Simpson eligible for the maximum punishment short of execution: life imprisonment without the possibility of parole.

Other than that I, like many, knew little about the case. I knew a great deal about Simpson's superstar role as an athlete, as the counter-jumping star of Hertz rental-car commercials, and in less-than-memorable motion pictures. The live "chase" down I-405 on television, however, was surreal. Police cars lined the on-ramps and off-ramps to the freeway to block traffic. Those on the freeways caught near the Ford Bronco were probably incredulous at the group of cruisers who were following it. Remarkably, coverage of the chase by news helicopters captured hundreds of people on foot lining the bridges across the freeway. As the vehicle headed farther south, I thought of my friend Mike Capizzi, the district attorney of Orange County. He was probably hoping that nothing would happen in his jurisdiction during the chase. Most of all, I began to pity the unfortunate prosecutor who would have to try this highly public figure. Simpson's fame would almost certainly create unique problems for the LA district attorney's office. The night ended with the Bronco's returning to Simpson's home. Simpson was arrested, jailed, and awaited his arraignment on the two murder charges filed earlier that day. It was the beginning of a truly incredible chain of events.

As the weeks passed and the case headed to trial, I learned about some of the other evidence in the case from a long-time friend, Rockne Harmon, a senior prosecutor with the Alameda County district attorney's office in Oakland, California. Harmon had a fascinating past. A native of New York City and a graduate of the U.S. Naval Academy, he had served during the Vietnam War on a gunboat, so it was easy to understand why he was fearless in court. He was an extraordinary resource when I was a prosecutor. During my legal battles over the admissibility of serology testing in the 1980s, he seemed to have an answer to nearly every problem I encountered. He had been through many of the same fights with similar testing methods in his own county. During those admissibility hearings Harmon provided me with a wealth of materials and advice. In the days before the Internet and e-mail, we would exchange transcripts of the testimony of expert witnesses by sending them by Greyhound bus, making a copy, then returning them on a bus the next day. Information technology at the time was, some would say, developing. Harmon had helped me many times with legal and scientific issues connected to DNA evidence and was able to give me a few inside details about the Simpson case when we talked over the telephone during the early summer of 1994.

The preliminary hearing in the case was televised. While at home one day, I watched and listened to the testimony of one of the LAPD investigators, Detective Mark Fuhrman. A good witness, I thought at the time. Very professional and smooth. The evidence began to come out: bloodstains had been found by lab personnel at the crime scene, in the Ford Bronco, on the driveway to Simpson's home, even on a glove recovered from behind the Simpson estate. It was already clear that DNA evidence was going to play a huge role in the trial. Another friend of mine was Lisa Kahn, a talented prosecutor in the LA district attorney's office; like Harmon and me, she specialized in DNA evidence. The LA district attorney's office had been even more aggressive in using RFLP evidence in 1989 and the years following than we had been in San Diego. Kahn had fought a number of admissibility battles to have RFLP evidence allowed at trials prosecuted by her office.

Much of the bloodstain evidence seized by LAPD crime-scene collectors in the Simpson case, it turned out, was either small or in degraded condition. The stains from the scene of the murders, for example, were littered with soil and leaves. Both made DNA difficult to detect, so PCR had to be used on many samples to obtain results. Because of the reliance of the LA district attorney's office on RFLP testing, however, they had less experience than we had in San Diego with the use of PCR techniques. Therefore, their lawyers—including Kahn—hadn't faced the same attacks on the technology and its use in trials.

I was happy to help with transcripts, scientific articles, and the same generous advice Harmon had given me for years. By 1994 we even had transcripts of DNA witnesses' testimony on computer disks and could ship them overnight. The days of the Greyhound bus paper shuttle were over. I wasn't carrying a caseload at that time that prevented me from helping another prosecution agency. Because of the extensive experience I had gained in teaching other prosecutors about DNA and other legal topics, I had been transferred in 1992 to my office's Training Division. That gave me more time to assist other deputy district attorneys in my own office with DNA cases as well.

The Simpson preliminary hearing was over. As July turned to August, the case never seemed to fade from public view. The murders had been particularly brutal. Prior 911 calls made by Nicole Brown Simpson to police describing previous attacks against her by Simpson were made public. The problems of domestic violence were constantly being raised in medical, legal, and media circles.

Then one day in August, my boss, Chuck Nickel, was out of the office. He had always been one of my most influential mentors and fully supported my efforts to have DNA evidence used in cases in both San Diego and other jurisdictions. Our legal assistant, Karen St.Charles, was busy answering phone calls from prosecutors looking for Nickel's advice. That was the norm in the Training Division. The state district attorneys' association had my full attention that day with a bill seeking to change California laws that governed extra credits prison inmates could earn to reduce their prison sentences. Not the most riveting topic, but one I had taken an interest in. As with many legislative proposals, changes had to be made, and as was usually the case, they had to be made now.

St.Charles and I fielded the telephone calls, juggled the legislative changes, and wished Nickel was back in the office. That afternoon, I was standing by the printer in her cubicle waiting for a draft of the bill to print. Her phone rang. She answered it and looked shocked. "Woody," she blurted out, "It's Marcia Clark. She wants to talk to you!" I had met Clark, the prosecutor in the Simpson case, just a few months earlier at a seminar held in Northern California about death-penalty cases. As usual, I spoke to the group about DNA. Then I had the opportunity to listen to Clark lecture about how to get capital juries to decide on the death penalty. I was extremely impressed with her knowledge and her ideas about convincing jurors to impose the ultimate punishment. She was an extremely quick thinker on her feet. She had also captured the instant attention of the media in the Simpson case. Clark had been to the scene of the murders of Brown and Goldman within hours of the crimes. LA district attorney Garcetti immediately assigned to her the prosecution of Simpson. She had tried several murder cases and was more than qualified to be the lead prosecutor in the Simpson trial.

Clark said she needed my help. I told her that it seemed to me that she had things under control. "No, I mean it," she pleaded. "I want you to come to LA and take care of the DNA evidence." Come to Los Angeles? I wasn't sure exactly what Clark meant. She explained that Simpson had hired Barry Scheck and Peter Neufeld to deal with the DNA results the LAPD had already gotten from testing they had done. Scheck and Neufeld were known internationally in DNA circles. They had both formed the famous Innocence Project in New York and had convinced a judge to disallow RFLP evidence in a Manhattan murder case years earlier. Harmon and I had met and become acquainted with both of them at FBI meetings.

Timing was also a factor. Kahn was pregnant, with her first child due later that year; her office would be deprived of its DNA expert prosecutor for a trial that was shaping up to be the most famous in its history. Combined with heavyweight DNA lawyers Scheck and Neufeld coming in to challenge the evidence, Clark and Garcetti wanted reinforcements. They wanted to take every step necessary to ensure that all their evidence would be heard by the jury that would eventually decide the fate of Simpson.

Harmon had already agreed to help, Clark told me. "By the time this is over you and I will be like brother and sister," she laughed. I told her that of course I'd help. I didn't know that my own district attorney, Ed Miller, had already agreed with District Attorney Garcetti to loan my services to Los Angeles County. But for how long? The good news was that Harmon and I would answer the admissibility challenges and, win or lose, be back home to watch the trial on television. Or so we thought.

Kahn, Harmon, and I began to talk on the phone every day. By September Harmon had already gone to LA to look at some of the mounting reports and raw data from DNA testing that had been completed. Some of the results were complicated. Others were straightforward. I spent much of my time focusing on the PCR portion of the case because that would apparently be the main legal battleground. By the fall of 1994 little controversy surrounded RFLP testing, apart from fights about the statistics that analysts provided for matching DNA profiles. PCR evidence was newer and was certain to be the technology on which Simpson's lawyers would focus their attack in order to keep the evidence from ever being heard by the jury. I had prepared an extensive legal brief—called *points and authorities* in legal circles—on PCR and updated it when new cases were published by state appellate and supreme courts, as well as federal courts. I freely shared that brief with prosecutors around the country. I would frequently incorporate their suggestions as well.

But first things first. I went off to Lake Tahoe in August to crew for my older brother, Willie, in a seventy-mile run around the circumference of the lake. All I had to do was scout out the locations where I would park and await his arrival during the foot race, then make sure he got a chair and something from the ice chest. When he took off again, I would drive to the next rest stop. I had borrowed a cellular telephone from my office to have with me for the trip. I knew Kahn and I would need to talk, probably a few times. The phone even worked during a round of golf. She wasn't amused when she tracked me down and found out I was on the course. Scheck and Neufeld, she said, were already filing motions in court demanding to have part of the original evidence in the case sent to them.

Normally, physical evidence in criminal cases belongs to the government. Law enforcement, frequently with input from the prosecutor's office, decides what to test and with what techniques. Sometimes defense attorneys want access to the evidence to conduct their own testing. Generally, prosecutors and police agencies aren't too concerned about sharing evidence with the defense. Either the police crime lab has already gotten results from its own testing or the prosecutor doesn't care about results the defense gets from other evidence items the crime lab didn't test. And given the extraordinary sensitivity of PCR testing—notwithstanding cases like that of Willie Ray Roberts (Chapter 6)—it usually doesn't require using up all of a sample to get results. But, again, much of the biological evidence in the Simpson case was either small in quantity or in a degraded condition. Giving the defense a portion of all the bloodstain evidence was out of the question.

But Kahn was caught in a fight in court about which items of evidence Simpson's lawyers would get a portion of. Simpson's primary lawyer at that time, Shapiro, could be persuasive in court. Judge Lance Ito, to whom the case was assigned for both the trial and pretrial motions, had been on the bench for about seven years, the last five as a superior court judge. A former prosecutor in the LA district attorney's office, he had been involved in a number of complex criminal trials, including presiding over the trial of Charles Keating for the Lincoln Savings and Loan fraud scandal in 1988.

Ito, Kahn assured me, would look at the issues and the law carefully. He wanted to make sure that Simpson had every right the law granted him with regard to DNA testing. That led Ito to order a hearing into the blood-stained items and how much DNA existed in each. His goal: to determine item by item whether there was enough DNA to give the defense a portion of it. Scheck and Neufeld also took part in the hearing and were relentless on behalf of Simpson. Their goal was to get as much of the evidence as possible for their own purposes. The scope of the hearing was remarkable. Day after day the judge heard evidence about the extent of testing that had already been conducted on each item, as well as the prospects for getting further results from what was left.

Although Harmon and I were surprised at the amount of time the hearing was taking—we did not believe the law even provided the defense a right to such a hearing—we weren't overly concerned. We were confident in the extraordinary reliability of DNA testing. To the collective knowledge of the most prominent DNA analysts in the field, defense testing of the same evidence had never produced a DNA result that was inconsistent and irreconcilable with the government's own results. Despite that confidence, we weren't in the middle of the war that Kahn was fighting. I assured her that I was coming home from Tahoe in two days and would be in LA first thing the next week. I sensed the urgency; Scheck and Neufeld were tenacious litigators.

That following week I drove to LA to become acquainted with the prosecution team and to start work on what was rapidly being called by newspaper and television commentators the "Trial of the Century." The charges were two counts of murder. The death penalty wasn't even being sought by the prosecutor's office. I walked into the Criminal Courts Building on West Temple Street in downtown LA and thought nothing seemed particularly unusual. Kahn met me in the reception area on the eighteenth floor and introduced me to Bill Hodgman, the director of the Central Operations division of the office, which tried most of the serious felony cases. He had tried Keating in front of Ito. I had met Hodgman at a state district attorneys' association meeting a few years before. I remembered that he was easygoing and seemed to be a very knowledgeable prosecutor.

I was briefed about the case. The evidence against Simpson was strong. The prior domestic violence, Simpson's movements around the time of the killings, and, above all, the DNA evidence painted a picture of an enraged Simpson, facing the permanent loss of his wife, brutally killing both her and an innocent man who had simply offered to return the eyeglasses she had left at a restaurant minutes earlier.

Kahn made the rounds with me, introducing me to a host of new colleagues. The prosecution team, I learned, was larger than normal. "Team" was an understatement. Including Harmon and me, there were over ten prosecuting attorneys working exclusively on the case. Add another ten or so law clerks, several investigators from the district attorney's office, support staff, and detectives in the LAPD. A cubicle in the office had my name on it, albeit hand-printed on a folded piece of paper. My cubicle was in the maze of offices nicknamed the "War Room." The same offices had been used in the ill-fated prosecution of the McMartin preschool child-molestation defendants a few years earlier. I was assured it was going to be different this time.

Harmon and I thought we'd at least be sworn in as temporary LA deputy district attorneys. But no oath, no certificates, not even an identification card to put in our scrapbooks. However, the hospitality was warm. The other attorneys in the office, the investigators, and the staff went out of their way to make us both feel at home. After staying the first two trips at the New Otani and Intercontinental hotels, both not far from the courthouse, Harmon and I were assigned living quarters in the Grand Promenade apartment building on Bunker Hill, a short drive from the Criminal Courts Building: two bedrooms, a living room, a kitchen, and the top floor no less.

The case against Simpson was developing and taking quick turns. Harmon and I touched base with Clark on my second trip to LA. I asked her how she thought the case was going so far. She was upbeat; but something seemed different. We'd learn later what that something was.

As with many homicides, the case against Simpson relied on circumstantial evidence. DNA testing was a critical component of that evidence. Clark knew how to tell a story to a jury. I could tell that from the first time I had met her at the death-penalty seminar months earlier. That skill would be essential to convince the jury of Simpson's guilt.

Harmon and I knew that the crimes had occurred in Brentwood, west of the city center. Why, we wondered, was the case transferred to downtown LA instead of being tried in the nearby Santa Monica branch court? We were told that, first, by court rule, any criminal case predicted to last several months had to be heard downtown, and, second, the Santa Monica courthouse would not hold the expected crush of media cameras and personnel. We learned early on that in this regard, at least, LA was a city completely unlike either Oakland or San Diego. On my second trip to the Criminal Courts Building, Harmon and I were taken by the district attorney's press spokesperson, Suzanne Childs, to the media room. I was astounded by the number of people packed into a room roughly the size of an average courtroom. Reporters, photojournalists, technicians, and audio-video equipment took up every available foot of space. It was a scene more reminiscent of a circus than a courthouse. That observation alone should have been an omen.

As my weeks in LA went by, fall turned toward winter. But time also brought additional DNA results that all pointed to Simpson as the killer. The prosecution was also aided by the fact that two of the most experienced and accomplished homicide detectives in the country were in charge of the LAPD investigation. Phil Vanatter and Tom Lange, senior members of the Robbery-Homicide Division, had worked countless homicide cases before. Vanatter, a tall and imposing man nearing retirement, reminded me of John Wayne. He was intimidated by nothing. What's more, he knew how people reacted to stress. He was perfect for the case against Simpson. Lange, a quiet, thoughtful man, provided a perfect complement to Vanatter's tough exterior. When the situation called for a reasoned and subtle approach, Lange had the edge. Harmon and I developed a close relationship with both men. They took us under their wings and told people we were "their lawyers."

All the DNA evidence provided a mountain of information. The results were separated into five areas: the crime scene outside Brown's condominium on South Bundy Drive, the Ford Bronco, Simpson's Rockingham home, a pair of socks in his bedroom, and a glove found behind his estate. The results were powerful. Both RFLP and PCR techniques were used in the analysis. Several labs collaborated in the testing, starting with the LAPD's own crime lab, which was able to do PCR DQ-Alpha testing. Cellmark—a lab that both the LAPD and the district attorney's office were familiar with—was involved in both RFLP and more advanced PCR testing. In addition, the California Department of Justice had been enlisted to help with the use of both technologies.

Testing of bloodstains found immediately outside Brown's home on Bundy provided significant results. A drop of blood next to the bodies of Brown and Goldman, as well as several drops that appeared to form a trail toward the parking area behind the home, matched known samples collected from Simpson. Three bloodstains found on the rear gate leading to the parking area from the trail of drops matched Simpson's samples as well. The chance that someone other than Simpson left one of the drops on the walkway was about one in 170 million. The probability that someone else left one of the stains on the rear gate was even less: approximately one in fifty-seven billion. The differences in the statistics were due to the fact that more genetic information could be gleaned from the testing that had been done on the gate stain than on the walkway stain.

Bloodstains in the Ford Bronco were generally small, and only PCR testing was possible. However, the results were important. Stains on the inside driver's door-handle opening, instrument panel, steering wheel, center console, and driver's side floor carpet were all consistent with Simpson's blood, although only limited DNA information could be obtained from them. Blood found on the driver's side carpet, however, matched that of Brown. Several DNA mixtures were discovered inside the vehicle. On the console a mixture was consistent with the blood of both Simpson and Goldman. Three other stains from the same console provided results that were compatible with mixtures of the blood of Simpson, Brown, and Goldman.

The trail of blood leading from the driveway up to and into the foyer of Simpson's home was analyzed. Four different drops of blood were tested, and all were consistent with having come from Simpson. One drop found in the foyer produced both RFLP and PCR matches to Simpson.

Two black socks that appeared to be identical were found at the foot of the bed in Simpson's bedroom during detectives' initial search of the home. One of the socks had a bloodstain that matched Simpson's profile. Even more significant, the same sock had a bloodstain, analyzed weeks later, that was matched using both RFLP and PCR testing to Brown. The chance that someone other than Brown had been the source of that blood was one in billions.

The leather glove that was found behind Simpson's home turned out to have numerous bloodstains on it, including one that proved to be an RFLP match to Goldman. Other stains on the glove led to RFLP or PCR results that were consistent with mixtures of the bloods of Brown and Goldman, Goldman and Simpson, or all three.

The blood samples that matched Simpson from all the locations were particularly important. When he was detained by Detectives Vanatter and Lange after his return from Chicago, Simpson was found to have a fresh cut on the knuckle of the middle finger of his left hand, the same hand that would fit inside the door handle recess of the driver's door of his Ford Bronco. The DNA evidence seemed insurmountable. The task fell to Kahn, Harmon, and me to make sure the jury would hear that evidence. Scheck and Neufeld had filed a motion that was inches thick, seeking to bar the evidence, particularly the PCR results. But we were convinced that we were ready for the challenge.

One day, while I was in the LA office preparing for the upcoming battle on the admissibility of the DNA results, I sensed someone in back of me and looked up. A tall man reached down to pick up a paper cup he had apparently dropped next to the water cooler. I recognized him from watching the preliminary hearing on television months earlier. It was Detective Fuhrman. Fuhrman had become the primary target of Simpson's lawyers' attack on the LAPD. The allegation: that Fuhrman had planted the bloody glove found behind Simpson's Rockingham estate. Fuhrman smiled at me and didn't miss a beat. "I'm very careful about what I pick up now," he said in a deadpan voice. I broke out laughing. So did Fuhrman.

I got my first glimpse of Judge Ito and the courtroom where the trial would take place in the first few weeks of my work on the case. A motion needed to be argued about the relatively minor issue of Simpson's lawyers getting access to information about the DNA testing that had already been performed. We all went to court on a morning when several legal questions were to be heard by the judge. The scene was part reality, part movie, and part circus. Just walking the thirty feet or so from the elevator to the courtroom was an ordeal. The security screening devices were tame compared with the gantlet of reporters and others who crowded the hallway.

Then we entered the courtroom. Simpson was seated in a chair at the defense table, closest to the bailiff, dressed in a suit. Although in custody, he was permitted to dress in civilian clothes even for the pretrial hearings. Shortly after, Simpson's lawyers entered from a side door. I was introduced to Shapiro and then to Johnnie Cochran. Cochran was a relatively recent addition to Simpson's defense team. He was engaging and obviously had a strong presence in a courtroom. He was wearing a beautifully cut and expensive suit. During the trial it seemed as though he wore a different suit every day, each equally elegant. I thought to myself he must have one very large closet at home to hold them all! My issue was the last on the day's agenda, but that was of little consequence. The courtroom remained packed and full for the entire day, a sign that this case was dramatically different from any other I had been involved in. And the world was watching. Hodgman made sure that I noticed the small television camera mounted on the wall, high above the empty jury box. At that point it was impossible to understand the influence that camera would have on the Trial of the Century. A trial that hadn't yet even begun.

*I*n an unusual decision for a case of this nature, Ito had ordered that the selection of the jury would start in October. Clark and Hodgman pleaded with Ito to delay jury selection until after completion of the pretrial motions, especially the one that was likely to be the most time-consuming issue—admissibility of the DNA evidence. Ito stood his ground, and Clark and Hodgman were forced to devote their attention to the jury process. They had to read extensive questionnaires filled out by potential jurors, and then engage in the often dull and time-consuming process of interviewing those jurors individually in court with all the attorneys and the judge present. The process is normally slow and tedious. With the additional questions that needed to be asked about how jurors felt about the defendant's celebrity status, the whole procedure slowed to a crawl. We didn't mind having the extra time to prepare for the DNA hearing. The jurors eventually selected, however, would have to be sent home to await the litigation of all the remaining motions. That could, conceivably, take a month or more.

Because we thought we were thoroughly prepared for the upcoming DNA hearings, Harmon and I spent much of our time on details of the chain of custody of all the biological evidence seized by the LAPD and sent to the various laboratories. Prosecutors always want to be sure that the exact movements of each piece of evidence are recorded in order to prevent problems with a jury's confidence in the results. Because Scheck and Neufeld would seize on any shortcomings in the handling of evidence, where each sample went and who received it at each stage were critical pieces of information. Harmon and I wanted to be ready for every eventuality that might come up during the hearing. We knew that we had to be aware of missing or weak links that would cause problems for Clark and Hodgman when they presented the DNA evidence to the jury at the trial. We talked about how watching that part of the trial on television from our offices in Oakland and San Diego was going to be a fascinating experience.

But plans have a way of going awry. Clark and Hodgman were unhappy with the selection of the jury. There was apparently a severe shortage of jurors with higher education backgrounds. Clark had tried many murder cases, but this panel of jurors seemed to her different from others. The prosecution team was worried. We felt the case was going to demand jurors with at least a rudimentary understanding of time lines and scientific evidence and the ability to comprehend and remember key details from extensive testimony.

As December arrived jury selection was nearly completed. Because the hearing on DNA would soon begin, the often-difficult process of scheduling expert witnesses to testify was necessary. Fortunately, the experts we needed were largely at our disposal. They knew that this hearing would showcase DNA evidence in front of much of the country and world, and they wanted to put DNA's best foot forward.

Once the jury was picked and sworn in, it was time to litigate whether our DNA results would be allowed at the trial. Suddenly, Cochran and Simpson's defense team astounded both the district attorney's office and Judge Ito by deciding to withdraw their motion requesting the court to prohibit testimony about the DNA results. We were caught by surprise. Why would the defense pass on not only an opportunity for the judge to possibly exclude the most damning evidence against Simpson but also the chance to question under oath some of the witnesses who would later testify at the trial? The answer, they told Ito, was that they wanted to go to trial immediately and not wait the month or more that would be consumed by a DNA hearing. The real reason? Only Simpson's lawyers know. But it was obvious that they were content with the jurors and alternate jurors who were already selected to try the case. Further delay would surely result in the loss of some of those jurors and the need to select others. We convinced Clark and Hodgman that the wisest course was to make sure that Simpson himself agreed with his attorneys' decision to give up his right to an admissibility hearing. After some legal wrangling and court hearings, we were finally satisfied that the defendant agreed with his attorneys' strategy. Harmon and I then turned to the logistics of packing and heading home. We had written some fairly extensive outlines of the anticipated testimony of the DNA experts. Clark, who had presented DNA testimony in a prior murder case, would be fully prepared.

What we weren't prepared for was an unexpected request to meet with Clark and Hodgman. They asked that we stay and put on the DNA evidence ourselves at the trial because they had been so occupied with jury selection that they had had little or no opportunity to prepare the many civilian and police witnesses for their testimony at the trial. We were reluctant to take this job on and tried to boost Clark's confidence. With her knowledge of the area and the background work that Kahn, Harmon, and I had already done, she could handle it smoothly. Hodgman pleaded with us to stay on the case. The defense had managed to keep the court in session on the case from the beginning and had effectively deprived them of the opportunity to prepare their case for trial. Most defendants charged with murder take every opportunity to delay the trial. Not this time, however. We relented and agreed to stay. Privately, we felt that as time went by in the trial, Clark might decide to put on the evidence herself. We never did get a chance to pack our bags for the final trip home to watch the case on television.

The trial began on the first court day of 1995 with opening statements by the attorneys. Leading off, Clark described, in compelling detail, the case she and Hodgman would present. Cochran's opening statement was a direct attack on the LAPD. A "rush to judgment," he declared to the jury, had led to the arrest of Simpson, a man totally innocent of the killings of Brown and Goldman. Cochran's assault included a denunciation of the LAPD's crime laboratory, which he labeled a "cesspool of contamination" that ultimately produced blood evidence that he alleged was "corrupted, contaminated, and compromised." His alliteration was impressive.

The biggest worry, I thought, was that the jurors warmed to the way Cochran spoke to them. Harmon and I knew that his claims were scientifically weak. But the effect on the jurors of merely mentioning the claims was noticeable. Our work was going to be more difficult than we had anticipated. Still, we should have expected nothing less from what the press and other media were now calling the "Dream Team" of defense lawyers. Cochran was clearly relying on the expertise of Scheck and Neufeld.

The trial had barely begun when, during legal arguments about the defense's opening statement, Hodgman suddenly suffered chest pains and was taken to the hospital. Forced to leave the courtroom team, he helped direct the case on the sidelines from his office. Chris Darden, a fellow prosecutor who had taken part in the investigation of Al Cowlings, the Ford Bronco driver during the slow-speed chase, was immediately called in to take Hodgman's place.

Other problems plagued the trial. One of the most immediate was the fact that the jurors and alternate jurors hearing the case were ordered sequestered for the entire length of the trial. They were housed in a hotel, prohibited from going home, and forced to lead a cloistered existence for what was expected to be months. They resided at the Intercontinental Hotel, immediately across the street from the apartment where Harmon and I stayed. Within a few weeks, several of the jurors complained about their being isolated, their living conditions, and the divisions that had already developed among them. On several occasions Judge Ito had to interview individual jurors who felt unable to continue to serve on the jury. Although a few of the protesting jurors were excused, the rest were forced to remain.

Months went by as testimony was taken from civilian witnesses, police officers, and detectives. Finally, in April, testimony started with the two LAPD crime-lab technicians, Dennis Fung and Andrea Mazzola, who collected the biological evidence at each of the key locations. Hank Goldberg, another deputy district attorney, was assigned the task of questioning them. The defense strategy was apparent. Alternating, Scheck and Neufeld questioned Fung and Mazzola for days, directly criticizing the way the evidence was collected, handled, packaged, and preserved. The entire month was taken up with the testimony of just those two witnesses.

Finally, in early May, my turn came. Once the defense had finished questioning Mazzola, I stood up and announced to Ito that the People called Dr. Robin Cotton as the next witness. Cotton, from Cellmark in Maryland, took the witness stand. Fortunately, Cotton was a good friend as a result of our working on cases in San Diego. We had discussed several times before that day the general topic of DNA, the RFLP and PCR methods, and the results her lab had gotten on the various pieces of evidence from the Bundy scene, the Bronco, Simpson's home, and the socks and glove. Cotton was always a delight for any lawyer to question on direct examination. Her qualifications were impeccable, her knowledge of DNA unmatched, and her knack for talking to jurors in a simple, direct manner was obvious. Our only problem was a difference in approaches between Clark, on the one hand, and Harmon and me on the other. After dealing with DNA evidence for a few years, we were confident that the simpler the approach, the stronger the testimony. As the power of DNA testing slowly became part of the general knowledge of most jurors, it no longer seemed necessary to explain the scientific basis of the testing techniques to them, if it ever was. But as my questioning of Cotton progressed, Clark wanted me to give additional explanations. Harmon tried to run interference for me with Clark, but she wanted the details.

I did as Clark requested, but the testimony started to drag. We never even got to the results until the third day of Cotton's testimony. I found some satisfaction in the coverage given the case that same day by our local newspaper, the *San Diego Union-Tribune*. The front page described Cotton and me as the DNA equivalent of Ginger Rogers and Fred Astaire. At least that explained why Fred Astaire always looked so good, I thought to myself. Within a few hours my bubble burst. Harmon and I turned on the *Tonight Show* with Jay Leno for a little relaxation. At the top of the show Leno and the "Dancing Itos" did a skit to the tune of the rock group Bee Gee's hit song "Staying Alive." The theme: how boring the DNA testimony has been. The name of the skit: "Staying Awake." At least I could laugh.

By Thursday of that week, Cotton had testified to some of the most damaging DNA results of the case. That evidence delivered some serious body blows to Simpson's defense. We all thought that for once the "corrupted, contaminated, and compromised" theme had suffered a setback. On Thursday Neufeld started his cross-examination of Cotton. Neufeld was aggressive, as was his nature. But Cotton was a tough nut to crack. Neufeld scored points with some concessions Cotton had to make about the inability to get RFLP results from so many of the samples that otherwise seemed to have enough blood. Just maybe Fung and Mazzola had not used the best techniques to collect and preserve the samples. But that concession didn't mean the results were wrong, only that not as much information could be gleaned from the tests. If they had been able to collect and preserve more of the DNA, we all thought, the jury would have heard results that were even more damaging to Simpson.

Late in the day, Neufeld tried to attack Cotton's testimony with a letter written to a scientific magazine that was critical of the methods used to calculate the probabilities that she had testified to. I knew that Neufeld was about to bring up the letter, which Ito had ruled earlier was hearsay and not admissible evidence. Ito didn't recognize the document Neufeld had in his hand and asked him what it was. In front of the jury, Neufeld declared, "It's a letter to *Nature* signed by twenty-five scientists." Worried that Neufeld might use the already-prohibited letter to mislead the jurors, I barely hesitated. "Your Honor, that was rejected and never published." Ito was instantly furious and abruptly slammed his hands down onto the bench. Cotton, startled, jumped up in her seat on the witness stand. Ito ordered the jury out of the courtroom. As soon as they had left, he angrily looked at both Neufeld and me and announced that we were both sanctioned $250. "Get your checkbooks out," he ordered. According to Ito, Neufeld made an improper argument to the jury; I had made an inappropriate "speaking objection." Panic set in. I had no checkbook. I had about twenty dollars in cash. I asked Harmon how much he had. He was as short as I was. Just then Darden got out of his chair, reached into his back pocket, and pulled out an envelope. He opened the envelope and, in full view of the court camera, grabbed three hundred dollar bills and gave them to me. Sheepishly, I marched over to the court clerk and paid my part of the sanction.

The jury was brought back, but because the end of the day was at hand, they heard only a few minutes more testimony. The trial then recessed until the following Monday. I rushed upstairs to telephone my boss, District Attorney Paul Pfingst, back in San Diego. I wanted him to hear about what had happened from me first, not from a news reporter. Sanctions are rare, and I had never been fined or held in contempt before. If anything, most of my bosses had always wanted me to be more aggressive in court than I normally was. I was patched through to Pfingst's office and could hear him on his speakerphone. He and several others were laughing in the background. I breathed a sigh of relief. Pfingst explained to me that they had already formed an officewide "Free Woody Fund" and were taking collections for me. I had to hand it to my colleagues. They had circled the wagons to help within minutes.

The bottom line of "The Sanction," as it later came to be known: from the money contributed by prosecutors and staff in the San Diego district attorney's office and unsolicited contributions I began to receive from people around the country, I repaid Darden his $250. At the end of the case I had several hundred dollars left and contributed them to a San Diego crime victims' fund. I then made it standard practice to carry my checkbook to court.

*H*armon and I called a few other DNA witnesses, including analysts from the California Department of Justice. Scheck and Neufeld continued to attack our evidence during their cross-examination, but their criticisms seemed to be reserved mostly for the PCR results. That tactic should have been a warning to us, especially because their occasional assault on even the RFLP testing didn't cause us any anxiety. It seemed they were adopting a shotgun approach, trying to raise whatever questions they could in jurors' minds.

The prosecution's case against Simpson finished in early summer. Then it was the defense's turn to call witnesses. In August, Scheck called the person who was the defense's showcase DNA witness: Dr. John Gerdes. We knew Gerdes was likely to testify, based on reports written by him that were provided to us earlier by Simpson's lawyers. The essence of those reports: Gerdes was sharply critical of the way that PCR testing was done in the LAPD crime laboratory. His main complaint was that the laboratory was, in his view, a pool of contamination. From his examination of the laboratory records, Gerdes believed that the analysts were novices when it came to PCR testing. Looking at the lab's data from testing that was done in the weeks both before and after that in the Simpson case, he observed that test samples seemed to be frequently contaminated. In fact, as part of the process of learning the technique and testing practice samples, some analysts did get results showing contamination from other sources. However, the results from testing of the samples in the Simpson case were remarkably clean. In addition, the LAPD evidence collectors—Fung and Mazzola—had used a technique carried over from the old days of ABO testing: the use of unstained controls. Unstained—also known as substrate—controls were usually collected in the 1970s and 1980s, before DNA testing had even been developed. A portion of a surface immediately next to, but outside, a bloodstain or semen stain would be collected as a separate evidence item. The purpose: to allow analysts to test that sample as well to determine whether any ABO types were present on the surface. If so, then testing of the stain might not reveal the correct types of its donor. If not, results from the biological fluid stain were most likely from the person who left the stain.

Despite the fact that DNA testing made the use of such controls largely unnecessary, Fung and Mazzola had collected them. They proved to be a bonus in the Simpson case. Every unstained control showed absolutely no evidence of DNA. Scientifically, that made the claim of contamination by Simpson's lawyers pure speculation. But Gerdes's testimony clearly influenced the jury. Enlarged photographs and other graphics were used to support his points about the contamination the lab had experienced in their practice samples. It was clear that I was going to have to go over each piece of evidence that was tested in the Simpson case to try to dismantle the claim of contamination. It would be tedious, but necessary.

I started my cross-examination of Gerdes on a Thursday, which was usually our last day of trial each week. I had plenty to talk about with him. For example, he did not work in a forensic laboratory and never had. Instead, he was the director of a lab in Colorado that specialized in immunological testing, normally used to compare tissue samples for transplants, transfusions, and other clinical purposes. Gerdes and I had faced each other before. In a case in San Diego he had testified similarly, criticizing the use of PCR testing in criminal cases. The basis for his opinion was his belief that samples taken from crime scenes were too susceptible to contamination, which could lead to inaccurate test results. I had reviewed transcripts of other cases in which Gerdes had testified and had some statements by him that I knew would contradict some of his earlier testimony in front of the Simpson jury. Those would have to wait until the following week.

As I drove home to San Diego that Thursday evening, I turned on the radio. Because the radio received only AM stations, my choices were limited. But in surfing the dial I tuned in a station that was talking about the case. A panel of lawyers was discussing the questions I had asked Gerdes earlier that afternoon. One of the attorneys said that it was obvious that I was going to question Gerdes on Monday about how his own laboratory didn't use some of the safeguards used by the LAPD lab. I hadn't even thought of that point. Of course I'm going to ask those questions, I said to myself in the car. At least now I was. Needless to say, the car radio stayed tuned to that station for the rest of the trial. I also made sure I had a notepad and pen on the passenger seat next to me for the drives to and from Los Angeles. I welcomed inspiration, no matter the source!

Then, suddenly, the trial took an excruciatingly painful turn for the prosecution. Audio tape recordings turned up that directly contradicted earlier testimony of Detective Fuhrman about his use of a racial epithet. Suddenly, Simpson's lawyers mounted an all-out assault on Fuhrman, characterizing him as a racist bent on convicting an innocent African American man. Their earlier claim that Furhman planted evidence had seemed empty at the time; now it had renewed life and threatened the entire prosecution. The tapes changed the whole approach of Simpson's attorneys to what was left of the trial. In his later closing argument, Cochran hammered home to the jury the obvious contradictions between Fuhrman's testimony and the audiocassettes, which told a different story about Fuhrman's testimony, character, and attitude.

The defense's claims of the unreliability of the DNA results lost much of their importance. After all, the results were accurate if Fuhrman had indeed planted the evidence. Experts were called in the closing days of the defense case to try to show that the bloodstains found on the rear gate at the Bundy crime scene could have come from a specific vial of Simpson's blood that was taken from him by detectives at the time of his arrest. The testimony was extremely technical but could sway one or more jurors who might already be skeptical of the case against Simpson.

The evidence portion of the trial ended with barely a whimper. Both sides basically agreed that it was time to stop. In part that decision was based on the fact that some of the remaining jurors had been replaced by alternate jurors. The reasons included illness and violations of the rules governing juror conduct. With only a pair of alternate jurors left, even Clark and Cochran agreed to bring the case to an end. I, for one, was certain the jurors were ready.

I drove home the week before closing arguments were set to begin and went into my San Diego office on a Saturday. Coincidentally, District Attorney Pfingst was there with his wife. Pfingst knew criminal cases and was an extraordinary trial lawyer. The two sat down in my office and asked how the case was going. Pfingst proceeded to give me an impromptu, twenty-minute closing argument for the Simpson case. I was impressed. Looking back, I wish that I had tape-recorded it for Clark's benefit. The theme of his mock argument was that, without even talking about the results, the fact of the matter was that there was blood where there shouldn't be blood, at least not if Simpson was innocent of the murders. His point wasn't lost on me. The blood stretched from the scene of the murders, out the back gate, into Simpson's Bronco, from his driveway into his house, and even on socks and a glove at his estate. The cut on Simpson's left-hand finger fit the scenario. Although in his initial interview with police Simpson said that he had cut it on a glass while talking on the phone with police, the coincidence seemed too great. I later passed this argument on to Clark.

I headed back to LA before dawn on Monday, thinking the end was in sight. But not before even more surprises came our way. The first was comical. CNN reported over the weekend that I was going to make part of the closing argument for the prosecution. I took it as a compliment but knew better. The other was that Judge Ito had ordered that the closing arguments would go into the nighttime. That was unusual. But his reasons were good ones. A real danger existed that we would run out of jurors. Because the jury would continue to be sequestered during the arguments and deliberations, Ito wanted to finish the arguments as soon as possible.

Clark and Darden would divide the prosecution's first closing argument. In criminal cases, the People argue both first and last and the defense is allowed one argument in the middle because the prosecution has the burden of proving the truth of the charges beyond a reasonable doubt. Clark delivered her opening argument in a calculating, methodical manner that detailed what she called the "mountain of evidence" that pointed to Simpson as the killer. Darden reiterated the strength of much of the evidence, focusing in particular on the record of incidents of domestic violence and Simpson's physical abuse of Brown. I thought his closing seemed a bit apologetic. Like a seasoned prosecutor, he tried to make the seriousness of the case paramount. But, in doing so, he told the jurors that deciding the fate of Simpson would be difficult. Clark had just finished telling the jury that it would be easy to arrive at the verdict because the evidence was so conclusive. I only hoped that the jurors weren't going to be put off by the apparent mixed messages.

Cochran and Scheck shared the single defense closing argument. Although they talked about many parts of the case and were critical of the LAPD's handling of the physical evidence, Fuhrman was their focal point. If Fuhrman lied, the theme went, Simpson should be found not guilty. One of the phrases Cochran used—based on a request by Darden earlier in the trial for Simpson to don the glove found at his home—still rings in my ears: "If it doesn't fit, you must acquit."

Darden and Clark delivered the prosecution's final argument to the jury. They countered each of the major points brought out by Cochran and Scheck. Ito read the court's instructions to the jury on the law, and on Friday, September 29, 1995, the jury finally was sent out to deliberate the case. It didn't seem possible that "the coin was in the air," as trial lawyers frequently say.

Everyone was exhausted and went their separate ways. I drove home and had the three-hour commute to think about the case. No murder prosecution had ever received the attention and scrutiny this case had. Television allowed anyone interested to see almost everything that had gone on in the trial. An entire jury was forced to live separated from their families and everyday existence for nearly a year. It was difficult to predict how those forces would combine, no matter how strong the evidence.

I went into my office in San Diego Monday morning. That afternoon I received a telephone call from Pattijo Fairbanks, the LA district attorney's assistant who had looked out so well for Harmon and me. The jury had reached a verdict and it was to be taken tomorrow morning, Pattijo said. A verdict that soon? That just might be good news, I thought optimistically. I walked quickly to my car and was caught on Broadway in San Diego by a local news reporter and cameraman. "What do you think the verdict is?" the reporter asked. "We'll find out tomorrow," I told her. I couldn't think of anything else to say.

I drove home, grabbed a suit, and jumped into the car with my wife, Michele. One of our investigators from the San Diego district attorney's office heard about the verdict and caught me before I left the office. He was kind enough to offer to drive me up to LA for the verdict and to make sure we were safe. Many in LA were concerned about the potential for riots if Simpson was convicted. I told the investigator how much I appreciated his offer, but I was convinced we'd be okay. The two of us drove up Interstate 5 to downtown LA and into the underground parking at the Grand Promenade. We took the elevator upstairs to the apartment. Harmon was already there.

The next day the three of us drove to the Criminal Courts Building a little earlier than normal. Investigators at the district attorney's office had let us know that they wanted all of us up on the eighteenth floor and gathered well before the verdict was scheduled to be read. When we got there, the atmosphere in the War Room was electric. As a lawyer, you get used to waiting. But most of the law clerks had never even worked on another case. The Simpson case was all they knew, and they were nervous. For that matter, so was I.

Clark, Darden, and a few of the others went down to court. Most of the prosecution team, including Harmon and me, watched the reading of the verdict from the War Room. We separated into groups in front of several TV sets and waited. And waited. Finally, the camera in the courtroom focused on Judge Ito. The verdicts were given to him and were then handed to the court clerk, the same court clerk who had taken my three hundred dollars for the sanction and said with a chuckle that she didn't have change. In less than a minute she announced that the jury had found Simpson not guilty of the murders.

The groans of Goldman's father, Fred Goldman, could be heard on the television. The gasps in the cubicle in which fifteen of us were watching were immediate. A few of the clerks immediately walked away in near shock. Michele and I looked at each other. No words were necessary. District Attorney Garcetti asked that all the attorneys and law clerks come to his office. We went down the hall and gathered in the huge room. A few of the clerks were sobbing. Others were standing by themselves, staring into space. There was going to be a press conference any minute. I walked over to Garcetti, who was sitting behind his desk reading a small stack of index cards. He looked up at me and said, "Woody, I haven't practiced this one." I knew what he meant. He had another stack of three-by-five cards ready for a press conference if the verdicts had been guilty. The one in his hands was for the other outcome.

A few minutes later we all walked through a side door leading to the conference room. We literally marched in like soldiers in two lines, stopped when the person ahead of us did, and made a military-style left turn. As luck would have it, I ended up standing in the second row, immediately behind Garcetti, who was at the podium. Because of the bright lights, cameras, and microphones, I could only see one person in the audience: Maria Shriver of NBC News. The press conference was short. The jury had reached a unanimous decision and had spoken. DNA provided results that shaped what seemed to all of us to be one of the strongest circumstantial-evidence murder cases in recent history. But many would later offer the opinion that DNA was given a black eye in the Trial of the Century.

What caused twelve jurors to acquit Simpson? Only those jurors know for sure, but I believe several decisions and events factored into the verdicts. Moving the trial from suburban Santa Monica to downtown LA changed the character of the jury and the atmosphere surrounding the trial. Distrust of the LAPD—particularly following the videotaped beating of Rodney King only four years before—was still palpable in urban LA. The smooth investigation narrative by Detective Fuhrman was followed months later by damning evidence contradicting his previous testimony. The prosecution failed to introduce evidence about the Bronco chase and the numerous contradictions in Simpson's initial statements to police. A glove allegedly worn by the killer was tried on the defendant in front of the jury and, when it failed to fit, proved to be a nightmare for the prosecution. The collection and handling of the physical evidence so crucial to the later DNA results were shown to have been, at best, adequate. At worst, the procedures followed were contrary to lab policy and guidelines. The DNA testimony, like that involving the evidence collection, was long and often tedious. DNA results that provided strong evidence of guilt were undercut by the emphasis the defense put on the way in which that evidence was gathered and preserved. The LAPD laboratory, through which all evidence was funneled, had experienced problems with contamination both before and after the Simpson-case samples were processed. Human performance arguably damaged the effectiveness of science.

Moreover, the defendant was a sports and entertainment celebrity who made his home in LA and who had become, at least during the trial, one of the city's most famous—or notorious—residents. The human factor in the trial can't be ignored, particularly because American culture seems to be obsessed with celebrity and that obsession can skew the way reality is perceived. It is impossible to gauge the relative importance of each of these factors. But in a case that rested on the identity of the killer, DNA results that pointed to the man charged with two brutal murders fell short of convincing a jury of his guilt.

CHAPTER NINE

Back Home in San Diego

AN UNUSUAL RAPE CASE

———•———

San Diego seemed quiet compared with Los Angeles. Prosecutors and staff in my office, judges, and other lawyers were extremely supportive. The assistant district attorney, Greg Thompson, asked me what I wanted to do after the ordeal of the Simpson case. Thompson was the former number-two prosecutor in the Los Angeles district attorney's office in the late 1980s and had been enlisted by District Attorney Paul Pfingst to take the same position in San Diego when Pfingst was elected in 1994. Thompson said he already had a slot in our felony-trial division waiting for me.

The cases ranged from drug sales to robbery, burglary, and even sex cases. DNA, thankfully, was taking a back seat in my career for at least a little while. But early in 1996 I was asked to prosecute an unusual rape case. Detective Norma Dormann of the San Diego Police Department came to my office while the victim sat in our reception area. Dormann, a sex-crimes investigator, prepared me for what she said at the outset was an odd case. First, the victim was an eighty-five-year-old woman. Uncommon, but not that unusual, I thought to myself. Second, the suspect was in his forties. That was more peculiar. The rape of an elderly victim by a young man is not extraordinary. But the same attack by a forty-six-year-old man is rare.

Dormann went over the facts with me as the victim had already described them to her. We then walked out to the reception room. She introduced me to the victim, who was named Addie. Addie moved a little slowly and used a walker to get around because of arthritis, but she showed the graciousness of a woman who had lived most of her life in the South. Her accent reminded me of Tennessee, but she was probably from Virginia or the Carolinas. I invited her into my office.

We all sat down and chatted about the weather and a few other easy topics. We turned to the case and the suspect, Stephen Nocilla. Sexual-assault victims aren't easy to pigeonhole. Although some are extremely emotional about what they have been through—and understandably so—most victims in my experience are able to calmly recount their ordeals. Addie defied any previous experience. It must be something about having seen that much life. Addie didn't have to vamp anyone. She knew what had happened to her and wasn't about to clam up.

The facts of her case were as unusual as Addie was herself. She lived in an apartment in the Golden Hill area, a popular, improving area of San Diego a stone's throw from downtown. One morning in January she was downtown for an appointment with her dentist. After her dental visit, Addie started toward the Woolworth's store on Broadway. While she was standing on the sidewalk with her walker, Addie began to feel faint and started to fall. A middle-aged man threw his arms around her and kept her from falling to the sidewalk. Commendable—here was a gentleman helping an elderly lady in distress. They bought some food at McDonald's. Addie paid—it was the least she could do as a gesture of appreciation, and besides the man claimed he had no money. His name, Addie found out, was Stephen Nocilla.

As they left the restaurant, Nocilla asked Addie where she was going next. Addie told him that she was headed home and was going to flag down a taxi. Nocilla insisted on accompanying her home to make sure she got there safely. He was also adamant that they take the bus. Addie told Nocilla that she was afraid. She hadn't used the bus in more than three years because of the stairs she would have to climb to board. Nocilla insisted that he would help her with the steps and that they would have no problems getting to her home. The two of them sat on a bench and talked for a few minutes. Nocilla prevailed on Addie, and the two of them took the bus to Addie's Golden Hill home. Addie and Nocilla walked approximately two blocks from the bus stop to her apartment, a small single-bedroom cottage. Nocilla entered the apartment with Addie, and the two sat down in the living room and talked for several hours. Addie proudly showed Nocilla her photo albums. She later told Detective Dormann and me that she thought that Nocilla was a nice man and that he seemed well-mannered.

The day turned to late afternoon, and the two of them began to watch the four o'clock news on television. Addie wanted Nocilla to leave her apartment before dark. She was going to thaw some frozen chicken for her dinner, but realized that it would take too long. Addie asked Nocilla if he would be willing to go to a nearby Kentucky Fried Chicken restaurant and buy dinner.

She told him that she had ten dollars and would be willing to buy his meal as well. Nocilla agreed. Addie was convinced that he would simply take the ten dollars and leave for good.

To Addie's surprise, Nocilla returned with the chicken about twenty minutes later. Addie warmed up some beans and made a salad and cornbread to go with the chicken. They ate dinner between 4:30 and 5:00. After dinner they returned to the living room of the apartment. About thirty minutes after dinner, Addie began to feel sleepy and asked Nocilla to leave. He did as she asked. But about a half hour later Addie's doorbell rang. She opened the door a few inches, but it was pushed open the rest of the way by a man at the door. It was Nocilla. He immediately walked into Addie's home. Addie hadn't gone to bed yet; she had been watching television in her bedroom. Nocilla told her that he didn't have a place to sleep and had been living on the street. He asked Addie whether he could sleep on her floor. Addie felt sorry for Nocilla and knew how dangerous it was for people to sleep on the streets. Addie told Nocilla that he could sleep on her living room couch. She got a pillow and a blanket for him.

Before she went back into her bedroom, Addie told Nocilla not to come into her room. She told him that she had a gun and showed it to Nocilla. She went into her bedroom and wedged a doorstop against her bedroom door so that Nocilla couldn't enter. Addie then went to sleep. She was wearing her nightgown with white and red striped shorts underneath it.

Addie awoke some time later and felt something heavy on top of her. She couldn't move her head either to the left or to the right. She opened her eyes and saw Nocilla on top of her. He angrily told her, "Don't make a sound. Don't cry out. Don't do anything loud." Addie cried and begged him, "Don't do this to me; please don't do this dirty thing to me." Nocilla said, "I'm hurting. I haven't had sex in weeks. I'll just be a minute. I'll be through in a minute. I'll be out of here, and I'll never come back here again." Nocilla, not wearing any pants, had pulled Addie's shorts down. He was rubbing his penis against Addie's vaginal area. She tried to keep her legs together so that he couldn't rape her and tried desperately to push him off. She just didn't have enough strength. Addie would later describe Nocilla's "mean and evil look" during the attack.

Nocilla ejaculated on Addie and her clothing. Addie wasn't certain that he had penetrated her vagina. She had last had sexual intercourse over thirty years earlier. Nocilla left immediately, but before leaving he asked Addie where her gun was. She refused to tell him. Nocilla mockingly laughed at Addie. She got up and tried to use her telephone. The headset had been disconnected from the phone, and Addie was unable to make a call. She decided not to go outside to use a pay phone. She placed her nightgown—on which Nocilla had left his semen—into a bucket of water to soak. She cleaned herself with a towel and then lay back down until daylight came.

At sunrise, Addie dressed, walked to a nearby café, and ordered a cup of coffee. While there, she saw a policewoman she was familiar with. The officer asked Addie how she was. Addie told her she had been raped and robbed of her gun, and she began to cry. The officer took Addie back to her apartment and took her story of the assault. Officers seized the bed linen from Addie's bedroom. Addie agreed to be seen at Villa View Hospital, a local facility where victims of sex crimes are treated. The examination is done by a sexual-assault response team, which combines police, medical personnel, and nurses who specialize in the treatment of sex victims. The nurses who dedicate their practice to rape exams are also specially trained in the collection of evidence. The results of Addie's exam revealed tearing, bruising, and bleeding in her vaginal area, all consistent with her having been sexually penetrated.

Two sheets taken by police from Addie's bed were closely examined in the San Diego Police Department crime laboratory. Three semen stains were found on the sheets. Although no sperm could be seen in an examination of the stains under a microscope, it was clear they contained semen. Each was tested for DNA by both the San Diego Police Department and Cellmark in Maryland. Despite the apparent absence of sperm, PCR testing revealed the semen donor's types at six different genetic markers, or "loci." Only about one in thirty-four million people would be expected to have those same types.

At about 9:30 the same evening Addie was attacked, a clerk at a nearby convenience store reported to police that a man had come into the store. The man told the clerk that he had just found a .22-caliber handgun next to a dumpster behind the store. He then put the gun on the store counter. Police came and collected the gun. While the police were still there, the clerk saw Nocilla and pointed him out to police as the man who had left the gun. Nocilla was questioned briefly. The next day, after Addie reported her attack to police, it was determined that the gun from the store belonged to her, and Nocilla was arrested. Testing of a known sample of Nocilla's blood showed that he could not be excluded as the source of the semen on the bedsheets. Nocilla had two prior felony convictions, including a 1993 conviction of assault with intent to commit rape. Under California's one-strike rape law, Nocilla faced a sentence of life imprisonment for what he was charged with having done to Addie.

Each time I spoke with Addie I gained more respect for her. She had been forced to endure a terrifying attack that resulted from her offering to help a man who was down and out—an offer that was repaid with the ultimate act of degradation.

The charges against Nocilla included rape, burglary, and the theft of Addie's gun. Allegations that I filed against him included the charge that he had raped Addie while committing the burglary. The burglary count and allegation were somewhat novel. After all, once he was inside Addie's apartment she had permitted him to spend the night in the living room. However, he entered Addie's bedroom without her consent. From my review of California law, it appeared that Nocilla's entry through her bedroom door was enough to make it a burglary. The allegation was important. Under California's one-strike rape law, if the jury agreed that Nocilla had committed a burglary, the penalty that he could receive would be twenty-five years to life in prison. Because he had been convicted previously of the crime of assault with the intent to commit rape, under California's three-strikes law that punishment would increase to fifty years to life just for the rape of Addie.

The preliminary hearing of the charges against Nocilla was held in late February. Addie testified at the hearing and detailed what Nocilla had done to her that night. After I had asked Addie my last question about the attack, she looked directly at the judge and said, "I thought he was a nice man, but he turned out to be a dog." When Addie said the word "dog," it sounded as though it were spelled "dawwwwg"—a little humor in what otherwise was a depressing set of facts. The judge decided that there was enough evidence to justify a trial, and a date was set.

Nocilla's jury trial started on June 13, 1996, and was assigned to Judge Joan Weber. I had never tried a case in front of Weber, but I knew that she ran an efficient courtroom. Have your witnesses ready, don't waste the jury's time sitting in the hallway, and you would be okay. The attorney representing Nocilla was Steve Cohan from the public defender's office. I had gotten along with Cohan well enough since the charges were filed against his client, but I could sense that there was going to be a problem. In particular, getting discovery of reports of expert witnesses who were likely to testify on his client's behalf was becoming difficult. In California, since the passage by the voters of Proposition 115 in 1990, prosecutors are entitled to reports of interviews with defense witnesses who are likely to testify at trial. In addition, reports by any experts the defense intends to call at trial also have to be provided to the prosecutor. The reason for these requirements is to prevent trials from being conducted by ambush and to avoid delays while prosecutors review for the first time documents in the possession of experts who testify at a trial.

The issue in *People v. Stephen Nocilla* wasn't going to be mistaken identification. Addie had spent plenty of time with Nocilla, and he had even turned her gun over to the store clerk a short time after the crimes. Rather, it was obvious to me that his defense would rely on the rape's never having occurred. Nocilla would probably also argue in the alternative that when he entered Addie's bedroom, he didn't intend to rape her. If the jury agreed, then the punishment Nocilla faced would be a fraction of the life sentence that he otherwise was exposed to.

Nocilla's lawyer and I talked about a possible plea bargain, but the discussions didn't go far. Both his past record and what he had done to Addie concerned me. Some defendants are genuine dangers to society, and I felt Nocilla was one of them. It was clear to me that he had mental problems of some sort, but that didn't justify what I was convinced was a planned attack that was a horrible violation of the trust Addie had placed in him.

After the jury was sworn in, I gave my opening statement. Wanting to get the jurors' attention as soon as possible, I talked about Addie. The jury already knew what the charges were but didn't know much about the victim. The first witness I called to the stand was Addie. I almost always had the victim of a sex crime testify first, while my opening statement was fresh in jurors' minds. Plus, I knew Addie would be a compelling witness. Showing the jury her southern background, how she felt about helping others, and how the defendant had betrayed the trust she had placed in him were important right out of the starting gate.

Cohan's cross-examination of Addie was necessarily careful. Any implication that Addie wasn't telling the truth would probably be detrimental to his client's defense. At the same time, Cohan had to place the seeds for his theory of the case and, ultimately, for the closing argument he would give to the jury. His questioning of Addie went about as far as was safe. Cohan emphasized how Addie had spent time with Nocilla both before and after they went to her cottage and how she had made dinner for him and they had talked for hours. He tried—I thought without success—to portray his client as someone who had mental problems. I knew that defense was going to come later, although I still hadn't received much in the way of reports from experts that Cohan was likely going to call. I was given a report by a mental health expert that indicated Nocilla was estimated to have an intelligence quotient (IQ) of about 70. The report, however, did not include any raw data, notes, or other documents that supported the opinion. Nonetheless, it was clear that Nocilla's defense was going to rely on that information.

I then called Debbie Kilgore, the sexual-assault nurse who had examined Addie at Villa View Hospital. Kilgore described her qualifications and the extensive experience she had with victims of sex crimes. I had Kilgore describe the whole process of a sexual-assault exam and how the procedures had changed after 1990. Before that, victims of rape were forced to wait in hospital emergency rooms to be seen by a physician. The wait could be hours, as emergency-room doctors were forced to deal with life-threatening cases first. Only when time allowed were doctors able to see sex victims.

The sexual-assault response-team (SART) system was put in place in many jurisdictions around the United States to fulfill the needs of both victims and the criminal-justice system. Kilgore felt strongly that the SART program was a success. She detailed her entire examination of Addie, including the evidence she collected and the injuries she had observed. Addie had told Kilgore about soreness in her vagina, and photographs of her genital area were taken to document what Kilgore had seen. She observed some bleeding, a small tear, and bruising in Addie's vaginal opening.

The police officers then testified, describing the initial contact with Addie at the coffee shop after the attack, their interviews with her, and the collection of the bed linen and clothing. The convenience-store clerk identified both Nocilla and the gun. Then came the DNA testimony. I had two analysts ready: Annette Peer of the San Diego Police Department crime lab and Dr. Charlotte Word from Cellmark. Word, like Peer and both Lisa Forman and Robin Cotton at Cellmark, was an accomplished scientist and a compelling witness. At the last minute, Cohan took me aside and said he was willing to agree to, or what's known in the law as "stipulate," to the DNA results and eliminate the need for the testimony of the DNA experts. In prior cases, I usually refused to stipulate to DNA evidence, mainly because the results are simply read to the jury instead of being described by live witnesses. I disliked DNA stipulations because much of the impact of DNA evidence is lost when a cold set of results is read to a jury. I made Cohan a counteroffer: if the stipulation included the fact that the semen was from his client, I would join in it. That statement would avoid any concern about the jury understanding the statistics that came with the DNA results. It had become obvious by this time in the trial that Cohan wasn't going to argue to the jury that his client hadn't ejaculated while he was on top of Addie. The stipulation was read to the jury. Three stains removed from the two sheets collected from Addie's bed contained semen. Each stain contained a mixture of DNA from Addie and DNA from Nocilla. I rested my case.

Cohan began to call witnesses in Nocilla's defense. One witness described seeing Nocilla and Addie downtown, while another saw them at the apartment. Nothing important, as far as I could tell. The defense then called a physician, Dr. Steven Gabaeff. A former emergency-room doctor, Gabaeff, it turned out, had been retained by Cohan to study Kilgore's findings and photographs. Gabaeff's credentials were impressive. Not only did he have more than thirty years' experience in the field, including exams of hundreds of rape victims, he was even appointed to a local advisory board on sexual assault by my boss, Paul Pfingst. Gabaeff was harshly critical of both the SART system and Kilgore's findings; he testified that in his opinion no one had sexually penetrated Addie. For the first time, I was concerned.

Two events worked in my favor; one I was ready for, the other blind luck. I had spoken to Gabaeff a couple of days earlier on the telephone. He was at least willing to talk with me before his testimony. We discussed the photographs and observations by Kilgore. Gabaeff insisted they were not necessarily the result of penetration by Nocilla. I could tell that he was not familiar with the law of rape, which prohibits the slightest penetration of even the vaginal lips. I asked him whether there was any indication of just slight penetration of Addie's external genitalia. He agreed that there was. And he conceded as much during my cross-examination in front of the jury, although minimizing the extent of the contact that could have occurred.

Gabaeff was adamant, however, that instituting the SART system was a mistake and that nurses were not nearly as qualified as medical school-trained physicians. His point appeared to be having an effect on the jury. But Gabaeff made a mistake that probably cost him his believability. I was being aggressive in my cross-examination because I thought Gabaeff was appearing arrogant in his criticism of Kilgore. We fenced on the issue of whether some vaginal bruising that was seen in the photographs of Addie could possibly have been the result of a chronic condition that existed prior to her contact with the defendant. Gabaeff lost his patience and said that any experienced physician would have simply had Addie undergo another exam after any injuries from the incident would have healed. Such an exam would show whether the bruising was related to the incident or not. I knew he was in a corner, and he didn't even realize it. I asked him just what was involved in such a follow-up exam. Gabaeff had never seen Addie and didn't seem to know how difficult it was for her to walk even a few steps. "All she would have to do is just jump up on the table and put her legs in the stirrups," he answered quickly. Several of the jurors, I later learned, visibly jerked in their chairs. I had no more questions for the doctor.

Nocilla's defense turned to his mental condition. Dr. Thomas Mac-Speiden, a San Diego psychologist, testified. He described his review of extensive materials about Nocilla, including his prior arrests. He administered a number of tests to Nocilla and came to the conclusion that Nocilla was a frotteurist. I had never heard the term before. MacSpeiden proceeded to describe a documented mental condition that impels males to engage in frottage—to rub their genitals, usually while they are clothed, against women, especially in public places. As a result of that condition, MacSpeiden told the jury, it was likely that Nocilla was simply rubbing himself against Addie and had no interest in raping her.

His assertion seemed at first a little comical, but MacSpeiden was dead serious. Frotteurism was, indeed, recognized by mental health professionals. However, it was also not very common. After some investigation of my own of the condition—done at the last minute as a result of getting MacSpeiden's report just before he testified—I set about cross-examining MacSpeiden, including asking about some of the other opinions in his report. MacSpeiden was forced to describe what he knew about other crimes for which Nocilla was arrested but not convicted. He had also considered the opinions of a couple of other psychologists who had examined Nocilla before he had. They had concluded that Nocilla had an antisocial personality. I asked MacSpeiden if that was the modern term for a person who had been previously called a sociopath and, before that, a psychopath. He agreed that it was, but he believed that the other psychologists were incorrect about Nocilla.

I also confronted him with the opinions of the other examiners that Nocilla's IQ was higher than MacSpeiden believed it to be from his testing. I thought the most damaging questions I asked MacSpeiden were about the relationship between even mild retardation and crimes. I asked him whether the fact that a person has an IQ of 70 causes that person to rape women. He agreed that it did not. I thought the point was made. MacSpeiden also agreed that frotteurism doesn't cause a person to commit rape.

We turned to closing arguments. I emphasized the facts testified to by Addie and supported by the testimony of the officers, the store clerk, and the DNA results. I talked briefly about smokescreens, but waited to hear Cohan's argument. Cohan talked about Nocilla's mental condition, his poor mental functioning, and that he had never learned appropriate sexual conduct. He also told the jurors that the evidence they had heard shouldn't be enough to convince them either that Nocilla had raped Addie or that he intended to do so when he entered her bedroom. Finally, Cohan argued that Addie's behavior had been flirtatious and may have been misunderstood by Nocilla.

I decided not to take long in my final argument. I spent most of my time reminding the jury of Addie's testimony, how Nocilla had violated her in her own bedroom, and the photographs and findings that supported the rape's having occurred. I ended with two points. The first dealt with retardation. Even Forest Gump, I told the jurors, wouldn't feel compelled to attack an elderly woman. The second point was about taking responsibility for a violent attack on one of society's most cherished members: a senior citizen.

On June 24 the jury returned guilty verdicts on all the counts, also finding to be true the allegations that made Nocilla subject to punishment under both the one-strike and three-strikes laws. Because of his prior conviction for assault with intent to commit rape, Nocilla was sentenced to a term of sixty years to life in prison. He would probably spend the rest of his life inside prison walls.

Addie was honored several months later by Pfingst as the San Diego County District Attorney's Office "Victim of the Year" for her courage and bravery in seeing her attacker brought to justice. Watching Addie slowly make her way to the podium to accept the award deeply moved both Dormann and me at the luncheon. Another memory of this case was a gift that Addie had for me. Once Nocilla's sentencing hearing had ended, Addie wanted me to have one of her proudest possessions: a King James Bible with her name inside. It still sits today on the shelf next to my desk. I make sure it doesn't get a chance to collect dust.

But I find myself unavoidably thinking about the entire spectacle of the Simpson trial—an early version of reality TV shows—and the vast resources committed by the prosecution only to have the jury acquit Simpson in the face of what most probably consider damning DNA and other circumstantial evidence. Addie was a poor, elderly, and brave woman. The district attorney's office committed the resources necessary to ensure that just punishment would be meted out for the crimes committed against her. Two cases, then, involving DNA—but how great the social and financial differences between the victims and their assailants.

CHAPTER TEN

When a Match Is Not a Match

———•———

Many of the other deputy district attorneys in my office, along with prosecutors across California and the country, were becoming accustomed to using DNA evidence. I always found it interesting at the outset of my lectures to ask how many of the prosecutors in attendance had tried a case that included DNA evidence. As the years passed, the number of hands that went up kept increasing. The technology was clearly playing an increasingly important role in trials all over the United States. But even the most experienced deputy district attorney could be tripped up. All one could do was hope that it didn't happen in the middle of a serious trial.

Mike Carpenter, my team leader at the time, was the unlucky prosecutor whom lightning struck. Carpenter had a serious case. Four different women were sexually assaulted between September 1994 and January 1995. The facts were disturbing. The first victim, a woman named Merle, worked as a lingerie model and nude dancer. The rules of her job permitted her to dance and to provide escort services for clients, but she was specifically prohibited from taking part in sexual acts. At about three o'clock one morning in September, she received a call to go to an apartment in Spring Valley, several miles east of San Diego. She went with her cousin, who customarily drove Merle to her clients, accompanied her until Merle was comfortable with the situation, and then waited outside while she performed. Merle knocked on the door of the apartment. A man answered and let her inside. The two discussed the fee; Merle was given $135 by the man, who signed a contract that Merle had brought with her. She went outside and told her cousin that everything was all right. The cousin stayed in the car while Merle returned to the apartment. Once inside, she used the bathroom to change into lingerie. When she came back into the main room, the man masturbated while

Merle danced. The man offered to pay her for sex, but Merle explained that she was forbidden to. She told him that she could perform a "hot show" for an additional tip. The man gave Merle an additional forty dollars for a hard-core show.

Merle began, but the man grabbed her and knocked her down to the floor. The two struggled. The man told Merle that he was a police officer and threatened to handcuff her if she didn't do what he wanted. Merle pleaded with him to take her to the police station. The attacker forced Merle into the bedroom and tried to rape her but was only able to partially penetrate her. Merle screamed, but the man put his hand over her mouth and threatened to shoot her with a gun. Merle continued to struggle with the man, who then tried to suffocate her. He slapped Merle on her face and turned her over and tried to rape her again, slightly penetrating her. He ejaculated on Merle's buttocks and thighs and then wiped her with a pillowcase. Merle was able to free herself from his grip and ran out the door. She told her cousin what had happened, and her cousin drove her back to the office.

The owner of the company took Merle to a sheriff's substation in Spring Valley. Merle was examined at Grossmont Hospital. The exam yielded material from Merle's shoulder and the back of her thighs that turned out to be semen. Injuries to different portions of her vagina were consistent with forced sexual intercourse. A search warrant was obtained for the man's apartment based on the allegations by Merle. Sheriff's detectives seized a pillowcase from the apartment. That pillowcase later proved to have semen on it. Curiously, the man, whose name was John Ivan Kocak, telephoned Merle's employer that night to complain that Merle had stolen money from him.

April, the second victim, was trying to sell the condominium she shared with her husband in La Mesa, another bedroom community east of San Diego. On January 16, April returned home from shopping at about 9:45 in the morning with her seven-month-old daughter. After putting her baby in a swing, she returned to her car in the parking lot to get her groceries. She saw a man in the lot and the two exchanged hellos. April took one box of her groceries into her home and then returned for the second. The man—who would later be identified as Kocak—asked April the price they were asking for the condo. She invited Kocak inside and gave him an informational sheet about the home, which the two then went over together.

As April and Kocak went down the hallway toward the bedroom, he put his hand on April's shoulder. She screamed and then found herself on the bed with Kocak atop her. April struggled with Kocak and tried to strike him in the crotch area. She attempted to gouge him with her keys, but she was choked and shaken and eventually lost consciousness. April awakened in her closet and discovered that her wrists and legs were bound with her husband's neckties. Her jeans were unzipped and pulled open and her mouth was stuffed with her husband's shorts. Although she was also blindfolded with ties, April was able to lift them enough to be able to see Kocak, who was going through files she and her husband kept in the bedroom. Kocak ordered April not to look at him. He told her that he was simply going to take their computer. April's daughter was still in her swing, but Kocak had taken the swing and placed it in the closet on top of April after she was tied up. April told him that the only things of value that they had were her wedding rings and an ATM card. Kocak stepped over April to get the ring set; as he did so he groped her breast and kissed her on the lips.

April was able eventually to free herself from the bindings and ran to a neighbor's home. The neighbor didn't even recognize April because of the blood on her, the bruises she had suffered, and the swelling to her entire face. Other neighbors arrived and telephoned 911. April screamed for someone to get her daughter. Some of the neighbors ran to April's apartment and found the baby unharmed. Others carefully removed the ligature around April's neck, taking care not to cut her because she was bound so tightly. She was taken to Grossmont Hospital, where doctors could see that she had significant bruises on her face and neck, which were visible for several weeks. One of her eyes was swollen closed. When her husband eventually came to the hospital, he could barely recognize April.

Five days after the assault on April, a woman named Patty was alone in her University Town Center apartment when she heard a knock on her door. When she asked what the person wanted, a man asked to see David. Patty told him that no one named David lived with her and gave him directions to the leasing office. About twenty minutes later the man returned and again knocked on the door. Believing that it was her husband, Patty this time opened the front door. The man, Kocak, again asked to see David and then grabbed the victim's neck with his hand and stepped into the apartment. He told her not to yell, but she screamed. Kocak ran away from the apartment, dropping his keys as he ran. He immediately returned to retrieve the keys. Patty continued screaming. Several neighbors came to her aid and called 911.

Finally, just three days later a businesswoman, Ann, returned to her University Town Center apartment after stopping at a store. She operated a real estate and mortgage-lending business from the apartment. After she was inside the apartment, Ann changed her clothing and was in the midst of a business call on her telephone when she heard a knock on the door. She placed the call on hold, looked through the peephole in the door, and saw a man. The man told Ann that he was staying in an apartment down the hall with friends and had locked himself out of the apartment. He asked to use Ann's telephone. Ann let the man into the apartment and handed him a cordless phone. She told him that she was in the middle of a long-distance call and went back into the bedroom that she used as an office.

Once Ann finished her call, the man threw her to the floor, where she landed on her face. When she screamed, he threatened to use a knife on her if she didn't stop. Ann stopped screaming. She was terrified and was convinced that the man was going to kill her. The attacker opened Ann's shirt and ripped off her bra. He then used the bra to gag Ann and ripped her shirt into strips that he used to tie her hands behind her back. The man stuffed some of the clothing into Ann's mouth and also placed a blindfold on her. He then removed her jeans and pantyhose. The assailant also tied Ann with her pantyhose across her chest and arm. He asked her questions to find out whether she was married or had a boyfriend.

The man then penetrated Ann's vagina, first with his finger, then with his penis. She believed that the man had ejaculated, but she didn't feel any semen on her. He also kissed her in her breast area. The man told Ann that if she cooperated he would leave her apartment in ten minutes. He tied a belt around her ankles and wanted to know where Ann kept her purse, money, and credit cards. He went through drawers and closets in the apartment. The man eventually found some condoms and then returned to Ann. He placed her on her back and tried to rape her, but the belt he had placed around Ann's ankles was too tight. He loosened the belt and then rolled her onto her stomach. He then attempted to sodomize her but was only partially successful. The man then raped Ann from behind. When he was done, he wiped her with something that felt to her like a towel or a shirt.

The attacker then tightened the bindings on Ann. She was now tied at the mouth with her bra, her hands were bound behind her back, and she was hogtied with her feet linked to her hands. Additional items the man used to tie Ann included an extension power cord, a bungee, and a vacuum-cleaner cord. He told her that he needed two hundred dollars and wanted to know where she kept her car keys. He told Ann that he would go to an ATM machine and if the PIN number she had given him did not work, he would return. Before he left, Ann heard him clean up areas of the apartment. She could tell that he was wearing rubber gloves during the cleaning. She was able to later determine that her rubber washing gloves were missing. The assailant then tied Ann even more tightly, turned the radio and television both on loud, and left.

Ann was able to pull the telephone down with her mouth from the desk it sat on. She turned on the speakerphone with her foot and then dialed 911 with her toe. She had to yell into the telephone because of the noise from the television and radio. She asked the operator to telephone her boyfriend and gave the operator his phone number. Within ten minutes Ann's boyfriend arrived. Police were right behind. Ann was untied; she was crying hysterically. Several items were missing from her apartment, including three rings, a necklace, a camcorder, a check, credits cards, her ATM card, and her car. A beauty-pageant medallion was also missing.

Ann was immediately taken by police to Harbor View Medical Center. She was examined and found to have abrasions on her arms, shoulder, lips, and vaginal area. Numbness in her arm lasted for one week after the attack. A criminalist from the San Diego Police Department collected evidence from Ann's apartment the same day as the assault. Among the items seized was a portion of a sweatshirt found in the bedroom that Ann used as her office. The crime laboratory determined that the fabric had a semen stain on it, as well as bloodstains. Using the PCR amplification process, the laboratory copied DNA from the semen stain and eventually typed it at the DQ-Alpha genetic marker, as well as at five additional DNA locations named Polymarker, which had been developed by the Cetus Corporation and its successor, Roche Molecular Systems. The result was a series of types that would be expected to be found, on average, only in one in forty-six hundred people. At the time, the police had no suspects in the case. Other DNA found on the fabric matched Ann's DNA. Ann, however, was never able to identify Kocak as the man who attacked her.

The identification by police of Kocak as the man who assaulted April and Ann was slowed by the fact more than one law-enforcement agency was involved in the investigations of the attacks. The initial assault on Merle in September was assigned to the Sheriff's Department because it had occurred in an unincorporated area of San Diego County. The fact that the victim was a nude dancer who had gone to the apartment consensually made the case difficult to prosecute. Then, several months later, the incidents involving the three additional victims took place within a period of only eight days.

Ann's case was assigned to Norma Dormann, the San Diego Police Department sex-crimes detective who had put together so well the case of eighty-five-year-old Addie (Chapter 9). Dormann had a hunch that whoever stole the jewelry from Ann would pawn the items at the nearest pawnshop, which turned out to be a few miles away in the Pacific Beach area of San Diego. She telephoned that store and was mistakenly told they had received no similar items. Dormann then gathered drawings made of the jewelry by Ann's brother, and they were entered into the police department's computer database. Shortly after, a hit was made to a gold chain and two rings pawned the next day by Kocak at the same Pacific Beach pawnshop Dormann had telephoned. That put Kocak at the head of Dormann's suspect list. The assault on Patty had been close in distance to Ann's, so Dormann was able to tie together the two attacks. Finally, by talking to sheriff's detectives and remembering a flyer they had distributed a week earlier about the attack on April, she was able to tie Kocak to that assault and then to the September incident with Merle.

Two weeks after the assault on Ann, Detective Dormann and police searched Kocak's apartment in the University Town Center area. Found inside were April's computer, her husband's clothing, the camera, and some of the other property stolen from their apartment. Also found were some pawn slips. Kocak admitted to police that the items belonged to April. He had also used her ATM card at a bank to get three hundred dollars in cash and tried on other occasions to get additional money. Police had collected fingerprints from the swing that April's daughter was in and determined that they matched those of Kocak. PCR testing of blood discovered on the computer was found to be consistent with Kocak's DNA. The DQ-Alpha types shared by the blood on the computer and Kocak are found in only about one in thirty people.

Kocak was arrested for the four incidents. DNA results from the sample of his blood that was taken were tested and compared with the semen stain left on the fabric that was used to wipe Ann after she was assaulted. Kocak's DNA matched the profile found in the semen stain. He was charged with over twenty crimes, ranging from assault to attempted murder, rape, robbery, sexual penetration with a foreign object, sodomy, and vehicle theft. Allegations were included in the complaint that, if proved, would result in Kocak's being sentenced to prison for life.

After a preliminary hearing of the charges, a judge decided that the evidence presented was enough to require a trial. After several continuances, that trial was set for November. Deputy District Attorney Carpenter knew the case was a strong one for several reasons: the three eyewitness identifications of Kocak, the circumstantial evidence that tied Kocak to the attacks, the fact that a jury would hear the story told by each of the victims, and Kocak's possession of the property taken in two of the incidents.

Carpenter also knew that the match that had been made by the San Diego police crime lab of the semen on the cloth in Ann's case and Kocak would be important at trial. Its significance was magnified by the fact that Ann couldn't identify Kocak as her assailant. But Carpenter wanted additional evidence. We talked about his case, and I told him that a new set of genetic markers that were just beginning to be used in criminal cases might be just the boost he wanted. At that time, the DQ-Alpha genetic marker, the five Polymarker locations, and even a few additional DNA loci that had been developed for use in crime labs still couldn't prove that no one else in the world could have left a piece of evidence. Forensic scientists wanted a set of genetic markers that were amenable to PCR testing yet were sufficiently individualizing to tell everyone in the world apart. In other words, they wanted the luxury of using PCR on very small samples and the power of RFLP typing to get results that were tantamount to identification.

The genetic markers that met these requirements were short tandem repeats, or STRs. Scientists investigating human diseases in 1990 discovered a set of markers characterized by short, repetitive sequences of DNA. Like those locations tested using the RFLP technique, STR markers are similar in that people repeat the same sequence of DNA differing numbers of times at each locus. Unlike RFLP markers, however, STR repetitions are very short. They are thus far less susceptible than RFLP markers to degradation, or even destruction, of the DNA fragments and can successfully be tested in small and older samples. Further research showed that many of these loci were not linked to any particular disease, and, importantly for forensic testing purposes, they varied in humans. Although an individual STR genetic marker by itself was not very powerful in telling people apart, testing several different locations would allow a forensic examiner to obtain results considerably more powerful than those typically obtained from testing existing PCR markers.

Scientists initially determined that a series of three STR loci was reliable for forensic testing. The technique used to test samples at those markers was similar to the earlier RFLP procedure. The data from which results were interpreted consisted of banding patterns, which were then compared with patterns from known samples, and exclusions or inclusions were then determined. As with each of the previous DNA technologies, statistical databases were then used to make estimates of the rarity of matching profiles. The three STR loci were already being used in the real world. During the Persian Gulf War in 1991, the U.S. Armed Forces Institute of Pathology used STR testing to identify the remains of dead Americans. When traditional identification techniques—including fingerprint and dental comparisons—failed, DNA testing was used. And when soldiers were killed in explosions or by other means that rendered regular DNA tests impossible, STR technology could be used.

I told Carpenter about the three new STR markers that could be tested in his case. He was enthusiastic. The laboratory that we would use was Cellmark, a lab known to both of us. Carpenter had done his own *Kelly-Frye* hearing in a rape series in 1989 using the earlier RFLP technology. He was comfortable with the scientists at Cellmark and their testimony. The decision was made to forward to Cellmark a portion of the fabric that had been used to clean Ann. Cellmark received the evidence and went ahead with STR testing at the three genetic-marker locations. Cellmark concluded from the testing that at each of the three STR loci DNA from the fabric matched the DNA of Kocak.

Carpenter and I discussed the results. We agreed that the defense in his case would probably object to the results and demand a *Kelly-Frye* hearing to try to convince the trial judge not to allow the Cellmark results to be admitted at Kocak's jury trial. For that matter, I mentioned, it was likely that the attorney representing Kocak would object to even the DQ-Alpha and Polymarker results that also implicated Kocak in the attack on Ann. But Carpenter was confident. I helped him prepare for the expected hearing by giving him a copy of a legal brief I had kept up to date on the admissibility of DNA testing; I frequently added to it as new technologies were introduced in criminal cases. I also prepared for him copies of scientific articles that described the use of the STR technique on the same genetic markers that were used at Cellmark. Carpenter put in hours of preparation for the hearing that we both knew was likely to happen.

The case against Kocak was assigned to Judge Richard M. Murphy for trial. Murphy was known as a fair judge who would carefully weigh both sides of a case and wasn't afraid to make a ruling that he felt was right. Kocak, through his attorney, Deputy Public Defender Ray Aragon, did indeed object to the jury's hearing the STR results from Cellmark. Kocak and his attorney also objected to the San Diego Police Department Polymarker results, which were also consistent with Kocak.

Murphy agreed that an admissibility hearing was necessary. As part of that hearing, Carpenter called an expert from Cellmark to testify about the lab's STR results. The expert described for Murphy the STR testing process and its development and validation, and provided an opinion that the technology was generally accepted in the scientific community. The scientist's testimony stretched into a second day and included descriptions of the results that Cellmark had gotten from its testing of the cloth.

Suddenly, during that testimony, the expert appeared to be stunned while glancing at some of the lab's data that were spread out on the witness stand. Carpenter knew something was wrong. Because it was time for the mid-afternoon recess, Murphy agreed to call a break. Carpenter and the witness marched up to the district attorney's offices on the seventh floor of the county courthouse. Carpenter found me down the hall. I could tell there was a problem. The expert broke in and gave me the news. In looking at the raw data and supporting material from the testing done by Cellmark on the fabric, the expert realized that the results didn't support the conclusion of a match between the DNA found on the cloth and Kocak. Instead, the results showed only that the evidence matched the victim, Ann. In the preparation of the report that was issued and provided to both the district attorney's office and the attorney for Kocak, the names of Ann and Kocak had been accidentally reversed. Cellmark's results, in reality, proved little or nothing. As the three of us talked during the recess, the course of action became obvious. Aragon and Judge Murphy would be notified immediately of the error in the report. A new report would be prepared once the Cellmark scientist returned to the laboratory, reviewed all the pertinent data, and tried to determine how the mistake had been made.

That afternoon, after the judge and Aragon were informed of the mistake, the hearing continued. But the expert from Cellmark was no longer needed. Carpenter told Murphy that he would not present that evidence to the jury. The hearing did continue in regard to the Polymarker testing that had been done by the San Diego Police Department on the same cloth. Ultimately, Murphy decided those results would be admissible at the trial. He found that the Polymarker technology was, indeed, generally accepted in the scientific community.

A jury was selected, and Kocak was tried on the charges that had been filed against him. The victims all testified, the circumstantial evidence of Kocak's involvement in the attacks was described to the jury, and the DNA results from the police crime lab were set out in detail. Those results implicated Kocak in the assault on Ann, as well as in the incident with April. In his defense, Kocak took the witness stand. He told the jury that his sexual encounter with Merle was consensual. As to April, Kocak testified that the two of them had a consensual sexual relationship that April turned around to report was forced. He claimed that she changed her mind about their relationship when he told her their affair was over. She then feigned a robbery to explain her injuries. Kocak denied having any contact with either Patty or Ann. He testified that he had gotten the property he pawned from a man at a bar. The jury convicted Kocak of three counts of rape; two of sodomy; one each of oral copulation, foreign-object penetration, and attempted rape; two counts of robbery; three of residential burglary; and other charges. The jury also found true allegations that he committed the burglaries with the intent to commit sex crimes. Judge Murphy sentenced Kocak to state prison for the term of one hundred years to life.

But the effects of the mistake that had been made in the laboratory's DNA report didn't disappear. Later testing by Cellmark verified that its earlier results for the DNA types on the evidence and the samples from Kocak and Ann were all correct; the DNA from the cloth matched Ann's. Just as important, a jury never heard the mistaken report's conclusions. Apparently, an expert hired by Kocak's attorney to review the testing data from Cellmark didn't catch the error himself. But some scientists and lawyers pointed to the case as an example of how DNA labs were capable of making mistakes. And therefore, they alleged, DNA results should be suspect, or the statistics of the rarity of matching DNA profiles should be modified to reflect the fact that labs make mistakes. But everything involving humans is subject to mistake. Fortunately, the error in the Kocak case was discovered by the very laboratory that had made it. And it was discovered prior to trial and ultimately had no effect on the trial's result.

Nevertheless, the controversy that surrounded the lab's mistake in report writing continued unabated for several years. Kocak's convictions and sentence were appealed and turned down by California's appellate courts. As we will see in Chapter 13, years later the opportunity would present itself to take a fresh look at the same evidence that gave rise to the error in reporting DNA results, an opportunity that would result in putting to rest any questions that might remain about a case in which a match was not a match.

CHAPTER ELEVEN

Exonerations, Databases, and STRs

Scientists were busy in the 1990s finding additional locations on the DNA molecule that could be tested with PCR-based methods. The fact that these techniques could be used on small samples, as well as the speed with which the testing could be accomplished, led to an explosion in the popularity of PCR technologies. DQ-Alpha was joined by the five different genetic markers that were known as Polymarker, followed by the addition of three STRs that increased the ability of forensic scientists to tell people apart. Nationwide, more prison inmates—like Ricky Daye (Chapter 6)—asked courts for DNA testing in their cases. The Innocence Project of Barry Scheck and Peter Neufeld at the Benjamin Cardozo School of Law in New York was inundated with requests from convicts for its lawyers to take their cases. A technology that could be successfully used on samples that were twenty or more years old provided hope to hundreds for possible exoneration and release from prison. And that hope eventually became reality for many. By 1996, more than fifty prison inmates had been exonerated by DNA testing and released from prison. Mostly, their convictions were from trials that took place many years before DNA testing was available. The issues that arose in those cases were often difficult and troubling to prosecutors, victims, and courts.

In many states, obstacles to having testing performed in old cases were enormous. Some jurisdictions required that for an inmate to even have an application for DNA testing considered the request had to be brought a short time after the inmate's conviction. Newly-discovered-evidence motions in some states were legally barred after as little as thirty days following the original trial. DNA testing had not even been conceived at the expiration of many of those mandatory periods. Scheck, Neufeld, and other attorneys who represented inmates seeking DNA testing often turned to writs of habeas corpus and other legal means to try to convince prosecutors and courts to allow access to testing. Prosecutors often fought those requests with all the fervor they could muster. Undoing a conviction obtained at great time, cost, and emotional expense was not going to happen without a fight in most instances, even when DNA testing could resolve doubts about the inmate's guilt.

Another major hurdle to asking for testing was the obvious requirement that the evidence to be tested had to still exist. Local police departments, sheriff's offices, state police, and even courts were overcrowded with physical evidence. Once cases were upheld on original appeals, the temptation to clear room for evidence in new cases was great. And, in most jurisdictions, that temptation was a necessity. But a large number of agencies kept the evidence, often locked away in corner offices, file cabinets, and shelves that normally gathered little other than dust. Even when evidence had been destroyed or couldn't be located, creative attorneys and investigators would comb other possible locations. Hospitals, coroner's offices, detectives' desks, and even court reporters' offices sometimes proved to be a source of important biological evidence. But, because of intentional destruction or other loss, in as many as 75 percent or more of those cases in which DNA testing might establish innocence, the evidence couldn't be found.

A review of the old cases in which DNA testing has led to exoneration and release is eye opening. The clear majority of those cases involved verdicts that relied on eyewitness identification, statements of the inmate, testimony of jailhouse or other informants, or the use of subjective sciences or technical evidence. In many cases, a combination of these types of evidence was used. An inmate may have been convicted at a jury trial, for example, based on evidence provided by a snitch, a general description of the attacker, and a microscopic hair comparison.

Even if evidence was located, getting access to that evidence was often a battle. Sometimes that battle deserved to be fought by both sides. One of the most difficult determinations in the review of an old case is the effect DNA results might have on the question of the inmate's innocence. For example, if testing on a swab taken from a rape victim revealed someone else's DNA, would that fact prove the inmate had not committed the attack?

The facts of each case vary. In a sexual assault of a small child, in which clearly only one person has committed the crime, DNA results that point to someone other than the inmate as the person who assaulted the victim normally show that the inmate is innocent. In the case of a rape of an adult woman, exclusionary DNA results may provide scant information about innocence. A husband, boyfriend, or another consensual partner—or even a second attacker—can be the source of the evidence, and thus the DNA results might shed little light on an inmate's innocence. Some types of evidence, however, are unlikely to provide any exonerating information. A hair found on a murder victim lying on the floor of a busy office, for example, like a fingerprint on a hotel-lobby door, is unlikely to provide helpful information because it very likely came from someone who had nothing to do with the crime. Not that all testing had to be able to conclusively show that the inmate was innocent. Early on, a few states, such as Illinois and New York, decided to permit testing if exclusionary results would provide material evidence. That standard meant that if those results would have been important for the jury to know, the inmate might be entitled at least to a new trial that could then include that evidence.

Courts sometimes struggled with interpretation of the statutes, rules, and case law that applied to deciding whether to order testing. Fortunately, a significant number of prosecutors across the country agreed to testing without the need for a court to decide. Because of the power of DNA to resolve questions that simply couldn't be answered at the time of the original trials, testing was often mutually agreed to. The possibility of having convicted an innocent inmate was—and continues to be—a great concern to everyone inside and outside the criminal-justice system.

The opposite, but perhaps equally important, consequence of PCR's power was the prospect of solving cases in which there was never before any information about the identity of the person who committed the crime. By testing biological evidence recovered at the crime scene or found on a victim and comparing it with databases of DNA profiles from known offenders, previously unsolved cases can be resolved. Early on, the FBI recognized the potential for identifying attackers in this way. For decades, the FBI had stored and maintained fingerprint records of anyone arrested in the United States for a felony or a jailable misdemeanor. Those known fingerprints were digitized and routinely searched for comparison with unknown fingerprints collected at crime scenes. DNA profiles are much easier to incorporate into a national database system than fingerprints because DNA types are simply numerical information. The only major issue is which groups of people should be required to provide samples of their DNA for inclusion in databases.

Fortunately, many states already had laws in place that required convicted offenders to provide samples of their blood after conviction. Most of these statutes had been enacted during the days of ABO and other serological testing but appeared to permit DNA testing as well. Other states passed legislation that was specific to DNA data-basing and collection of samples. Before long, all fifty states and the federal government enacted laws that required defendants convicted of certain felony crimes to give samples. Typically, the crimes that trigger collection are rape, other sex offenses, and murder. Some states added other crimes as well.

A small few—especially Virginia—mandate that defendants convicted of any felony must provide samples for testing and data-banking. The Virginia approach seemed revolutionary when it was enacted. No one questioned the fact that violent criminals have a high rate of reoffending, particularly when compared with the general population. The wisdom of collecting and data-basing DNA profiles of violent criminals seemed obvious. But what about those who were guilty of simple drug possession, forgery, or auto theft? Virginia was willing to try collecting data from them also.

Passing laws was one thing. Funding an infrastructure for collecting and testing samples was another. At the same time, the question of who was going to test the samples that were sitting in police evidence lockers had to be answered. Crime labs were already overburdened with testing evidence in cases in which the suspected attacker was known and already arrested. DNA analysts and crime-lab personnel were unable to keep up with testing that was needed in cases that were about to go to trial. Adding to that burden was unthinkable. But databases were started, and small numbers of unsolved cases were examined. The potential was great. PCR testing of six different genetic markers wasn't going to set the scientific world on fire and couldn't identify an assailant from a database search even the way fingerprints could. But it was a start, and that start would shortly enjoy a boost that few would have envisioned.

Everyone realized that the power of PCR testing of small samples in criminal cases would eventually render the RFLP technique obsolete. Not only did PCR provide results with limited evidence, but retesting by defendants was available in most cases. The desire to maintain a portion of evidence for later retesting pervades both the scientific community and the criminal-justice system.

The FBI early on recognized that STR testing would provide a unique means of identifying the donors of DNA samples; STR was going to exceed even the power of previous RFLP techniques. In addition the FBI had already been given the task of developing and administering the national DNA database system. Although that task was originally limited by the fact that pre-STR technologies proved cumbersome for data-basing, some successes had been encountered with database matches in unsolved cases. Nicknamed

CODIS, the FBI's Combined DNA Index System had been years in the making. The Bureau had the benefit of its extensive experience with fingerprint databanks. But a successful DNA database would require extraordinary cooperation between state and local law enforcement in the collection of samples from qualifying offenders, the testing of those samples, and the DNA typing of evidence in unsolved cases. The process was slow to become a reality.

Because the FBI knew that a DNA database would rely on STRs, it sponsored a committee of forensic and other DNA scientists to select those STR genetic markers, or loci, that would form the core of its CODIS database system. In 1997 the committee announced its selection of thirteen STR genetic markers that from that point on would be the language spoken by its database system. The committee thereby charted the course to be taken by crime labs across the country. A few state appellate courts had already declared that STR testing results could properly be heard by juries in criminal trials. Massachusetts, Nebraska, and California early on approved the admission in evidence of results from testing of the three STR markers first used in casework. That approval was likely to pave the way for approval of the other ten markers and their results.

The FBI's selection of the thirteen genetic markers meant that manufacturers of the "kits" used to perform STR testing had to scramble. Since the original PCR and DQ-Alpha days, kits had been routinely used by crime labs and even in hospitals. Like disease-diagnosis clinics, crime labs find it efficient and economical to purchase chemicals and other ingredients for DNA testing in kit form. Kits were already available for the three STR markers that were in use in many crime laboratories. New kits would be needed to allow those labs to test some or all of the thirteen markers declared to embody the future of forensic testing in the United States.

Manufacturers of the new kits that would ultimately test all the CODIS markers encountered a few obstacles. Most labs used kits that tested just nine of the thirteen markers. After a period of time, many of those laboratories added the additional four loci to their stable of STRs. However, testing had to be split between the original nine and the remaining four. Thus two separate amplifications of DNA had to be accomplished to get results at all thirteen loci. Nonetheless, results from the use of even just the first nine markers proved astounding. Matching profiles at just nine STR locations meant very small probabilities of coincidental matches. Typically, the chances of someone matching an item of evidence seized from a crime scene were one in billions or even trillions. If all thirteen locations were used and led to matching results, the probability was even smaller.

As a result of these often small probabilities, some laboratories, including the FBI's own lab, adopted policies permitting experts to give an opinion in court that a sample came from, for example, a defendant. That opinion often took the place of giving a statistical estimate of the rarity of the DNA profile that was the same for both the defendant and the evidence that had been tested. Sometimes, however, attorneys felt the effect on juries was greater when testimony was presented that the statistical chances of the match were "one in ten trillion" instead. Some lawyers preferred to have the expert witness describe both, trying to impress on jurors the extraordinary power of the test results.

STR testing provided another important benefit. Mixtures of DNA from more than one person are common in casework. The mixture may be an anticipated combination of DNA from an attacker and the victim in a rape case, or it may be an unexpected mix of blood from two persons in a single stain. Previous PCR techniques, including those using the DQ-Alpha and Polymarker loci, were frequently ineffective in obtaining complete information about the profiles of each contributor to a mixture. STRs, because of the number of different types that are possible at each marker, give analysts the opportunity to provide investigators with much greater information.

As time passed, STR results were used increasingly in court. Other than in a few trial courts in a handful of states, STR typing was uniformly approved, including by appeals courts. Unlike the more uneven legal path negotiated by RFLP testing, PCR-based techniques encountered little rejection by higher courts. STR testing and offender databases were clearly going to assist law enforcement in its fight against violent crime. It was next necessary to get those tools in the hands of police, sheriff, and state-patrol labs. Sometimes the impetus for change is a graphic showing of the results of new approaches. In this case, the wait for that showing was a brief one.

As STR technologies made their way into crime laboratories, the San Diego Police Department was faced with many of the same issues confronted by crime labs across the United States. Additional money would have to be spent to implement those technologies in a working laboratory, especially when expensive new equipment was needed to perform the testing. The first method used to type the three original STRs required little additional equipment in an existing casework lab. However, science never stands still. Automated machines were designed and created to conduct the entire STR typing process formerly manually performed by DNA analysts. Inside a desktop machine about twice the size of a kitchen microwave oven, a sophisticated set of miniature tools can determine the STR profile of both evidence and known samples.

Analysts still had to interpret the results. However, use of the new automated equipment allowed analysts to examine more evidence items and locate more potentially important biological material that could be tested. But the problem of too many cases and not enough analysts was acute. To make matters worse, prosecutors facing trial in serious cases knew that juries expected to hear DNA results. Not testing a piece of evidence seized during the investigation of a crime would be to run the risk of alienating one or more jurors. If DNA testing was so important, jurors might ask, why didn't the police test all the evidence? The pressure to test more and more evidence stretched laboratories thin.

The San Diego Police Department was no exception. Because prosecutors in my own office were making requests for testing in record numbers, the lab sought help. Assistant Police Chief Nancy Goodrich, crime-lab manager Mike Grubb, and DNA Supervisor Patrick O'Donnell asked to meet with Assistant District Attorney Greg Thompson and me. They explained the problem. They had two requests: that I be made a buffer between prosecutors and the crime lab, and that I review each request made by a San Diego deputy district attorney for DNA testing. Grubb and O'Donnell were convinced that I had the experience and knowledge of DNA techniques to screen out much of the testing that prosecutors were asking for. In a perfect world every item seized would be tested. In the real world, only a fraction of those samples could be typed. Thompson and District Attorney Paul Pfingst agreed. From now on, any DNA testing requested by a prosecutor would have to be cleared by me. It seemed a good idea, and it didn't appear that it would take that much of my time. I felt like a diplomat with my new title of Crime Laboratories Liaison. Most important, I would still take cases of my own.

One of those cases came through my door in March 2000. Deputy District Attorney Dan Lamborn, a long-time friend and confidante, was sitting in for the chief of our felony-trial division. San Diego Police Department Homicide Detective Joe Cristinziani had told Lamborn on the phone that he had a sexual-assault case from 1995 that had just been solved by a match in the police department DNA database. Lamborn got a brief description of the case from Cristinziani and decided that I should review it. Cristinziani walked down the hall to my office and introduced himself. I recognized him, but the first question that came to mind was why a homicide detective had a sex case. He explained. He had been assigned to sex crimes in 1995 when the case occurred, and he had kept the case all that time, even after he had been reassigned to the homicide division. The case had always troubled him, and Cristinziani wanted to do whatever was necessary to solve it. DNA had allowed him to do that. We sat down and started the chronology. It was fascinating.

Sandra, a student at the University of San Diego, was temporarily living with three other coeds in one unit of a duplex a short distance from the university in the community of Linda Vista. At about 10:00 the evening of March 9, 1995, Sandra left school, where she had been studying in the library. She was driven home from the school by a university police officer. Sandra entered the two-story townhouse and first spent some time searching for her identification, which she had apparently misplaced. Sandra intended to join several of her friends who were in the Mission Beach area that evening. She searched for her identification for almost forty-five minutes, but she couldn't find it. Sandra then telephoned one of her friends, telling her that she would be unable to join them that evening. Sandra was always asked for her identification at bars, even though she was twenty-three years old.

A little later, at about 11:30, Sandra heard noises coming from the upstairs area of the townhouse, which consisted of a large bedroom and a connected bathroom. She went upstairs but saw no one on the second floor. Sandra walked inside the bathroom and turned on the light. She was examining herself in the bathroom mirror when she suddenly heard a noise, which caused her to look to her right. She immediately felt a blow to the right side of her head and face. The sheer force of the blow knocked her to the floor of the bathroom. She felt a body come over her while she was on the floor and could tell that hands were covering her face. At that moment Sandra was convinced the person was a male. She was unable, however, to see the man's face because the light in the bathroom was now off. Sandra was scared to death.

The man said something and Sandra instinctively replied that she would do whatever he wanted. She pleaded with him not to kill her. The man dragged her from the bathroom floor to the bedroom. The bedroom had two beds, located on opposite sides of the room. The bedroom lights were all off. Sandra still couldn't see her attacker's face. He picked up Sandra and threw her on the bed that was closest to the bathroom. The man then removed her dress. Sensing the worst, Sandra asked the man whether he had a condom. He answered that he didn't and then asked Sandra why she had asked. Sandra lied, telling him that she had herpes. She desperately hoped that the man would end his attack on her. Sandra then heard the man pulling a zipper on his own clothing. He got on top of Sandra and began to rape her. Sandra was in great pain and prayed to God that the attack would stop. Some time during the assault the man asked Sandra when her roommates were coming home. She told him that she had no idea. At another point, her attacker asked whether there was any money in the residence. Sandra pleaded that they were all students and never had any extra money.

Crying because of the pain, she pleaded with the man to stop. He got up off the bed, went to the other side of the room, and then came back. Sandra ended up on the other bed in the room, next to her assailant. She still couldn't get any view of his face. The room was pitch black. The man tried to force Sandra to give him oral sex, but she was able to push her head away from him. He ended the attempt, but then raped Sandra a second time. He eventually ejaculated on Sandra's chest and face. Without even thinking, she tried to wipe it up with the bedsheet.

Her attacker then ordered Sandra to get on her knees on the bed. Sandra froze and was terrified at what she thought he was going to do. She pleaded with him to let her go, but he raped her a third time. The man then directed Sandra to the other side of the room by the first bed. She still couldn't see his face because of the darkness. He tied her hands behind her back with her sundress. He then went into the bathroom and turned on the light. Sandra thought about looking up at him but was too scared to even try to get a look at his face. He returned from the bathroom and hogtied Sandra's legs to her hands. At some point after that, the attacker violated Sandra again, this time with his fingers. After her legs were tied together, he dragged Sandra across the bedroom carpet while on her stomach, causing painful scrapes to her knees.

The man told Sandra that he needed time to leave the residence, and she believed he reentered the bathroom. Within seconds, Sandra heard the sound of footsteps going down the stairs. After waiting a few minutes, she untied herself, went to the phone, and tried to call the police. The telephone was dead. Sandra clumsily put on some clothing and went to the next-door neighbor, who immediately called the police. San Diego police officers quickly arrived and took down Sandra's crying description of what had happened to her. She was then driven to Villa View Hospital for a sexual-assault medical examination. There, Sandra was treated for her injuries and samples of evidence were collected from her body.

The next day Sandra was interviewed by Cristinziani, who was assigned to investigate her assault. At the time, Cristinziani was a novice sex-crimes detective. But he had two important characteristics on his side: a good head on his shoulders and common sense. Sandra repeated to him the same description she had given patrol officers the night before. The procedure of multiple interviews of sex-crimes victims frequently seems unnecessary and unfair to victims of sexual assaults. Nothing could be further from the truth. Victims of sex offenses are usually traumatized by the attacks. Smaller details of the attack are sometimes jumbled, confused, or simply not recalled at the time victims are interviewed by patrol officers who arrive at the scene. The space created by a day or two after the assault typically allows the victim to remember additional details of an attack. Despite the recollection of additional facts about an incident, the descriptions given by victims who have been sexually assaulted are normally remarkably consistent. That consistency is extremely helpful in proving the guilt of defendants who have committed sexual assaults. An allegation that a crime is simply being made up by a victim can often be successfully rebutted by proving to a jury that the victim repeated the same general description of her attack on several occasions.

Sandra's brutal attack was most likely committed by a stranger. Cristinziani asked the San Diego Police Department crime lab to perform DNA testing on evidence that was collected from her. Using PCR, the lab developed a genetic profile from the semen found on swabs that were taken from Sandra's genitals, neck, and chest area. The same DQ-Alpha and Polymarker profile was found on the fitted sheet from the second bed she was attacked on. Cristinziani combed the area of the duplex where Sandra had been attacked. Neighbors were interviewed. Records of the police department about similar assaults in the general area were reviewed. Sex offenders known to live in a wide area surrounding the duplex were looked at and considered. Several possible suspects were interviewed, and their DNA samples were tested. None produced a lead on the identity of Sandra's rapist. Sandra couldn't even provide a description of her attacker because she couldn't get a good look at his face. The case turned cold.

But unknown to Cristinziani, another crime would eventually prove to be the means for identifying the man who had forced Sandra to undergo her ordeal. Seven months after the assault, a woman was tanning herself in a salon a few miles from Sandra's duplex. Minutes after beginning her tanning session, the woman felt a wet substance on her right hip and thigh. She sat up and saw the backside of a man leaving her tanning room. The woman realized that someone had ejaculated on her and screamed. An employee immediately went to the room, found out what had happened, and telephoned police.

The employee, just before she heard the scream, had seen a man standing outside the room in which the victim was tanning. The man had turned away. The employee went to clean another room and then returned to the reception area. Once she called the police, the worker looked at a video monitor that displayed images taken from a video camera in the salon hallway, including the area outside the victim's room. She saw the same man she had seen earlier; this time he was moving quickly toward a staircase leading outside the salon.

San Diego police officers answered the phone call and learned from the victim that seven dollars was missing from her purse, which had been inside the room. The officers also recovered the semen left on the victim. A suspect was eventually developed by detectives because a license plate was observed on the vehicle in which he had fled. PCR testing was done on a portion of the semen that was collected from the victim. A known sample was obtained from the suspect, a twenty-five-year-old man named Paul Vasquez. The crime lab determined that Vasquez matched the DQ-Alpha and Polymarker profile from the semen on the tanning-room victim.

Vasquez was arrested and charged with the incident in the tanning salon. He was also charged with a similar act in which he had exposed himself to another woman six months earlier at the same salon. The date of that crime was April 3, 1995—less than a month after the brutal attack on Sandra. Both this victim and the salon employee identified Vasquez. Before his trial, Vasquez pleaded guilty to two misdemeanor indecent-exposure charges that had been filed by prosecutors against him. He decided to go to trial on the remaining felony counts of burglary and theft. He demanded a trial because he had three prior convictions that qualified as strikes: two 1988 home burglaries that he had committed when he was eighteen and one 1991 robbery. Vasquez had escaped the harsh, life-imprisonment provisions of the three-strikes law because it had not gone into effect in California until 1994. But his 1995 crimes now exposed him to that punishment as long as he was convicted of any felony—including the theft of the victim's seven dollars.

Vasquez was convicted at his jury trial of the theft charge. The judge decided to dismiss two of Vasquez's previous convictions and sentence Vasquez to prison for a total of eight years instead of the life term he could have been given under the three-strikes law. The judge noted that the only felony crime Vasquez was convicted of by a jury was the theft of the small amount of money. Were it not for his prior convictions, the crime would have been a misdemeanor, just like the indecent exposures to which he had already pleaded guilty.

Vasquez began serving his prison term in 1996. As long as he behaved himself and did the work assigned to him while he was in prison, he'd be released sometime in 2001. Vasquez had dodged a bullet when the judge decided to give him only eight years in prison. Little did he know that the second shot would be right on target.

Brian Burritt appeared to be a quiet and reserved man, but I was always convinced he knew exactly what he was doing. I met Burritt at the California Department of Justice DNA laboratory in Berkeley in the mid-1990s. He was an analyst who had a penchant for databases, to the point that he even used his own laptop computer to compare DNA profiles from unsolved cases to those of convicted offenders who were required to provide their own blood and saliva. To some, Burritt was a computer nerd. To others, like me, he was a modern-day Sherlock Holmes.

Fortunately for the San Diego Police Department, Burritt was interested in moving to San Diego. He applied for a DNA position and accepted the department's later offer. Burritt and his wife moved to San Diego. While he settled in with the police lab, his wife joined the San Diego sheriff's crime laboratory. By the spring of 1999 he had become intimately familiar with how the San Diego Police Department maintained its DNA profiles. Equally important, Burritt began to input profiles into the CODIS database to enable the comparison of DNA results from casework. On June 20, 1999, Burritt contacted Detective Cristinziani. He had breathtaking news. Burritt had determined that a match existed between the DNA profiles of the unidentified rapist of Sandra and another case that had also been worked on in the lab. That case was the incident at the tanning salon involving Vasquez.

Cristinziani was excited. He was now a detective in the department's homicide division and had honed his skills since he started the investigation of Sandra's attack four years earlier. Finally, he had a real lead in determining who had committed the brutal assault on Sandra. The fact that the match included a relatively common profile (one in 2,600 people) didn't deter Cristinziani. Once he retrieved the tanning-salon case file and examined it, he knew that Vasquez was his man. Not only had Vasquez been paroled to San Diego from a previous prison term only a month before Sandra's assault, but the tanning case was obviously sexual in nature.

Cristinziani quickly found out that Vasquez was still in prison as a result of his sentence in the tanning case. To be sure that Vasquez was the right person, Cristinziani asked for a search warrant to obtain new samples of Vasquez's DNA. One year before, in 1998, Cristinziani had forwarded one of the vaginal swabs taken from Sandra to Cellmark for RFLP testing. He had requested the RFLP testing so that a more discriminating profile than the original one could be obtained for later comparisons with any suspects. RFLP testing on the swab by Cellmark had produced a clear profile from the semen donor. A new sample was needed from Vasquez to enable Cell-mark to determine whether he was indeed that man. Together, Cristinziani and I wrote a declaration in support of a search warrant detailing the entire investigation, including the match to the tanning case discovered by Burritt. Cristinziani signed the declaration, and a San Diego superior court judge is-sued the warrant.

On August 31, 1999, Cristinziani drove to North Kern State Prison in Central California. He was eventually led to Vasquez. Cristinziani explained to Vasquez why he was there. Vasquez said little. Cristinziani personally took oral swabs from Vasquez. Those swabs would contain millions of epithelial cells from the lining of Vasquez's mouth that would allow analysts to determine his DNA profile. Cristinziani sealed the swabs into containers and drove home to San Diego. The San Diego Police Department crime lab shipped a portion of the known sample of Vasquez's DNA to Cellmark. A few months later, RFLP testing of the sample produced a complete match to the profile Cellmark had determined the year before from the vaginal swab. The probability of a chance match was extremely remote: about one in twenty-eight billion.

Cristinziani was now ready to charge Vasquez with the attack on San-dra over five years before. Cristinziani brought Sandra into my office, and the three of us spoke for a couple of hours. Sandra was now a law student at an east coast university but was home during a break in school. We discussed her life and how she felt about her attacker's finally being identified and lo-cated. Sandra was tentative but obviously felt relief that police now knew exactly who her assailant was. She was apologetic about never being able to provide any description of the man. We assured her that the fact she never got a good look at her attacker wasn't important. The science of molecular biology had provided all the information that was needed. We shared a laugh at the thought that none of us had taken much science in school.

We had Sandra recount what she remembered of the night of March 9, 1995. Her description of the events was remarkably consistent with her pre-vious narratives. Purposely, neither Cristinziani nor I showed Sandra any photographs of Vasquez. We wanted to wait for Sandra to see him in court. A no-lose situation, I thought. If Sandra recognized Vasquez from the attack, there would be additional evidence of his guilt. If not, her believability to the jury would probably be increased. If Sandra were to be accused of lying by Vasquez's eventual attorney, why wouldn't she simply identify him as her assailant?

Cristinziani and I explained to Sandra what the process would involve, including at least two trips to San Diego for court. She understood and was willing to assist. Remarkably, she showed no outward contempt or hatred for the man who had brutalized her in the duplex. Rather, she felt he deserved forgiveness for the way he had treated her. I immediately thought of Addie and what she had told me three years before about Stephen Nocilla (Chapter 9).

I filed formal charges against Vasquez for the crimes he had committed against Sandra: two counts of rape, two counts of sexual penetration, and other crimes. The complaint also alleged that he had committed the sex crimes during the course of a burglary. If found to be true, those allegations would increase Vasquez's punishment for the sex crimes to twenty-five years to life. The complaint also included allegations of Vasquez's three prior strike convictions, which could elevate his possible sentence. If convicted of all the charges and allegations, Vasquez faced the prospect of spending the remainder of his life in prison. The preliminary hearing was held on May 12, 2000. Sandra came to court and testified to the entire set of events that took place on the night she was attacked. She was calm but began to cry when she described the rapes. At a break during my direct examination of Sandra, I took her aside. Did she recognize the defendant, I asked her. She didn't. All Sandra could say was that there was nothing about Vasquez that was inconsistent with the little she knew about her assailant. Sandra was concerned. Cristinziani and I told her not to worry. Evidence much stronger than eyewitness identification had told us who her attacker was.

The judge who presided over the preliminary hearing ordered Vasquez to stand trial. The judge was forced to dismiss some of the lesser crimes because the statute of limitations had run from the time of the 1995 assault. In other words, too many years had passed between the time of Sandra's attack and when those charges were filed against Vasquez. Limitations statutes exist to require that charges be brought against a person who has committed a crime within a certain period of time. The more serious the charge, the longer the particular statute permits charges to be filed. The sex charges, the sex allegations, and the previous strike convictions that were alleged in Vasquez's case all survived.

A trial date was set for July 21. Vasquez's attorney, Deputy Public Defender Albert Tamayo, was a veteran of serious cases. He knew that time would be needed to thoroughly investigate the case and closely examine the DNA results that he recognized were likely to be compelling evidence at trial. Tamayo casually asked if we'd consider a lesser sentence if his client were to plead guilty. I told him no. Vasquez's record of prior convictions and the severity of the assault on Sandra cried out for no plea bargain. Unless his client wanted to plead guilty to all the charges and allegations, a jury would have to decide his fate. Trial dates were continued a few times because of Tamayo's trial schedule and the need to have his expert review the DNA data from both the San Diego Police Department and Cellmark. Finally, on August 21, 2001, the case was ready for trial. I knew the trial would probably go quickly because we were assigned to Judge John Thompson. His courtroom was, to say the least, efficient. But he was also a very fair judge and one who wasn't afraid to make a decision.

I began by making an important request, or motion, to Thompson. I asked him to allow the two victims of the tanning incidents to testify about what Vasquez had done to them, even though Vasquez had already been tried on those charges. California law permits evidence of other sex-related crimes by a defendant to show that the defendant has a predisposition to commit such crimes. Thompson refused to allow my evidence. He felt that the testimony from those victims would unfairly prejudice the jury against Vasquez.

I thought Judge Thompson was wrong, but he had given me a fair hearing, and I respected his decision. The irony of the whole subject was probably lost on everyone else involved in the case. The Evidence Code section of the law allowing that type of evidence—along with a companion law in domestic-violence cases—was enacted in response to the not guilty verdicts in the trial of O. J. Simpson. At least I had contributed to proving sex and domestic-violence cases by helping to lose the Trial of the Century.

Also, Tamayo offered to stipulate that the semen that was collected from Sandra's neck and vaginal swabs came from Vasquez. I agreed, especially knowing how Thompson liked to move cases along. Plus, I wouldn't run the risk of some question being raised in the mind of a juror from all the DNA testimony. It had worked in the Nocilla trial. But the stipulation should have been a clue. There's an old expression that goes something like: "Fool me once, shame on you; fool me twice, shame on me." I fell victim to that old saying.

After we picked a jury, I gave my opening statement, setting out the evidence that I was convinced would show that the man who committed the violent attack on Sandra was Vasquez. Given an opportunity to give his opening statement, Tamayo "reserved" his opening so that he could give it after all my witnesses had testified. Sandra was my first witness. She testified to the acts that her attacker had forced her to undergo. Alternately reserved and crying, Sandra answered the questions I put to her about exactly what the man had done to her. I showed Sandra enlarged photographs that

had been taken of the injuries to her head during her sexual-assault examination a few hours after the attack. The photos revealed a cut and large
bruising around her right eye and temple. Sandra cried. The jury was clearly
moved. Finally, I asked Sandra whether she recognized Vasquez, who was
sitting next to attorney Tamayo. She answered that she did not. I asked her
whether anything about Vasquez's appearance indicated that he could not
have been the man who had brutalized her. "No," she answered, "he could
be the man."

Tamayo was measured and controlled in his cross-examination of Sandra. He wasn't about to run the risk of alienating one or more jurors by being
aggressive and confrontational. Unless the defense is going to try to convince
the jury that a victim is lying, a kid-gloves approach is usually called for.
Tamayo appeared to adopt that approach. I wasn't surprised. The case, I was
convinced, was clearly one of who did it, as opposed to whether or not it
had happened. A "whodunit" rather than a "what was it," as prosecutors and
defense lawyers are prone to say. There were serious injuries to the victim,
both to her head and to her genital area. This wasn't going to be a consent
defense; the police weren't even able to locate the attacker for several years.
Or so I thought.

I marched on with my other witnesses: the campus-police officer who
had driven Sandra to the duplex; the patrol officer who had taken Sandra's
statement at the scene; then the SART nurse who had examined Sandra at
the hospital. Finally, Cristinziani took the stand. The bulk of his testimony
involved his interviews with Sandra and their consistency. The jury was
read the stipulations about the DNA evidence. Sandra's neck swab contained
the defendant's semen. The swabs from her external vaginal area contained the defendant's semen. The swabs from her internal vaginal area
contained the defendant's semen. I rested my case.

Tamayo called his only witness to the stand: the defendant. I was surprised, but not shocked. After Los Angeles, nothing shocked me anymore.
We all knew that if he testified Vasquez would have to answer my questions about his prior convictions. The jury would hear about his burglaries,
but the robbery would have to be referred to as a "theft-related" case. The
law of evidence sometimes allows a criminal defendant to soften the blow
of having a criminal record. As to exactly what Vasquez would testify to,
I was in the dark. Unlike other witnesses, a defendant doesn't have to give
reports of his own anticipated testimony to the prosecutor ahead of time. All
I was confident about was that he would somehow try to explain how his semen got on Sandra. The most likely explanation he would give was that he

had consensual sex with Sandra, then left the house. Someone else must have broken in the duplex and attacked her.

I was half-right. The other half was a good old-fashioned surprise. Vasquez testified during his direct exam that he was walking toward a liquor store near the University of San Diego in March 1995 when a young woman approached him and asked whether he would buy her some booze. Vasquez identified Sandra as that young woman. Sandra, he testified, told him that she was underage and needed help getting some alcohol. Tamayo asked him what happened next. Vasquez told the jury that after buying her the liquor, she invited him back to her apartment. They went to the duplex, entered, and then sat down on the couch. There, Sandra began kissing Vasquez and the two fondled each other. Sandra led Vasquez to a bedroom, where they laid down on the bed. Vasquez testified that she told him she wanted to have sex with him. And she told him she liked to have rough sex. That must be how she suffered the injuries to her genital area, Vasquez testified. When they were done, Vasquez said he left the home. He never saw Sandra again. "No further questions," Tamayo told the judge.

Judge Thompson asked whether I had any questions on cross-examination. I told the judge that I did. This was going to be different from the Kerwin Hall case (Chapter 5). No narcissistic ladies' man, Vasquez was fighting to avoid prison for the rest of his life the only way he knew how to do it. And that way was to try to plant a seed of doubt in the mind of at least one juror about whether Sandra had told the truth. Tamayo had wisely brought out during his direct questioning of Vasquez that he had had problems with the law in the past. Taking some of the sting out of cross-examination by being upfront about a witness's prior convictions was usually the best course. I didn't miss the opportunity to bring them up again.

The heart of Vasquez's testimony was the incredible assertion that the acts committed against Sandra were with her consent. But he made a mistake. A big one, I thought. Vasquez never claimed that although he had sex with the victim, someone else must have attacked her. I grabbed the blowups of Sandra's face and head injuries. I asked Vasquez how the injuries had happened. I wasn't that concerned about his answer, expecting him to say that he didn't know. But Vasquez didn't shy away from the question. Sandra had told him to slap her, he replied. "She what?" I fired back. To my surprise, Vasquez told the jury that Sandra said she liked it rough and wanted him to hit her. I showed the jury the photos again. Without my even asking, Vasquez then said that Sandra told him to slap her some more. Sandra had also suffered scrapes to her wrists from being tied up. I showed Vasquez photos of her wrists and asked him how the scrapes had occurred. He answered that she told him that she wanted to be tied up. He had done what she asked him to do. I didn't have any more questions. After some brief redirect questions by his attorney, Vasquez left the witness stand and took his seat. Tamayo told the judge and jury that he had no additional witnesses. I had no rebuttal evidence. It was time for closing arguments.

I spent most of my first argument describing the evidence, the law about the crimes Vasquez was charged with, and how those facts proved his guilt. Tamayo focused in his argument on reasonable doubt and how his client's testimony should be enough to create doubt in the minds of the jury. I spent my final argument on one subject: Vasquez's testimony and how it simply made no sense. Sandra's description of what had happened to her, her injuries, the SART nurse's findings, the photographs, and the DNA results told a single, consistent story. The only contradiction: the testimony of the defendant. And that testimony was inherently unbelievable. "Slap me more" and "tie my hands," I told the jury, were the product of the defendant's desperate attempt to avoid being held responsible for an inexcusable attack on an innocent woman.

The jury was sent out for their deliberations and returned with verdicts the next day. Vasquez was found guilty of the charges against him, and the allegations that he had committed the sex crimes against Sandra in the course of a burglary were determined to be true. Vasquez admitted to the judge that the prior convictions were true. A month later, Judge Thompson sentenced Vasquez to state prison for a term of eighty-five years to life.

If the evidence from the tanning salon in October 1995 had not been collected and analyzed by the San Diego Police Department, the DNA profile of Vasquez would never have been in the hands of law enforcement in time for Burritt and his computer to link Vasquez to a vicious sexual assault seven months before. DNA testing had indeed entered the computer age. And DNA databases were here to stay.

CHAPTER TWELVE

A National Approach

———•———

*A*s we saw in the previous chapter, Paul Vasquez was caught and eventually convicted by DNA testing evidence. What perhaps stood out most about the case was his decision to testify in his own defense. Saddled with prior convictions for crimes that he knew the jury would learn about if he testified, Vasquez nonetheless decided to take the witness stand. The best explanation for his decision may have been that Vasquez felt trapped by science. His jury learned that rape evidence collected from the victim came from him. That evidence may have left Vasquez, in his own mind, with no alternative other than to try to explain how the evidence had gotten there. A case that traditionally would have been fought over who had committed the crime was transformed by DNA testing into a battle over how it had happened. For juries, those fights are usually easier to resolve.

But in the same way that DNA evidence was identifying rapists and murderers, it was increasingly helping wrongfully convicted inmates. The work being done by Barry Scheck, Peter Neufeld, and others at the Innocence Project was resulting in more and more DNA exonerations. The examples were so numerous and compelling that the federal government took an interest, and that interest would eventually lead to dramatic changes nationwide in how states treated prison inmates trying to get help.

Janet Reno was a prosecutor who knew the challenges of charging and convicting violent criminals. A native of Dade County, Florida, Reno was appointed state's attorney in Miami and served a total of six terms leading one of the nation's largest prosecutor's offices. Miami was a big city, and crime fighting was a big job. She knew very well that day-in, day-out battle. In fact, Reno knew it so well that President Bill Clinton appointed her attorney general of the United States in 1993. Unlike the two nominees who preceded her—Zoë Baird and Kimba Wood—Reno had no difficulties with nannies or taxes. She lived a quiet life dedicated to public service. Her honesty was perhaps her most endearing quality. Once when asked at a public meeting whether she liked men, Reno replied, "I'm just an awkward old maid with a very great affection for men."

After taking office, Reno was concerned about the growing number of DNA exonerations. She asked the National Institute of Justice (NIJ), the research and development arm of the Department of Justice, to take a close look at the whole area. The initial result of their review was a study of twenty-eight prison inmates released and exonerated as a result of postconviction DNA testing. *Convicted by Juries, Exonerated by Science,* published by NIJ in June 1996, chronicled the cases of those twenty-eight men—including Ricky Daye (Chapter 6); all had served ten or more years in prison until they were pardoned, their sentences were commuted, or the charges were dismissed. Their stories were remarkably consistent; they were convicted at trials that often included faulty eyewitness identification, informer testimony, and "soft" science such as hair comparison.

The goals of Reno and the Department of Justice included sensitizing those in the criminal-justice system to the cases and their common attributes so that steps could be taken both to correct investigations and trials and thus avoid wrongful convictions and, just as important, to ensure that DNA testing would become a routine tool in the hands of law enforcement. Statistics that were being produced by crime laboratories were astonishing. In over 25 percent of cases, DNA results showed that suspects who were believed by law enforcement to have committed crimes were excluded and exonerated. If not for DNA, many of those suspects would have likely been charged and some even convicted of those crimes.

The attorney general decided that a national commission was needed to undertake an extensive review of the entire area of DNA testing and the justice system. Under the direction of NIJ, she chartered a group that was to be composed of experienced attorneys and professionals in the areas of law enforcement, the courts, and DNA science. Their mission: to recommend to the attorney general concrete steps that could be taken to improve the administration of justice.

I remember my telephone call. It was the fall of 1997. Lisa Forman, who had left Cellmark the year before and was now working for NIJ as a program manager, wanted to know whether I was interested in joining the new commission, to be called the National Commission on the Future of DNA

Evidence. The group would be meeting at least quarterly, with additional meetings of smaller groups dedicated to specific issues. In Washington earlier that year I had taken part in a focus-group meeting in which a number of the participants tried to identify specific issues in forensic DNA testing that affected law enforcement and the courts. The transition to a larger, federal commission seemed natural and exciting. Here was an opportunity to have an impact on national policy in an area that had become the heart of my professional career.

I told Forman that I'd be honored, but that I would have to talk to Paul Pfingst, the district attorney. Pfingst and Assistant District Attorney Greg Thompson were extremely supportive. They knew that DNA testing was certain to have an even greater impact on criminal cases than it already had. They were also confident that having a representative on a national policy-making group could only help with legislation, funding, and other resources that could ultimately improve the criminal-justice system in California and San Diego.

Our first meeting was held in March the next year in the Great Hall of the Department of Justice in downtown Washington, D.C. I walked inside the building, went through two different security stations, and then entered the hall. It was a beautiful, two-story room, with art deco light fixtures and a terra-cotta tile floor accented with gray marble borders. A few television news cameras were positioned at the end of a huge U-shaped set of meeting tables.

I saw several familiar faces. Chris Asplen was originally a local prosecutor in Pennsylvania; afterward he joined the American Prosecutors Research Institute (APRI) in Alexandria, Virginia, as the head of its DNA unit. In that role he directed the training and education of prosecutors around the country in the use of DNA testing in investigations and court cases. He had recently left the DNA unit at APRI and joined the U.S. Attorney's office in Washington. We had become good friends, as I had frequently lectured at seminars he hosted in various cities across the United States. Reno appointed Asplen to be the executive director of the new commission because of his extraordinary knowledge of DNA testing and its unique legal issues. It was a perfect choice. Asplen and Forman then introduced me to the newly appointed chair of our commission, Justice Shirley Abrahamson. Abrahamson sat as chief justice of the Wisconsin Supreme Court. The first woman to ever serve on the Wisconsin high court, Abrahamson was nationally renowned for her knowledge of the law and her ability to achieve consensus on difficult issues. Her selection was an outstanding one, as I would later learn firsthand.

NIJ always attempted to include on its committees and commissions members who had varying views on matters affecting justice. By including as many different viewpoints as possible, NIJ believed that the value of conclusions and recommendations increased, even though the process might be difficult. The DNA commission would be no exception. Ultimately, twenty-two commissioners from a wide variety of disciplines took part in the process. Including Abrahamson, there were two judges, three crime-laboratory directors, a population geneticist, three police chiefs, a sheriff, a medical examiner, the mayor of Baltimore, a physician, three prosecutors, three criminal-defense lawyers, a law school professor, and the director of a national victims' group. The final member was William Webster, a retired judge and former director of both the FBI and the Central Intelligence Agency. It was an interesting group, to say the least.

Several members of the commission were long-time friends of mine: Dwight Adams, head of the FBI's DNA unit; Jim Wooley and Norm Gahn, prosecutors in Cleveland and Milwaukee; Jan Bashinski, chief of the California Department of Justice lab system; Barry Scheck; and Jeff Thoma, the public defender of Mendocino County in Northern California. Thoma had been an intern for the San Diego Superior Court; I had supervised him when I was a research attorney back in 1980. Thoma joined the San Diego Public Defender's office after law school and was the office expert on DNA evidence for several years.

After introducing ourselves, the group got down to business. The first item was to break into working groups to focus on the major areas that the commission was going to examine. The smaller groups would include commissioners as well as individuals not serving on the commission. For thirty minutes we worked on the names of prospective individuals to invite to join the smaller committees. The five working groups that were formed were research and development, crime-scene investigation, laboratory funding, legal issues, and postconviction issues. The postconviction group had gotten a head start on their work and had already met a few times. One of the highest priorities for the commission was the development of comprehensive recommendations for all involved in the criminal-justice system in the postconviction DNA testing area. I volunteered to serve on the lab-funding working group. Although commissioners were invited to take part in any or all of the five groups, I felt that funding was so important that any help I provided could have a critical and long-lasting effect. I had never been involved in any large-scale attempt to obtain money for justice projects and was excited at the prospect of learning firsthand how the process worked.

Later that day, the attorney general entered the hall and spoke to our commission. She described how extremely important she felt our effort was. We each had the opportunity to meet her after her comments. I was surprised at how tall she was. But she had a presence that made her height pale by comparison. She spoke to me as though we had known each other for years. Her honesty and integrity were obvious. It wasn't hard to see why the president had made her the top law-enforcement officer in the United States.

Over the next two years the full commission met eleven times, with nearly as many working-group meetings. So that no one would have to always travel cross-country, we met in cities that included Washington, Chicago, Boston, Dallas, and Santa Fe. Frequent-flyer miles were one thing. But the travel grew tiring. I learned one important lesson about air travel: there is no better place for uninterrupted work. I found that I was much more productive reading cases at 37,000 feet than in my office. Something about the absence of a telephone, I suppose.

We made progress. The laboratory-funding group that I took part in was a joy. Our chair was Paul Ferrara, the director of the Virginia crime-laboratory system. He was down-to-earth, knew about dealing with legislatures, and was head of the most successful state DNA database system in the country. The other members of our group included David Coffman of the Florida crime-lab system; Barry Fisher, head of the Los Angeles Sheriff's Department crime lab; Steve Niezgoda, manager of the CODIS national database for the FBI; Cecelia Crouse, a DNA analyst from Palm Beach, Florida; and Victor Weedn, formerly of the Armed Forces Institute of Pathology.

We approached the two major issues facing labs and their ability to process cases: dealing with active case backlogs and testing convicted-offender samples. To adequately make any recommendations, we realized that we would need to get a grasp on the scale of the problems we wanted to address. We had to know how many cases had not yet been analyzed, the number of new cases, and the quantity of existing and new offenders to be added to convicted-offender databases. Getting those numbers required surveying state and local laboratories to obtain rough estimates of the scope of the problem. Fortunately, NIJ was able to make the resources for those surveys available, and months later our group was presented with estimates of the numbers of cases and offenders. The statistics were staggering. Hundreds of thousands of rape kits sat on police property-room shelves. Another few hundred thousand samples from convicted offenders had not yet been tested. Most discouraging of all was an estimate of one million samples owed by offenders but not yet collected by law enforcement or prison officials.

Ferrara and I were discouraged but still hopeful. One of our approaches was to talk about the cost to society of a typical rape. NIJ had access to an estimate that had been previously made for the cost to a victim of being raped: $87,000. It seemed almost grotesque to try to put a dollar amount on a sexual assault, but the attempt served a function. With even a hundred thousand unsolved rape cases, the cost to victims was almost nine billion dollars. Under that light, not providing money to test all the backlogged evidence and offender samples seemed ridiculous. Estimates also have been made of how many times a typical rapist reoffends and commits another rape. The average: nine times. So, the reasoning goes, by identifying, arresting, and incarcerating attackers with DNA testing, the next victims are spared. But statistics are just statistics. Money still had to be pried away from legislators to meet this critical need. That point was driven home at one of our commission meetings. All anyone needed to hear was the story told by Debbie Smith.

*D*ebbie Smith seemed the unlikeliest of victims. She was inside her home in the middle of a spring day in a beautiful neighborhood in Williamsburg, Virginia, one of the safest towns in the country. Her husband, a police lieutenant, was at home. Smith was doing the family laundry when she had trouble with the dryer vent. She went outside to check it. When she reentered her house, she didn't lock the back door. She always locked that door but didn't this time because she was going to take the trash out in a matter of minutes.

But those minutes were enough to wreak havoc on her, her husband, and their family. A man wearing a mask confronted her inside the back door, grabbed her, and forced her to a wooded area near her home. He put a blindfold on her and raped her over and over. He told her that he knew where she lived and would come back if she ever told anyone. If he returned, the man said, he would kill her.

Her husband was asleep upstairs. He had worked overnight and, in fact, hadn't slept for more than twenty-four hours. The rapist eventually let her go, and she went to her bedroom. She woke her husband up and told him, "He got me, Rob. He got me." She was scared that if she told anyone, the man would come back and harm one of her family members. But her husband knew better. He knew that she had to go to the hospital because evidence from her assailant was undoubtedly left on her. They went to the hospital and what might turn out to be critical evidence was collected from her body. Like most victims of rape, Smith was devastated. She had trouble sleeping. Even the simplest parts of her daily routine were difficult. She was depressed and questioned her reason for living. But her family had to come first, she thought—no matter what the masked man had done to her.

For years, Debbie Smith worried about the man who had taken away so much of her life. The police department followed up every tip or lead, but no luck. Smith understandably became obsessed with security. She and her husband had an alarm system installed, including a necklace that she could push in an emergency. They added a security fence and motion detectors. But peace of mind still eluded her.

Then one day, over six years after her attack, Smith's life changed again, but this time for the better. Her husband handed her a composite drawing that had been created years earlier based on her description of her attacker. Her husband had kept the drawing with him the entire six years. As he gave the sketch to her, he told her they could get rid of it—her rapist had been identified.

A DNA analyst at the Virginia state lab—the laboratory system managed by Ferrara—had found a database match between evidence in her rape and a man already in prison for the kidnapping and robbery of another victim. Smith didn't have to worry about her attacker returning. At least not for some time.

Like Vasquez, who had assaulted Sandra in San Diego (Chapter 11), Smith's rapist had been sent to prison within a few months of his assault on Smith. It had taken so long for the match to be made between the evidence in her case and the convicted kidnapper for the very reasons identified by our working group: lack of money and resources.

Smith recounted in detail her ordeal to the full commission. It was as compelling as the testimony of any rape victim I had heard in a trial. Her final comments were an inspiration to all of us. She pleaded to the group in tears, "As a victim who has experienced both the before and aftereffects of this hideous crime, I implore you as a commission to do all that you can, as soon as you can." I went up to Smith and her husband during a break in the meeting. I introduced myself, thanked both of them, and praised her for her incredible courage. Her message was crystal clear. Don't wait because every day means more unnecessary victims and more heartache for those who were already victims of violent crime.

Our laboratory-funding group took Smith seriously, and our work met with success. In 2000 Clinton signed into law the DNA Analysis Backlog Elimination Act, authorizing forty million dollars for forensic DNA testing. The targets: unsolved cases and convicted-offender database samples. The legislation was drafted by our group, endorsed by the full commission, and heavily sponsored in both the U.S. Senate and House of Representatives.

The other working groups provided the commission with a host of issues to digest and debate. The postconviction group completed a comprehensive set of suggested guidelines for dealing with inmate requests for DNA analysis. Later entitled *Postconviction DNA Testing: Recommendations for Handling Requests,* the document provided guidance for courts, police, crime labs, prosecutors, defense attorneys, and victims. The commission was aware that many courts—especially those in the vast majority of states that had no specific postconviction DNA law—were likely to follow our recommendations. The commission discussed the way the subcommittee had grouped cases into categories. The classifications were important. If a case was considered Category 1, the court should order DNA testing. The other categories into which cases might fall provided for either discretionary testing or none at all. The recommendations also included a model statute addressing testing. Designed for those states without specific laws governing inmate DNA testing, the suggested statute was likely to be adopted by several. The exoneration of wrongfully convicted defendants was highly publicized, and many state legislatures were beginning to debate what type of law to enact.

One of the most controversial issues in inmate DNA testing is the standard courts should use when deciding whether testing is appropriate. Only a few states in the late 1990s even had laws on the books dictating when DNA typing should be ordered if a defendant has already been convicted and sentenced to prison. Those states allowed courts to order testing if the results of that testing might provide relevant and material evidence in the case that was never heard by the original jury that convicted the defendant. The majority of prosecutors across the country favored a different standard: testing would be allowed if the results might prove that the inmate was totally innocent of the crime.

The working group and commission debated the differing standards. Scheck and a few other commissioners favored the standard of relevant and material results, while a group of others believed the innocence rule was more appropriate. Each side had good arguments. To several of us, neither seemed the best rule. Borrowing from other areas of criminal law, the commission eventually decided to adopt a different standard: testing should be allowed if there is a reasonable possibility that there would have been a different verdict if the DNA results had been known. In other words, assuming DNA results were to provide exculpatory results from specific evidence, was there a reasonable chance that the jury would not have reached the guilty verdict or verdicts that it did?

The research and development working group examined likely future technologies that would be used on biological evidence. Automation, portability of typing machines, and the ability to test smaller and more degraded samples—as well as mixtures of DNA—were all described. The group recognized, however, that because state and national databases relied so heavily on the existing STR markers, they were likely to be used for many years.

The legal-issues committee reviewed many subjects that were at times hotly contested in appellate courts. One of the most controversial of those topics—and one debated by the entire commission—was what types of convicted offenders should be tested and have their profiles entered into databases. The scope of state laws governing the types of crimes requiring DNA testing was broad. Virginia was the best example of a state that required all convicted felons to provide blood and saliva samples for testing and inclusion in a state databank. Most states, however, mandated sampling and typing of only violent offenders. Typically, those offenses included forcible sex crimes, murder, and kidnapping.

However, the experience of Virginia over several years of testing unsolved cases and comparing the resulting profiles to its database of convicted offenders provided critical information. Virginia discovered that in most of their computer matches of evidence in violent crimes to offenders in their state database, the person was in the database because of having been convicted of a nonviolent crime. That revelation of violent crimes committed by heretofore nonviolent criminals surprised many. As a result, more and more states adopted the all-felony-convictions model. But the issues involved were important.

One viewpoint held by a number of commissioners was that DNA databasing of all felony offenders was an undue and inappropriate invasion of personal privacy. Felons, the law recognized, enjoy fewer rights than those who have not been convicted of crimes. However, requiring nonviolent criminals to provide samples and allowing their DNA to be tested and maintained in databanks went too far. Those samples could be misused by the government or stolen. Health or life insurers might obtain the samples, test them for genetic diseases, and deny coverage. Nevertheless, the effectiveness of taking and testing samples from all felons was inescapable. Ferrara's database successes in Virginia were impressive, to say the least. Why, I repeatedly asked during commission meetings, was DNA different from fingerprints? Typically, fingerprints are, and have been for decades, taken from anyone arrested for a crime, including most misdemeanors.

We heard presentations from representatives of the Forensic Science Service in England describing their experiences with DNA data-basing. The British take samples from everyone convicted of a felony. In addition, they actively fund and support both their offender database system and the testing of new cases. Unlike the United States—where "cold hits" were made at an average rate in 2000 of perhaps fifty per month—Great Britain was matching almost 250 cases per week to offenders in its databases.

The commission went around and around and never resolved the issue. However, I think it was clear to all that states were headed in the direction of creating all-felon databases. A couple of states had even authorized taking and testing samples from those simply arrested for a felony crime. Funding problems, however, prevented those states from being able to obtain the required samples for testing. The impetus for providing local and state crime laboratories with funds to support such an effort was there. But changes come slowly.

The crime-scene group similarly provided important information that was incorporated by the full commission. Recognizing the need for skilled crime-scene evidence collection, the working group produced a pamphlet and training CD, *What Every Law Enforcement Officer Should Know about DNA Evidence*. The goal of NIJ was to provide every law enforcement officer and deputy sheriff with a copy of the pamphlet and the CD.

But one of my personal highlights came during a discussion of the collection of unusual samples. Sometimes law enforcement has no legal basis to force a suspect to give a blood or saliva sample so that police can test and compare that sample with evidence in a case. Or police don't want the individual to know that he or she is a suspect. One of the methods used to get a sample under those circumstances is to recover a discarded cigarette, a drinking cup thrown in a garbage can, or even what's left of saliva spat on a sidewalk by the suspect. The question arose during our discussions of whether collecting spit was legal under search-and-seizure laws based on the Fourth Amendment to the Constitution. "Of course it is," I shouted out. The Fourth Amendment, I explained, allows police to seize anything that a person can't reasonably believe is protected from access by others. The legal standard frequently cited is whether a person has a reasonable expectation of privacy in the location police want to search. "Especially," I then deadpanned, "when there is no reasonable expectoration of privacy." The group went silent for a moment. Groans of despair were heard at my bad pun. Then it dawned on me that a court reporter was taking down everything I said.

CHAPTER THIRTEEN

The District Attorney's Office Searches for Innocence

———•———

*D*istrict Attorney Paul Pfingst and Assistant District Attorney Greg Thompson were interested in the progress of the commission. Although our work seemed to go slowly, at least we were making inroads into the problems of unsolved cases and postconviction testing. The president's signing of the backlog bill was a gigantic step forward. Pfingst and Thompson liked to hear about the topics that were the most hotly debated. They were both a little skeptical when I told them my belief that California would eventually collect DNA samples from every person arrested for a felony. At the time, California didn't even require samples from everyone convicted of, much less arrested for, a felony.

In Congress, bills were being introduced to deal with the whole area of postconviction DNA. Stories of inmates being denied testing because of restrictive time limits on newly discovered evidence were compelling. The most broad-based measure, titled the Innocence Protection Act, was sponsored by Senator Patrick Leahy of Vermont and a group of other senators. Introduced in February 2000, Senate Bill 2073 would reform how requests for postconviction DNA testing were handled at the federal level. Through the mechanism of federal funding, individual states would be required, under the bill, to enact similar legislation in order to receive monies in other areas dealing with criminal justice. Leahy's legislation not only was designed to address inmate testing but included several provisions for improving the representation of defendants charged with death-penalty crimes. In many respects, that aspect of the bill generated more controversy than the DNA-testing provisions. The standard for testing contained in the measure was familiar. Inmates would be entitled to DNA testing if they could show that it might produce results that would have been relevant and material in their earlier trial. The bill had broad support among both senators and members of the House of Representatives.

But opposition surfaced, particularly within the Senate. Judiciary Committee Chairman Senator Orrin Hatch of Utah introduced an alternative measure. Senate Bill 3130, named the Criminal Justice Integrity and Law Enforcement Assistance Act, provided a different standard for deciding whether to grant testing. The proposed rule: testing would be required only if it had the potential to provide evidence establishing the inmate's innocence. Noticeably absent from the Hatch bill were any provisions dealing with attorney representation of death-penalty defendants.

Months passed before hearings were held on the proposed legislative changes. In the interim, a whole new approach to looking at previous cases would be developed. The irony was that it was going to be devised in my own office. Pfingst, at the beginning of his tenure, formed a legal-policy committee to help guide the administration of the district attorney's office, which included nearly three hundred prosecutors. I took part in the group, mainly because of my work with the crime labs and the increasing role DNA and other forensic testing were playing in our cases.

Assistant District Attorney Thompson headed the committee and asked in April 2000 that I update the group on the work of the national commission. I decided to include in my remarks the recent debates about inmate DNA testing in Congress—or, as I had learned to call it from the laboratory-funding working group, "on the Hill." I described Leahy's introduction of the Innocence Protection Act and the problems with that bill. After I talked about the standard contained in the Leahy bill for postconviction testing, but before I was able to give my thoughts, Jim Pippin, my supervisor in the felony-trial division, broke in. "Why aren't we doing that on our own?" he asked. I looked at him with obvious questions written all over my face. Pippin was a longtime prosecutor who had tried many of the most serious cases in San Diego over the preceding thirty years. A bleeding-heart liberal he wasn't. As head of the division that tried the most serious cases day in and day out, he reviewed and made decisions on hundreds of violent cases every year.

But Pippin cared about whom the office prosecuted and for what. Pippin was always concerned about prosecuting an innocent defendant. Worse yet, he worried that an innocent person could be convicted and sentenced for a crime he or she hadn't committed. He knew about the cases that DNA had solved and how it had been used to convict defendants charged with rapes and murders. But he also knew about its use to exonerate wrongly convicted inmates like Ricky Daye (Chapter 6).

I stared back at Pippin. "Why?" I asked him rhetorically. I explained that we weren't even able to keep up with the DNA testing that was needed for our cases that were set for trial. Pippin didn't back down. He pointed out that perhaps the cases in which the office had already convicted someone were the most important and ripe for DNA. I told Pippin—and what at that point was a curious group of other committee members—that I thought it was a higher priority to solve the backlogged cases of rapes and murders whose evidence was still sitting in police property rooms.

We took a break in the meeting for coffee. A few minutes later we reconvened. We were joined by the district attorney, and Thompson turned the meeting over to him. He said he understood that we had been talking about DNA testing in old cases. He then announced that he wanted the office to perform such testing. Pfingst looked directly at me and smiled: "Woody, you're going to figure out a way to do it." I muttered to the deputy district attorney next to me that I didn't know how we were going to do what no prosecutor's office, to my knowledge, had ever even attempted. I turned back to Pfingst and pleaded with him that efforts to test our old cases would compromise any chances of having analyses done on the unsolved sex and homicide investigations. He didn't miss a beat. Figure out a way to get them tested as well, Pfingst answered.

Talk about marching orders. But Pfingst, Thompson, and Pippin knew the importance of the order. And they had a good point. In small counties, district attorneys could be confident in the reliability of their convictions in serious cases because they had probably personally tried those cases or were otherwise closely familiar with them. But in a large county like San Diego no one could know that much about each case. In addition, Pfingst had taken office in 1995, and he certainly knew little or nothing about cases that were tried before he became district attorney.

And how was such a program to be devised? "You and Lisa Weinreb will make it work," Pfingst said with a smile. Weinreb was a fellow deputy district attorney who had been assigned to assist Thompson with special projects. She had little experience with DNA, but if there was ever a project that could be deemed special, this was it. A few days later Weinreb and I sat down and talked about some general ideas. What cases would we review? How would we look at them? What would we decide in those cases? Would we just do testing in cases that seemed appropriate, or would we offer the testing to inmates first? How would we involve the attorneys who represented those inmates?

We had absolutely nothing to guide us other than our imaginations and my knowledge of the DNA exonerations that had taken place over the last several years. But we slowly put together a series of guidelines that would eventually govern our review of San Diego's old cases. To begin we had to decide which cases to examine. We rejected the idea that we would review all past felony cases from San Diego County. Besides the fact that the sheer number of those cases would make testing prohibitive, we saw no reason to look at drug possession, check forgeries, and similar crimes. DNA had little or no prospect of proving that defendants sentenced for those crimes had been wrongfully convicted.

In addition, the cases we wanted to target were those that were tried before DNA testing was available. We developed a set of criteria that we felt would weed out all but the cases in which DNA stood a chance of settling claims of innocence. We would look at every case from San Diego in which the inmate was still in prison and the conviction had been before 1993. By still being incarcerated for the crime, the inmate had to have been sentenced to at least a dozen or so years in prison. That would screen out the less serious felony cases that DNA testing was highly unlikely to shed any light on. Also, because the San Diego Police Department had begun using DNA in late 1992, testing was readily available beginning in 1993.

The next task was to devise a way to identify those inmates who qualified under our criteria. Fortunately, through the cooperation of both the California Department of Corrections and the Lifer Unit of the district attorney's office, we were successful. The Department of Corrections could query their computer system to identify those current inmates who had been sentenced to prison before 1993. They were willing to provide that information to us. The Lifer Unit of our own office kept detailed records on San Diego defendants who had been sentenced to life terms in prison—cases primarily of murder, kidnapping, and a few sex crimes. The unit also maintained records of every parole hearing that the inmate had taken part in while in prison. Those hearings included detailed descriptions of the crime and what the inmate had to say about what he or she had done. Those records would be important in our individual case reviews.

But we didn't want to totally limit our inquiry to cases tried before 1993. We decided to limit our proactive review to those inmates but if any defendant or his or her attorney wanted us to also examine a post-1992 case, we would be happy to do so. Later, we sent letters to the major bar associations and criminal-defense lawyer groups to let them know of our criteria and guidelines.

We waited to find out how many cases would be part of our proactive examination. The answer was just short of a thousand. Weinreb and I had guessed the number would be a few hundred less. But now that we knew the number of cases, we had to decide exactly how we were going to perform the review. Our concept was still vague, but one thing was crystal clear: we were going to need help to comb through each case. Just getting the old office files on the cases would require a good deal of effort. Gathering the required documents from those files to examine the cases in detail would take time. We would both have to fit the reviews of the thousand or so cases in with our other duties. The answer was clear to both of us: law students. Law students were plentiful. They liked working for law offices and gaining both experience and a foot in the door. Best of all: law students were cheap. Weinreb put out notices to the local law schools and scheduled interviews. Many students wanted the job of being a law clerk, particularly for a prosecutor's office. When they heard what the DNA Project—as we later named it—was about, they were enthusiastic. Never mind the low pay. The prospects of looking at the cases and the experience it would generate for them were attractive.

But exactly what were the law clerks going to do? When three of them were about to report for duty, we had to finalize precisely how the project was going to operate. Lists of convicted defendants would be obtained from the Department of Corrections and the Lifer Unit. Files would be ordered from storage. The cases would be reviewed, a checklist followed, and copies made of the important documents in each file. In addition, we wanted the law students to play a role in the case reviews. Weinreb and I had them compile all the records for each case, then write a summary, including their recommendation about whether DNA testing would be helpful. Deciding the order in which we would review the cases was particularly scientific. We settled on starting with inmates whose last names started with A and ending with those starting with Z. I was particularly proud of coming up with that idea.

We also had to determine the circumstances that would merit the offer of testing. We decided to follow the standard contained in the commission's model statute—if DNA testing were to provide results helpful to the inmate, is there a reasonable probability that the jury would have reached a different verdict? We later refined that standard to also permit testing if there was a reasonable probability that the inmate's sentence would have been less. Specifically, we would offer testing in any case in which the inmate had continuously claimed innocence, biological evidence still existed, and DNA testing of that evidence could resolve that claim. A continuous claim of innocence meant that the inmate had denied at each opportunity having committed the crime. We weren't interested in considering DNA testing in those cases in which the inmate claimed consent, self-defense, or that the crimes were an accident. With few exceptions, DNA is a tool to identify the perpetrator, not to determine how a crime was committed. However, we did not reject cases simply because at one point a defendant made a statement indicating involvement in the crime. For example, if an inmate claimed that admissions made to a police officer were coerced or that the only reason he or she admitted taking part in the crime was to get a lesser sentence, we would still consider the case. Also, the fact that a defendant had pleaded guilty to the crime did not disqualify the case from consideration. If that defendant received a significantly lesser sentence for entering a guilty plea or if in the plea the defendant did not admit the facts that were part of the case, an offer of DNA testing might still be made. One of the unfortunate facts of life in criminal cases is that defendants sometimes plead guilty to crimes they did not commit.

Next, what we would do when the determination was made that DNA testing had the potential to help an inmate? We decided that if we felt a case qualified for testing, we would have the law clerks determine whether the evidence seized in the investigation of the case still existed. If so, we would offer testing to the inmate through his or her attorney. If no attorney could be found who represented the defendant, we would contact the local public defender's office and they would speak to the inmate. The San Diego Public Defender's Office cooperated and appreciated the idea of a prosecutor's office undertaking such a review of its own cases. No defendant, we decided, would be forced to undergo testing. If the inmate decided not to accept our offer, we would go no further.

We also had to be concerned with who would test the samples in those cases in which the inmate accepted our offer. The good news was that the San Diego Police Department lab agreed to help. They believed strongly in using DNA to exonerate the innocent. The only assurance they needed from us was that I would continue to help prioritize their existing casework testing. Any postconviction cases we would forward to them would obviously have to be fit in around cases that were awaiting trial. But help came from another source. Shortly after announcing our program, our commission met for one of its last meetings. Dwight Adams, who had become the FBI's assistant director in charge of the laboratory division, stopped me at a break. He had heard about our program and offered the services of the Bureau in any case in which an inmate accepted our offer of DNA testing. The FBI shared our concern about wrongful convictions.

Finally, we decided that we would independently review each case submitted to us by the law clerks. Weinreb would decide whether the case qualified, then refer the case package to me. If I agreed, we would act accordingly.

If not, we would discuss the case further. If we were unable to come to the same conclusion, we would seek input from the major-case-review panel in the office. The district attorney had organized a group of San Diego prosecutors to make recommendations to him on whether the death penalty should be sought in pending murder cases. For our purposes, if a case was unusually difficult or troublesome, we could also solicit the input of the panel of experienced attorneys.

The evidence against Daye in 1984 had been strong. Eyewitnesses identified him as the attacker. Scientific evidence said the same. But Daye was totally innocent of the charges of which he was convicted. Weinreb and I liked to remind each other of that fact as we began to go through the hundreds of cases. The first batch of law clerks was excited. At varying times over the life of the project—which took more than three years to even near completion—between one and five law students assisted us. Dealing with nearly a thousand cases took time; time to get the case files, time to compile the documents and make a recommendation, and time for the two of us to review them. I found myself trying to review the cases in bundles; five here, another ten there. Flying to meetings and lectures was my most productive time. I sometimes wondered whether people sitting next to me on an airplane were looking over my shoulder. If so, they were getting an eyeful. The fact summaries were frequently awful to read, from brutal sexual assaults to torture murders. With time they would wear down even the most experienced attorney.

And the poor students. Several came to the project determined to find as many innocent inmates as possible. But within weeks they became jaded to the realities of violent crime. Nevertheless, they maintained their objectivity, which was so critical to the project's success. If just one innocent inmate was uncovered, the project would be an enormous success. If none was found, the district attorney and the community could have increased confidence in the reliability of the justice system.

Barely two months after we began, I received a telephone call from Rhett DeHart, counsel to Senator Hatch at the Senate Judiciary Committee in Washington. DeHart was working on the postconviction bill sponsored by Hatch. He asked whether I would be willing to testify about the bill in front of the Senate Judiciary Committee. Hearings on the legislation had finally been scheduled. DeHart thought my perspective would be helpful to the committee as a result of our examination of old cases. The decision was easy. Prosecutors were being portrayed as antagonistic to inmate DNA testing in much of the discussion about the competing bills sponsored by Hatch and Leahy. I could present an alternative view. Although I believed the stand-ard for testing contained in the Hatch bill was perhaps a little strict, the one provided in the Leahy bill was too loose. So I prepared a formal statement, forwarded it to Hatch's office, and awaited the trip to Washington for my tes-timony. I wondered whether I'd sit in the same chair that U.S. Supreme Court justices sit in when hearings are held on their confirmation.

A few weeks later I traveled to the nation's capital and the next day entered the Russell Senate Building adjacent to the Capitol. My name was on the witness list, and after negotiating the security stations I made my way to the Senate Judiciary Committee anteroom. DeHart was there and welcomed me. A few minutes later we all made our way into the busy com-mittee room. With a few glances I took in Senator Dianne Feinstein of my own state, Hatch, Leahy, Charles Schumer of New York, and Jeff Sessions of Alabama. I spoke to Barry Scheck and Jim Wooley of the commission, as well as Enid Camps of the California Attorney General's office, all of whom were present to testify as well. The session was called to order by Hatch, and everyone sat down. Senator Joseph Biden of Delaware took his seat. To my amazement, Senator Strom Thurmond entered and was helped into his chair. He looked old, but joked about having sat in the Senate longer than most of the committee members had been alive. It was a scene that seemed surreal. The same people I had seen on television for years were now three-dimensional. I thought back to the first time I entered Judge Lance Ito's courtroom during the Simpson trial.

The hearing itself was almost anticlimactic. Ten of us testified, half in support of the Leahy bill, the others—including me—touting the Hatch version. One witness was Dennis Fritz, a wrongfully convicted man who spent twelve years in an Oklahoma prison before DNA testing showed his in-nocence. I testified along with Scheck and Wooley in the second session that morning. Senator Hatch was gracious in his introductory comments about the three of us. He was a pro and it showed. Every witness is required to prepare his or her comments in advance and provide them to the commit-tee a few days before the hearing. Most witnesses read their prepared com-ments. I felt uncomfortable doing that because it was like reading an opening statement or closing argument to a jury—guaranteed to cause anyone to lose interest. I took my opportunity to talk about the relative strengths of the Leahy and Hatch bills and then described our new program in San Diego. The committee members seemed very interested. They were, understand-ably, skeptical that many other prosecutor offices would implement such a program. The senators were cordial, yet partisan. I thought to myself that they probably had no clue that here was a Democrat testifying on behalf of a bill sponsored by the ranking Judiciary Committee Republican. The hearing ended at noon. After lunch with a few friends, I headed home. It was a little heady having testified in front of the U.S. Senate Judiciary Committee. My only disappointment was not seeing Senator Edward "Ted" Kennedy in his chair. But that was more than made up for by looking Thurmond in the eye and realizing I was watching a piece of American history.

Back home we continued with the DNA Project. The law students were working hard and fortunately were able to perform their tasks with little supervision. Other than having us sign their timesheets and answer occasional questions, they were extraordinarily self-sufficient. The program was making progress, albeit slowly. One product of moving at a limited pace, although unintentional, was the fact that some of the nine hundred-plus inmates were being naturally released from prison. If we hadn't gotten to their cases yet, we did not consider them for DNA testing. We did receive a significant number of requests from inmates asking us to make sure that we reviewed their cases. Most were already on our list. Many were from counties other than San Diego. We referred their requests to the prosecutor's office in their own county.

One of the trends that surprised both of us was the number of cases in which the convicted inmate consistently conceded being the person responsible. Our early statistics were revealing that in over 70 percent of our cases the inmate had previously admitted being the individual who killed, had sexual relations with, or otherwise committed the acts against the victim. Those inmates claimed at the time that their actions were justified or that they were responsible only for lesser crimes. Their defenses were not unusual: in murders, that the killing was in self-defense, an accident, or without any intent to kill; in sexual assaults, that the victim consented to the acts; in others, that there was some justification for what they had done.

A letter we were sent early on caught our attention. An inmate housed at Donovan State Prison in San Diego County wanted to make sure that we looked at his case. He had been convicted of molesting a twelve-year-old San Diego girl years earlier and had been sentenced to nine years in prison. He claimed in his letter that he was innocent of that crime and named the man he said had assaulted the victim. However, he also told us in his letter that he knew we would discover that he was also serving a twenty-one-year sentence for another set of crimes. He wanted us to know that he had, in fact, committed those. His candor caught our attention. The other irony was that his last name began with a W. We had started with the As, so Weinreb and I laughed that he must have figured out our alphabetical strategy. We moved him to the top of the list and had the law clerks immediately look at his case.

We decided to offer him testing. The police department had already destroyed the physical evidence seized in his case because all his appeals had long been exhausted. The San Diego Superior Court, however, still had the evidence that had been made exhibits at his trial. We asked the court to release those exhibits, a request that was joined in by the inmate's attorney. The evidence was analyzed by the San Diego Police Department crime lab. Unfortunately, no biological evidence that DNA testing could be performed on was found. No relief was possible for the inmate.

The project began to receive national attention. Several prosecutor's offices wanted to know the details of our program so that they could implement it in their own counties. Susan Gaertner, the district attorney of Ramsey County, Minnesota, spent two days in San Diego learning our protocol. As a result, she implemented a similar project in her hometown of St. Paul.

Later in 2000, our own state Senate was presented with a bill to enact a postconviction DNA testing law in California. Sponsored by Senator John Burton, the bill would be one of the most far-reaching pieces of DNA legislation in the country. California Attorney General Bill Lockyer was concerned. The Burton bill, as it came to be known, would allow testing if it had the potential to provide relevant evidence for any inmate's case. That standard was, to say the least, a familiar one. Janet Gaard and Les Kleinberg, two of Lockyer's most trusted legislative aides, telephoned and asked whether I would help the attorney general with the proposed bill. The answer was yes. However, although I had spent a great deal of time on our commission's model statute and the federal Innocence Protection Act, I didn't realize how difficult California legislation could be. Burton was as powerful a legislator as anyone in the country. President pro tem of the Senate, he was savvy, smart, and surrounded by persuasive legislative aides. Lockyer's office proposed amendments to Burton's bill. His office countered that our changes were unnecessary.

It became obvious that Lockyer and Burton needed to meet personally, along with their aides. I flew to Sacramento for the meeting, expecting the worst. Both were highly experienced Democratic politicians but felt little compassion for each other. I entered the conference with Gaard, Kleinberg, and the attorney general. Burton joined us with his assistants. Within seconds, the fiery Burton and Lockyer were arguing. It was like coaches in a basketball game getting into a fight even before tipoff. I, for one, was speechless. Both left the room in a huff. The rest of us sat around wondering what to do. We decided to at least talk about the problems we had with the Burton bill. We made a little progress. Burton's aides, Mary Kennedy and Anthony Williams, were willing to listen to our concerns. Not long after that, Burton returned. Lockyer had gone back to his office down the street from the Capitol. Burton wanted to know our objections. We listed them. One by one he agreed with our changes. They weren't earthshaking, but they were provisions of the bill that genuinely concerned us. We turned to the heart of the bill: the standard that would guide judges in deciding whether to grant DNA testing. Burton wouldn't budge. The potential for relevant evidence, he insisted, was all that an inmate should have to show to get testing.

We all decided to separate but to talk again later in the day. Gaard, Kleinberg, and I returned to their offices at the Department of Justice. We ordered sandwiches and began to roundtable our position. Actual innocence wasn't going to get Burton's buy-in. Relevant evidence had no chance with the attorney general. The three of us chatted and talked alternatives. As though a light bulb had suddenly been turned on, I realized that we had a standard that had already been reviewed by experts from around the country. That standard was contained in the model statute recommended by the DNA commission. I discussed it with Gaard and Kleinberg. They liked it but wanted to discuss it with Ward Campbell. Campbell, a supervising deputy attorney general, was probably the office's premier expert on appellate litigation. If Campbell recommended against something, the wise course was to take another tack. We discussed with him by telephone the reasonable-probability standard for testing contained in the commission's model statute. He liked it. Attorney General Lockyer had no problem with it either. The next step was to see what Kennedy and Williams thought of the idea. Without their support, it would be an uphill battle to convince Burton. We dialed the number and Kennedy answered the phone. She laughed. They were just dialing us with the same suggestion.

That meant we had reached a consensus. It was obvious Burton wanted to see his bill passed. Getting the approval of the attorney general was important. Even the heavily Democratic-controlled California legislature didn't like the prospect of trying to enact laws that affected criminal justice in the face of opposition from the attorney general. Plus, Governor Gray Davis was never one to be soft on crime. The battle had been fought and perhaps won by both sides. Or, in reality, won by justice. California would help protect the rights of inmates who were convicted of crimes they hadn't committed—or, rather, those that DNA testing had the potential for exonerating. California Senate Bill 42 was passed by both the Senate and Assembly and was signed into law by Davis. Burton had gotten what he wanted. Law enforcement and prosecutors were satisfied with the result. Only inmates who truly deserved DNA testing were likely to have it ordered in their cases.

But what about our DNA Project? Over the course of three years the law clerks, Weinreb, and I read about and analyzed some of the most grotesque crimes that had been committed in San Diego's history. But we were slowly and methodically weeding out those cases in which DNA testing might have an effect. Unfortunately, we were having much the same experience as the Innocence Project. In roughly 75 percent of the cases for which Weinreb and I agreed DNA testing would be appropriate, the physical evidence had already been destroyed, usually because law enforcement didn't have the room to maintain it. Appeals and other legal attacks had long since been completed in those cases. There was no apparent reason to keep the evidence any longer. Although the policies of the sheriff's office and police departments around San Diego County differed, they were similar in many respects. In sexual assaults, for example, destruction after all appeals had been exhausted was common. Murder cases were different. In most of those cases, the agency in charge of the investigation still had the evidence that had been collected by its officers and lab personnel. In some instances, the evidence we were interested in was still in the possession of the court. Once an exhibit was admitted by a judge at a trial, that evidence became the responsibility of the court to maintain. Courts were hesitant to destroy evidence in the most serious cases, even after the appeals process had been completed.

One of the provisions of the Burton bill that survived our negotiations required law enforcement and the courts to preserve biological evidence. From the effective date of the bill, January 1, 2001, DNA evidence could be destroyed only if the defendant was released from prison or law enforcement provided notice to the inmate of its intent to dispose of the evidence. But that wouldn't have any effect on our cases in which the evidence had already been destroyed.

Weinreb and I were most troubled by the cases in which biological evidence wasn't capable of clearly showing a defendant's innocence. Although we embraced and supported the reasonable-probability standard for our internal review, it was sometimes difficult to apply. Take, for example, a murder case in which loose hairs are found on a victim's body. If we were to assume that DNA testing would show that one or more of those hairs couldn't have come from either the defendant or the victim, should testing be offered? Or because hairs are dropped and transferred so easily, are they likely to be unrelated to the crime and is testing then unlikely to be helpful? Each case had to be decided on its own facts. If a clump of many hairs clutched in the hand of a murder victim was collected, they could certainly be critical evidence and testing would be offered. If, however, the evidence was stray hairs adhering to the victim's body on the floor of a hotel room, our decision would likely be different.

Ultimately, the cases that we decided deserved testing under our program and that still had available physical evidence were interesting and challenging. In one case, a man convicted in 1990 of the sodomy of another male was serving a lengthy prison sentence. He had consistently maintained his innocence of the crime, from his arrest through his trial and sentencing. By checking the court exhibits, one of our law clerks determined that the victim's underwear was still in the custody of the court. The San Diego Police Department had tested the underwear at the time of its initial investigation and had found semen on it. No further testing was possible at that time. I contacted the public defender's office, and an attorney was assigned to communicate our offer of free testing of the underwear to the inmate. Within a few weeks we received our answer: no thanks.

The inmate's answer gave us more confidence in the correctness of the jury's verdict. But there were plenty of other cases to turn our attention to. Another case we offered testing in was challenging. A woman had been kidnapped from a rest stop along Interstate 8 in 1986. Her body was found a few days later in a lagoon near the Pacific Ocean, about twenty-five miles away from the location of her abduction. A suspect was questioned about the kidnapping and killing and made a few statements implicating himself in the crime. By the time of trial, he claimed the statements had been coerced from him by detectives. The man was convicted at a trial in 1991.

In the victim's car investigators had found a towel that was determined at the time to have semen on it. The woman had been at the rest stop because she was driving home from El Centro, one hundred miles east of San Diego. She had been there to spend the weekend with her husband, who was assigned to a naval air base in the desert. In an interview, the husband told detectives he had had sexual intercourse with the victim the day before the kidnapping. But the case qualified for testing. If that semen evidence produced results that were inconsistent with both the convicted defendant and the husband, a new trial might be appropriate. Ironically, the judge who presided over the inmate's trial had said at the time of the defendant's 1991 sentencing that even he still had a question about the defendant's guilt.

The offer of DNA testing was made to the inmate's attorney. Months later the attorney provided me with two letters written by his client, a man in his seventies. They were certainly the work of a crusty old salt and were a little contradictory, but they seemed to contain the man's consent to testing. His attorney agreed. The physical evidence in the case still existed—from the victim's underwear, which was found on her remains, to swabs taken from her body. Also included in the evidence was the towel from the victim's car at the rest stop. Only one piece of evidence provided any DNA results: the towel. It was then necessary to get a sample of the husband's DNA. Fortunately, he was still in the U.S. Navy, and a sample of his blood was forwarded to the laboratory. His profile matched that found on the towel. No results were generated that were helpful to the inmate, and he remained in prison.

Another case that resulted in testing being offered had been a controversial one for years. The case was that of John Ivan Kocak, the man who had been convicted by Deputy District Attorney Mike Carpenter of attacks on four victims in 1994–1995, as we saw in Chapter 10. The final victim, Ann, had been sexually assaulted in her home. Kocak had been linked by PCR DNA testing done by the San Diego Police Department crime lab to semen found on a piece of fabric collected from her apartment. Only about one in forty-six hundred people would be expected to have that same DNA profile. Before Kocak's trial, testing on another portion of the fabric was done by Cellmark using the first three STR markers that had been developed for forensic testing. Those results were reported by the laboratory to include the defendant. At the admissibility hearing demanded by the defendant's attorney, it was discovered by the analyst from the lab that a transcriptional error had been made in the report. In reality, the results were consistent with the victim's DNA, not Kocak's.

The mistaken reported results were never heard by the jury that decided Kocak's guilt. The legal controversy that accompanied the laboratory's mistake, however, continued. The case seemed perfect for inclusion in our project. Although the accuracy of the earlier PCR DQ-Alpha and Polymarker results that matched the inmate was not challenged, much more definitive testing was now available. If the semen could not have come from Kocak, a new trial would probably be appropriate. So the offer was made. Kocak accepted, and STR testing was arranged with the San Diego Police Department lab. A few weeks later the answer came: Kocak's DNA was identified at each genetic-marker location. The results were powerful: statistically, no one else in the world could have left that semen. Case closed.

Another murder case had intrigued San Diego for years. A twenty-year-old student at San Diego State University had disappeared one evening in 1986. A search resulted in the discovery of her body beneath a bridge adjacent to busy Interstate 15. To the shock of the entire community, the man arrested for the killing was a California Highway Patrol officer. The case was eventually tried, and the jury was unable to reach a verdict. The case was retried in 1988, this time by Pfingst, who was a deputy district attorney in the office at that time. The defendant was convicted of the murder of the young woman and sentenced to life imprisonment.

The trials had included serological testing of blood that was found on clothing and shoes recovered from the victim. The serology technology used at the time wasn't very powerful in telling people apart, but it did provide some results that failed to eliminate the Highway Patrol officer as the person who left the blood. PCR testing could be attempted on portions of those bloodstains that might remain from the testing performed fifteen years earlier. If results excluded the defendant, a new trial might be ordered. We decided to offer testing to the inmate through his attorney. At first, it appeared that our offer would be accepted. Eventually, the offer of testing was declined. A few months after the refusal, the former Highway Patrol officer appeared before the California Board of Prison Terms for a parole hearing. The prosecutor who had assisted Pfingst in the successful retrial, Joan Stein, attended the hearing. At one point she was permitted to ask the inmate why, if he hadn't committed the crime, he wouldn't agree to testing. He said nothing.

A couple other cases led to testing but failed to produce results that affected the inmates' convictions. A handful of cases would require more time to determine whether evidence still existed and whether the cases would ultimately qualify for testing. Eventually, the number of cases reviewed was reduced to 766. Some two hundred inmates were released from prison during the life of the project because their terms ended. Of that total of 766 cases, 759 were rejected for DNA testing. Although only seven cases resulted in formal offers of testing, another twenty or so would have if the physical evidence hadn't already been destroyed. But what was learned from the project was important. For one thing, it provided the district attorney of San Diego County an additional layer of confidence in the integrity of convictions of serious crimes in his jurisdiction. For another, it proved that an in-house DNA review of convictions could be done. Other prosecutor's offices across the United States began identical or similar programs.

Both Weinreb and I were asked to give presentations on our postconviction review effort. One lecture I was asked to make was particularly memorable. A seminar was scheduled at Harvard University while we were in the midst of the program. The meeting was a combination wrap-up session for the DNA commission and a symposium on DNA and the criminal-justice system. Sponsored by the John F. Kennedy School of Government, it proved to be a fascinating two days. The conclusion of the first day included an open-microphone question-and-answer session. The questioners: students at the Kennedy School; the answerer: Attorney General Janet Reno. The questioning, a tradition at the Kennedy School of Government, was no-holds-barred. These were students at one of the most famous schools in the world, and they were not shy. The attorney general was accommodating and answered any and all questions. When asked what she did wrong in the Branch Davidian incident in Waco, Texas, she was brutally honest.

The next day, during the seminar on DNA and criminal justice, the first speaker was Dr. James Watson: the same Watson who had shared the Nobel Prize in 1953 with Dr. Francis Crick for discovering the structure of the DNA molecule. After Watson's presentation, a student asked him a question about his work with DNA. The student didn't particularly like Watson's answer and began to argue with him. I sat in amazement, but Watson wasn't fazed. The next speaker raised the question of how jurors could be expected to understand some of the extremely small probability estimates attached to DNA results. He asked the audience how any juror was going to take into account and weigh a number such as one in five trillion?

My turn came next to speak to the group about postconviction DNA testing and our program. But the first slide I projected onto the screen was simply the words "1 in 5,000,000,000,000." I paused for a moment and then said to the audience, "Perhaps, unlike a juror, I understand exactly what the number one in five trillion means." The audience was curious. "This small probability of one in five trillion is precisely the chances that, after asking Dr. Watson a question about DNA, I would argue with him about his answer." The audience roared with laughter. I sneaked a peek at Watson in the corner of the auditorium. He liked it too.

CHAPTER FOURTEEN

DNA Takes to Television

————————

The search for innocent inmates wasn't restricted to the in-house work of the district attorney's office or that of the Innocence Project at Cardozo University. One day my telephone rang, and one of the most interesting conversations I had ever taken part in ensued. The caller was a man named John Bunnell, who explained to me that he was a close friend of a professional acquaintance of mine, Rod Englert. I had known Englert for years, our paths having crossed both in the prosecution of our San Diego criminal cases and at training seminars sponsored by the National College of District Attorneys. A detective, then a lieutenant, in the Multnomah County Sheriff's Department in Portland, Oregon, Englert was one of the most experienced investigators in the field of crime-scene recon-struction and was an internationally known expert on interpreting bloodstain patterns to determine how offenses had occurred.

Bunnell explained that he had formerly been in the Multnomah County Sheriff's Department with Englert. Now, he was host of the television se-ries *World's Wildest Police Videos*. Why in the world was he calling me, I thought to myself. The producer of his show, Paul Stojanovich, wanted to do a program on DNA, Bunnell said. My curiosity got the better of me. I told Bunnell I had spent quite a bit of time on the subject. He wanted to get together for dinner the next night with me and David Simons, an executive producer from Hollywood. I agreed to meet them at their suggested location: the Top of the Cove restaurant in La Jolla, a well-known eatery.

Getting some background information on Simons was irresistible. Thanks to the Internet, I learned that he had been producer and executive producer of several television programs. He had even been nominated for an Emmy award for a children's program broadcast by the Showtime and

Hallmark networks. What could he have in mind for a program on DNA? Dinner with the two revealed the answer. Simons envisioned a live, reality television program focusing on cases of prison inmates who claimed that they were innocent of the crimes for which they were convicted. The kicker: the program would include revealing the results of DNA testing to the convict live on the air; an immediate interview would be broadcast with the inmate's reaction to the news.

Bunnell and Simons could sense my disbelief at their idea. It might have been my blank stare. Simons asked whether I had doubts. I tried to explain that it wasn't particularly easy to interview an inmate in a state prison. But they were undeterred. Then I tossed out my opinion that no warden would be excited about the prospect of having a live television crew in a prison facility, particularly if an inmate might be surprised by information that could affect his status as a convicted felon.

Simons was still unmoved. If a live broadcast wasn't possible, why couldn't the inmates still agree to DNA testing and be interviewed in prison about the results? That was a little harder to take apart. "How would the cases be identified?" I asked him, given that there must be nearly a million prisoners in state and federal penitentiaries across the country. After thinking about the proposal, however, I told Simons and Bunnell that there might be a way to identify potential cases. The Innocence Project, run by Barry Scheck and Peter Neufeld, would be the place to start. Scheck and Neufeld had many cases that they thought deserved testing but no money to pay for the analysis. Simons interjected that they could pay for the testing.

It was getting harder to make fun of Simons's idea. I still couldn't get past what I knew would be roadblocks placed in the path Simons envisioned for the program. Prison authorities didn't answer to television producers. But he was insistent. What's more, he wanted my help in putting the program together. They already had a partner in the program: the Fox television network. I complained that I was a lawyer, not a TV consultant. They persisted. No one knew more about the field than I did, Bunnell insisted. They both asked that I think about the idea. At least I had a great dinner at one of San Diego's best restaurants. Everything else was, to say the least, unclear.

A week later Simons called and said he and Bunnell were in town again. He asked whether I would join them for dinner. Paying for testing would be no problem, Simons said. Getting cases from the Innocence Project made sense, so he asked whether I would talk to Scheck. Simons added that if I agreed to help with the program, I should also be ready to be an on-air expert for the broadcast. I told them that I thought their idea might just work.

As for being in the program, I suggested that we wait and see how the plans developed and cross that bridge if and when we approached it. Simons said that he would put his assistant, Mary Jo Blue, in touch with me. What for, I asked? To agree on a contract, he said with a laugh.

I wasn't sure what I had gotten myself into. Fox television. A reality program. And I still had a full-time job. I talked it over with my wife, Michele. I turned to my brother Peter for advice. Then I spoke to Assistant District Attorney Greg Thompson. Nothing prevented me from taking part in the program, even from getting paid for my work. As long as it didn't interfere with my duties as a prosecutor and I took time off for anything related to the show, I wouldn't be breaking any laws, regulations, or ethical rules. A check with the county's own lawyers verified that I could participate.

Blue called. I referred her to my brother Peter and decided to leave the negotiations to him. I sat down and thought about the best way to make the project a success. At the same time, I wanted to ensure an ethical, professional, and legal approach to the cases that would form the backbone for the program. I turned to Scheck. I knew that the Innocence Project was routinely inundated by more requests for postconviction DNA testing than could even be reviewed by its attorneys and law clerks. But I also knew that in a number of cases Scheck and Neufeld believed that testing was appropriate, but the inmate could not afford testing. Those cases would be ideal for the television program. Scheck, a little reluctantly, agreed to help. He would screen cases and identify those in which the inmate, though unable to afford testing, would agree to be interviewed for the broadcast. After a couple of months, about ten cases merited a detailed review.

But the legwork involved in researching the cases, deciding on witnesses and relatives to be interviewed, and scheduling production was daunting. Fortunately, Simons had quickly put together an impressive group of producers, researchers, and staff. Simons convinced Al Berman, a long-time CBS News producer, to executive-produce the program with him. To direct, Berman enlisted a veteran and fellow CBS News director, Don Roy King. Experienced freelance news reporters and segment producers were brought on by Berman to take charge of research for each of the cases. The group quickly went to work and rented private office space across the street from CBS Studios in Manhattan.

I began to talk regularly with the reporters and story producers, getting as much information as possible about each case. My assignment was to determine what evidence seized in each case had the greatest potential to prove the inmate's innocence. I reviewed police reports, lab data, and the trial court and appellate court opinions in each inmate's case. Most of my work was done at night and on weekends, although phone calls during business days were common. I carefully kept track of any work I performed for the program, so that I could take the time as vacation from my official position. I filled out timesheets that went down to the nearest minute, just to be safe.

Slowly the program was taking shape, but the logistics of several of the cases proved problematical. For one, some states absolutely prohibited interviews with inmates. That meant we had to focus on the other states. Just getting hold of the information needed for each case took hours of staff time in New York. Fortunately, the reporters were able to ferret out the details of the cases, of the police investigations, and of what had happened after the trials.

As Christmas arrived in 2000, the cases had been narrowed to a handful. Each had the potential for DNA testing that could affect the inmate's staying in prison. In a couple of cases, I needed to speak with the prosecutor who had handled the original case. My reception was usually lukewarm, at best. I suppose that wasn't surprising. Arrangements had to be made for obtaining the physical evidence, which the reporters had determined still existed. Usually, both law enforcement and the prosecutor's office ended up being cooperative. A couple of prosecutors later told me that my taking part in the program gave it enough credibility for them to agree to our requests for access to the evidence. Whether or not that was true, without the evidence the entire effort would have been futile.

We already knew who would be the on-air host of the program. John Walsh, who had gained fame as the host of *America's Most Wanted,* another Fox program, had signed on. In addition, the show would even be co-sponsored by the highly popular television show. Walsh had helped to find many of the nation's most dangerous fugitives from justice. After losing his young son Adam to a kidnapper and killer, Walsh had dedicated his life to helping others who had been the victims of violent crime.

The cases the program would concentrate on included that of Marty Tankleff, convicted in Suffolk County, New York, of the 1988 slaying of his mother and father. Hairs found on the bodies of his parents were still in existence and could be tested. From the moment of his arrest and charging, Tankleff had adamantly insisted that he was totally innocent of the murders.

In a second case, Ralph Armstrong was tried for and convicted of the 1980 sexual assault and murder of Charise Kamps in Madison, Wisconsin. Armstrong was an acquaintance of the victim and admitted being in her apartment prior to the crime. But Armstrong denied any involvement in her attack. Hairs found on the victim's bathrobe and on her bed had been located and were available for testing.

Wilton Dedge was first convicted in 1981 of the sexual assault of a seventeen-year-old Florida woman. His conviction was reversed by a Florida court of appeal because his trial had included dog-scent evidence that linked Dedge to linens collected from the victim's bed. The court that decided Dedge's appeal concluded that the dog-scent testimony was improperly allowed at his trial because it wasn't sufficiently reliable to be heard by jurors. In his second trial, Dedge was again convicted; that trial included the testimony of a paid jail informant. Evidence that remained from his case included slides of specimens recovered from the victim, as well as pubic hairs.

The fourth case was the 1985 kidnapping and murder of an eight-year-old New Orleans girl. John Francis Wille and his companion were arrested in an arson case in Florida two months later. During their interrogation, each confessed to killing the little girl but later claimed that the confession was coerced by police. It was determined that the companion had falsely confessed to another killing. Wille was arrested, charged, and convicted of the murder. Semen evidence on the victim's clothing and a nearby magazine, as well as hairs on the body of the victim, still existed.

The final case to be included in the program was more unusual than the other four. Albert DiSalvo, reputed for decades to be the infamous Boston Strangler, became the subject of intense attention in late 2000 because the body of his last reputed victim, who had been killed in 1964, had been recently exhumed. Her remains were in excellent condition, and forensic experts were able to retrieve evidence. That evidence might yield DNA results that either linked DiSalvo to the crime or exonerated him. Although our program was not involved in the exhumation or testing that might be performed on evidence from the victim, the story would be included. Relatives of the victim even agreed to be interviewed for the broadcast.

I was busy going over the evidence in the several cases, contacting laboratories, and making decisions about testing. The reporters, producers, and staff were working long hours researching the cases, interviewing witnesses and families, and getting their work ready for television production. The goal was ambitious: a two-hour prime-time broadcast devoted exclusively to the cases and DNA testing. But I was still uncertain about the role I would have in the production of the program. Despite Simons's talk about my being on the show, it seemed to me my best use was simply as a technical consultant. I had already exceeded my "fifteen minutes of fame" during the O. J. Simpson trial five years earlier. But Simons, Berman, and King had other ideas. It took a trip to New York City to make that clear.

Lecturing to groups about DNA was one of my passions. Despite the rigors of travel and missed time at home, I enjoyed spreading the word about the technology that had taken the criminal-justice system by storm. Even more, I felt an obligation not only to help prosecutors around the United States with DNA testing but also to let anyone and everyone know what it could reveal about the most serious criminal cases. District Attorneys Ed Miller and Paul Pfingst were both understanding and allowed me the opportunity to answer many of the requests they'd get for my help in educating prosecutors, defense attorneys, judges, and scientists.

In January 2001 I had promised to give a talk to the New Jersey state prosecutors' association in Princeton. I telephoned Berman at the television offices in New York City and let him know. He asked whether I'd have time to take the train into the city and meet the people involved in the production of the show. Up to that time, the only one whom I had met in person was Simons. It turned out that my talk in Princeton was scheduled to end in the early afternoon, so I could make the trip into Manhattan. Once there, I grabbed a cab to West Fifty-Seventh Street, across from CBS Studios. I walked into a building and found my way to the temporary offices of Helix Productions, the name given the company formed to produce the television program. As I walked in, I heard a familiar voice. It was Dave Fitzpatrick, one of the segment producers. Fitzpatrick was producing the stories on both Tankleff and Armstrong. He welcomed me and quickly introduced me to the other staff members who were in the offices.

It was getting close to 6:00 P.M., so Fitzpatrick suggested that we get something to eat in a Spanish restaurant down the street. A group of about eight of us from the DNA program joined him for dinner. The restaurant turned out to be a favorite spot for current and former CBS News staffers. Berman couldn't make it, but one of the other producers and several associate producers were there. We talked shop for a while. Near the end of dinner, I leaned over to Fitzpatrick and asked him whether he had any new information about my role in the program. He laughed. He said I was going to be the show's co-star with Walsh. He could see my surprise. I asked him how he or anyone else could know whether I'd even be able to talk in front of a camera. "You just passed the screen test tonight," he shot back. Fitzpatrick laughed some more. He explained that they had viewed videos of me from the Simpson case, network news, and other programs. They decided, he said, that I wouldn't have any problem with cameras.

Over the next few months, the program began to take shape. Arrangements were made to conduct the DNA testing in each of the cases. Consent forms were signed by the inmates that would permit their interviews with reporters. Decisions were made about other interviews, video segments, and several shorter stories. Two hours on television moved quickly, but that meant a great deal of preparation. In March Berman and Simons decided to tape-record the bulk of the "live" portion of the program from an actual state prison. Their choice: the East Jersey State Prison, commonly known as Rahway State Prison. Its location about an hour from New York City was convenient. Its architecture was even more compelling. Circular modules, reminiscent of 1950s' style brick-and-mortar, were straight out of the cinema. The prison had been featured in many television shows and movies over the decades. Prison authorities agreed to cooperate with us.

Dates were set for filming: a Sunday and Monday in the first week of April. Because the program would be broadcast as though it were live, filming would be at night at the prison. In addition, the results of DNA testing in the cases would be revealed to the inmates for the first time during their interviews, then played during the broadcast as if they were being interviewed live. The project was ambitious, to say the least. I would be at Rahway with Walsh. I would explain what DNA testing was all about, and then we would film my report of the results of testing in each case.

Michele wasn't about to miss a trip to New York City. We flew in on a Saturday and, after we did a little sightseeing Sunday morning, a driver arrived to take us to the New Jersey prison. Once there, I was amazed by the speed and efficiency of the movers who were unloading and setting up cameras, booms, lights, a crane, and video trailer-studios. Guards watched curiously from the front fence of the prison facility. I spotted a woman who seemed to be in charge. It turned out to be Blue. She invited us into a large motorhome. She asked whether I minded sharing the motorhome with Walsh instead of having one of my own. I asked whether she was kidding, but she wasn't. Laughing inside, I told her that one motorhome would be just fine. Not long after our arrival, Walsh entered the motorhome. I recognized him immediately and introduced both Michele and myself. Walsh was friendly and appreciative of my willingness to help with the show. That afternoon we met at different times with Berman, Simons, Blue, and King, the director, to talk about how the filming was to proceed over the next two nights.

At a break I wandered around the site and walked inside the primary trailer-studio, in which monitors, tape machines, and several of the production staff were housed. Sitting in the trailer was a man named Lane Venardos, who had been a long-time CBS News mainstay and was a senior producer on our program. He was one of the warmest and kindest members of the entire staff. Sensing my jitters, he told me there was no reason to be nervous. He had watched portions of the Simpson trial tapes. He said that I looked so calm in Los Angeles, he was sure this show would be easy for me. I thanked him, knowing he was just trying to make me feel better. The Simpson case was one thing; the television business was another. "Just be yourself," Venardos advised. Easier said than done, I thought. I wasn't even hungry when the buffet was set up during the evening. Everyone else was enjoying the food, which was laid out in the prison conference room.

Taping of Walsh finally began inside the prison walls. Those segments would be used at the beginning of the broadcast. Michele and I bided our time in the motorhome. Finally, as the clock neared 11:00 P.M., I was told to start my makeup. I was directed to the captain's chair at the front of the motorhome. "You can only do so much with this face," I joked to the woman. She laughed, but probably only out of courtesy.

Around midnight, I was called to the area in front of the prison gates that would be the set for my taping with Walsh. It was cool and began to drizzle. I was dressed in a business suit and was not used to the conditions. Simons, Berman, and King were all waiting. Clearly, this was now business. And with about fifty people working on the taping at midnight on a Sunday, I couldn't blame anyone for feeling that way. We had talked generally about what I would say during my portions of the program, but Berman didn't want me to have a script. They felt that my impromptu commentary would be more effective and more consistent with the live television concept. As a trial lawyer, I shouldn't have found speaking without a script a great leap. But this was a new experience. Just do it, I thought to myself.

My taping started. Walsh stood in his trademark leather jacket, seemingly impervious to what was rapidly becoming colder and wetter weather. I couldn't say the same. We would do several rehearsals for each scene and then tape at least two "clean" versions for each segment. They seemed to go well, but something wasn't right. For what was going to be broadcast as a "live" show later that spring, the weather seemed wrong. But we kept on until the night finally came to an end at 2:00 A.M. We rode back to the hotel with Blue. The next day, we were to start even later in the afternoon. Michele decided to stay in the city, so I ventured out for Night Two by myself. Taping was less eventful than it was the previous night, probably because the equipment was already set up and everyone had gotten used to the setting. We continued past midnight, but something did not seem right again. Only later would I find out what that was.

We flew home the next day and rejoined the real world. But, a couple of weeks later, Blue telephoned me and said they wanted to retape my portions. The problem that had nagged everyone was finally figured out. It just didn't make sense to have me describing DNA results at the same location where Walsh was introducing the stories of each inmate. Simons, Berman, and King wanted to retape my portions at a DNA laboratory. It was an obvious solution. I spent an entire Saturday at a laboratory in the Los Angeles area taping my segments. King and Simons were there to direct and produce. I had my own motorhome, or "star wagon," as I learned they were called.

We finished the taping and I waited for the program to air. On May 17, 2001, *Judgment Night DNA: The Ultimate Test* was broadcast on the Fox network nationwide. Michele and I watched the two-hour program, not sure exactly what to expect. None of the inmates was exonerated as a result of DNA testing. In Tankleff's case, results from the hairs recovered from his parents' bodies showed they were from either his father or his mother. In the cases of Dedge and Wille, testing failed to provide any significant results. Even the evidence recovered from the body of the victim in the case of DiSalvo, the alleged Boston Strangler, didn't produce any important scientific information.

The one exception was the case of Armstrong. Testing that was conducted on the hairs from the bathrobe of the victim and from her bed showed that neither Armstrong nor she was the donor of the hairs. On the program, I told Walsh that I thought Armstrong probably deserved a new trial. A few years later, Armstrong was indeed granted a new trial by the Wisconsin Supreme Court. His conviction was reversed based on additional DNA testing that showed that not only the hairs from the victim's body but also a semen stain could not have come from Armstrong. Also a few years after the program, additional testing was performed on semen recovered in the Dedge case. That testing excluded Dedge as the donor of those samples. He was released from prison, and charges against him were dismissed.

The day after the program aired, I couldn't help looking on the Internet for the overnight ratings. Unfortunately, our show was broadcast at the same time as the season's final episode of the NBC series *Friends*. Worse yet, we were opposite wrestling on the UPN network. I think we finished sixth for the time slot. There had been talk of a series being created from our program, but it was obvious to me that the work and investment that would be necessary for a series would be overwhelming. I quickly resigned myself to the fact that I wouldn't need to get a Screen Actors' Guild card.

STR testing had become an additional tool for scientists to use in the analysis of DNA evidence in criminal cases. But science never stands still. Another test would be developed for analyzing samples that traditional DNA testing wasn't capable of providing answers for. And that test would have an imposing name: mitochondrial DNA typing.

CHAPTER FIFTEEN

The Tragic Case of a Small Child

Eritrea, a small African country, found itself embroiled in civil war in 1984. A six-year-old girl, Frewoini, immigrated to the United States with her family to avoid the dangers in her homeland. Her life in the United States was difficult, even though she was living with her family. When she was sixteen, Frewoini left home, met a man, and was soon pregnant with his child. The two lived together for more than a year, during which Frewoini gave birth to a daughter. Frewoini and the child's father soon separated.

She later went to work for a call center and met another man, Lamont Johnson. The two dated for several months before Frewoini ended the relationship. She was introduced to another man and became pregnant with a boy, Thomas, who was born in January 2000. When Thomas was four months old, Frewoini again began to date Johnson. Although Thomas had been fathered by another man, Johnson seemed to Frewoini to be content with their relationship. Johnson would care for Thomas and his older sister when Frewoini was at work or away from home.

One day in July, Frewoini went to work. Thomas and his older sister were being cared for by Johnson. When Frewoini returned after her work day, Johnson told her that Thomas had fallen off the bed. Frewoini could see that Thomas's face was a little red, but he was alert, acting normally, and otherwise seemed to be fine. The next day, however, she could see bruising on his face and called a nurse on the telephone for advice. She was referred to Children's Hospital. When Frewoini spoke to someone at the hospital, she was told to bring Thomas in as soon as possible. Frewoini couldn't immediately drive Thomas to Children's because Johnson was away from home with the car and Frewoini couldn't contact him. When he did return, both drove

Thomas to Children's Hospital. The doctors there believed Thomas's injuries were not the result of a fall but were caused by abuse. Thomas was kept in the hospital overnight for observation and temporarily placed in protective custody.

Thomas was examined further and was found to have injuries to his face that doctors believed couldn't have been the result of a fall off a bed. However, his laboratory results and X-rays were normal. After staying in Children's for a few days, Thomas was placed temporarily in a foster home. Juvenile Court proceedings were begun, and Frewoini was granted custody of her son. She had to agree, however, not to continue to see Johnson or to permit her children to be in his company. But Frewoini didn't believe that Thomas's injuries were caused by Johnson, so she continued to have contact with him despite the agreement. In September, Frewoini and her two children went to Johnson's home to stay for the weekend. On one of those days Frewoini left the house at dinnertime to go to work at the call center. After she arrived, Johnson telephoned her and asked her to come home because, Johnson said, Thomas was choking.

Johnson was trained as a nursing assistant and was familiar with life-saving techniques. He even owned a pair of stethoscopes. Thomas's sister saw Johnson take Thomas into another room; she heard Thomas whine and cry, then stop. He then began to cry again, and once again he stopped. Johnson returned to the main room with Thomas, who seemed to his sister to be asleep. Johnson had the sister listen to the little boy's heartbeat with one of the stethoscopes. She could hear his heart beating quickly, but she thought Thomas was dead because his eyes were closed. Johnson then made his telephone call to Frewoini at work. Frewoini arrived home and saw that Thomas was neither moving nor breathing. His mouth was blue. Frewoini tried to administer CPR but she wasn't sure how to do it. Johnson stood nearby. Frewoini dialed 911 and ran outside the house with Thomas to try to find help. Paramedics arrived and found Thomas near death. He was taken to a hospital, but efforts to revive him failed, and he was declared dead.

When doctors tried to save Thomas, they removed his diaper and discovered a curly, pubic-like hair on his groin. Injuries were also noted to his anus. An autopsy revealed that Thomas had suffered tears to his rectum. Examination of his brain showed that he had both old and new bleeding in several locations that appeared by experts to be from shaking or striking the child with an object.

Johnson was charged by the district attorney's office with murder in the death of young Thomas. An allegation was added that, if found true by a jury, would raise the possible punishment to life imprisonment without the possibility of parole. After a preliminary hearing of the charges, a trial date was set. The case was assigned to Deputy District Attorney Dan Goldstein. Goldstein was the most successful homicide prosecutor in the office's Family Protection Division, a unit that specialized in domestic- and child-abuse cases. He liked to move cases along as quickly as possible and was well known in the San Diego legal community as a tenacious trial lawyer.

The trial of Johnson was sent to Judge William Kennedy, one of San Diego's best criminal judges. But before the trial started, Johnson's attorney, Brian White, wanted the court to hold a hearing on the DNA evidence that Goldstein wanted to use. That evidence was DNA results from the apparent pubic hair that had been found by the hospital doctors who had unsuccessfully tried to save Thomas's life. The judge agreed that a hearing was necessary because the results came from a new form of DNA testing. Its name: mitochondrial DNA. It linked Johnson to the hair found on Thomas's groin.

Mitochondrial DNA testing had been used only sparingly in criminal cases in the United States at that time. Mitochondrial DNA was normally turned to for the testing of hairs. The root of a hair often has enough DNA to allow testing using traditional techniques, such as DQ-Alpha, Polymarker, or even STR typing. However, when no root is present or a root doesn't have enough regular DNA—usually referred to as nuclear DNA— the shaft of a hair is all that can be tested. Hair shafts do not have enough nuclear DNA inside to produce test results. However, they do have mitochondrial DNA.

Mitochondrial DNA is different from nuclear DNA in several respects. Mitochondria, which contain the mitochondrial DNA, are found inside cells, but instead of being located in the nucleus of the cell they are located in the surrounding area, called the cytoplasm. Mitochondrial DNA is more plentiful in a sample of biological evidence than nuclear DNA. However, it is not capable of telling people apart with the same precision as nuclear DNA testing, such as STR typing. An individual's mitochondrial DNA profile is inherited from that person's mother only. That means all of a mother's children, grandchildren, and so on have the same mitochondrial types as the mother.

Also, in mitochondrial DNA testing the odds of finding matching profiles are not usually described with statistics like "one in" an estimated number or similar probabilities. Instead, if the mitochondrial DNA profile from a piece of evidence is the same as that from a known person, an analyst normally compares that profile to a database of results from several thousand persons who have already been tested. If the profile has been seen before, the number of times that it has already been observed is listed in the report of the lab's results. If it has not been observed before, that fact will be reported as well, along with the number of samples that was searched in the database that was used. That way some estimate can be provided of how rare the matching mitochondrial DNA types are. Again, the same profile would be expected to match any person who shared the same maternal relationship with the individual who was found to have matching results with the evidence.

The hair found in Thomas's diaper, which was determined to be most likely a pubic hair, was a good candidate for mitochondrial DNA testing. Goldstein and I had talked about the best plan of action. We already knew from a previous examination of the hair that the root could not be successfully tested. Pubic hairs are difficult to get nuclear DNA results from even with a good root attached. This hair had little or no nuclear DNA in the root location.

Goldstein wanted to know where we should send the hair for testing. A few labs offered mitochondrial DNA testing, but inevitably, in the case against Johnson, if results came back that implicated him, the defense would object to the evidence, and a hearing would be required. None had been held in our San Diego courts—or in California, as far as I knew—on the admissibility of mitochondrial DNA testing. I made a suggestion to Goldstein. I was familiar with a scientist named Dr. Mitchell Holland from scientific meetings where I had spoken. One of the benefits of taking part in those meetings was the opportunity to listen to scientists and to get to know firsthand the testing technologies they used and their successes—as well as their failures. Holland had gained extraordinary experience in the use of mitochondrial DNA while he did testing and research at the Armed Forces Institute of Pathology (AFIP) in Rockville, Maryland. AFIP had the responsibility of identifying the remains of American war dead and other military personnel who died in the service of the United States. When traditional techniques like fingerprinting and dental comparisons—and even nuclear DNA testing—were unsuccessful, mitochondrial DNA was turned to for the identification of human bodies or other remains.

I was aware that Holland had recently left AFIP and joined a private DNA laboratory in Springfield, Virginia, named the Bode Technology Group. Bode offered traditional DNA testing, but, more important for Goldstein's case, it also offered mitochondrial DNA typing. And Holland, I convinced Goldstein, had the education, training, and experience to make him the ideal witness for a *Kelly-Frye* hearing on the admissibility of mitochondrial DNA testing results. Goldstein agreed; the pubic hair was sent to Bode, along with known DNA samples including one from Johnson.

Bode performed its testing on the pubic hair and was able to determine its mitochondrial DNA sequence. Unlike nuclear DNA testing, mitochondrial testing reveals the sequence of the A, C, G, and T bases in specific areas of the mitochondria. When Bode's results were compared with the results of testing done on the known samples, the lab concluded that the hair could not have come from Frewoini or anyone in her maternal line. However, the hair's mitochondrial DNA sequence was the same as that found in Johnson's known sample of DNA. Bode did not have that sequence in its database of 4,142 people.

Judge Kennedy agreed with White, Johnson's attorney, that a hearing would have to be held on the mitochondrial DNA testing results. But Goldstein and I were confident. Not only would Holland testify, but I was ready to give Kennedy several published scientific articles that detailed the science underlying mitochondrial DNA testing and the reliability of the results that the technique provided. And I knew that it wouldn't hurt that it was the same technology that was used to identify American servicemen who died in combat.

I called Holland to the witness stand in the admissibility hearing. I went over his education and experience with mitochondrial DNA and the steps in its testing. He detailed the techniques used and compared them with the steps in traditional DNA typing, such as STRs, including the use of PCR to first copy the DNA. Holland told Kennedy that the differences occurred only in the typing phase, where the individual bases are determined rather than differing lengths of repeated DNA sequences. Holland gave his opinion that mitochondrial DNA testing was generally accepted in the scientific community and referred to several of the scientific publications that I had already provided to the defense and to the judge.

Christopher Plourd was enlisted by White to handle the admissibility hearing for the defense. Since the Willie Ray Roberts case (Chapter 6), Plourd had specialized in forensic-science issues, particularly DNA evidence, as I had for the district attorney's office. Plourd knew the issues, including those that were unique to mitochondrial DNA. He cross-examined Holland about the danger of contamination in mitochondrial DNA testing. Like other technologies that relied on the PCR process, mitochondrial DNA testing required careful attention to the possibility of contamination. Its ability to be used on small or particularly old samples made it more susceptible than other techniques to contaminating DNA from other sources, whether in the environment or in the laboratory.

Plourd also questioned Holland about a feature unique to mitochondrial DNA testing known as heteroplasmy. At certain locations of our mitochondrial DNA, referred to by experts as "hot spots," samples taken from the same person can occasionally reveal a different A, C, G, or T result. That fact, Plourd correctly pointed out, could lead to incorrect conclusions. Samples could be mistakenly declared to be from different individuals. More important, samples from different people could incorrectly be called a match.

On redirect questioning, I had Holland describe to Kennedy that the problem of heteroplasmy was well known to mitochondrial DNA testing analysts. Several procedures were implemented by laboratories to watch those known hot spots and to interpret results carefully. Repeat testing of different samples from the same person might be required. Guidelines were developed in the field to interpret results accordingly. Most important in our case, the results showed no need for any concern about either heteroplasmy or contamination.

Kennedy ultimately agreed that mitochondrial DNA testing was generally accepted in the scientific community and that our evidence met the *Kelly-Frye* standard, thus allowing the evidence at the trial of Johnson. Kennedy also decided that the criticisms that Plourd had raised during the hearing about the possibility of contamination and heteroplasmy did not require exclusion of the evidence. Rather, they could be brought up during the trial, and the jury would ultimately decide what weight those complaints should carry in their decision about the significance of the evidence.

A jury was selected, and Goldstein presented his case against Johnson. That jury ultimately failed to reach a verdict, and a mistrial was declared. The vote was 11–1 to convict Johnson. Before a retrial could be held, Goldstein ran for judge and was elected to the San Diego Superior Court. In his place, Deputy District Attorney Sharon Majors-Lewis was assigned to retry the case. Majors-Lewis convinced a new jury that Johnson was indeed guilty of murder in the first degree. The jury also agreed that the allegation was true. Kennedy later sentenced Johnson to life imprisonment without the possibility of parole.

Kennedy's decision allowing the hair mitochondrial DNA evidence was used by both prosecutors and defense attorneys in cases that followed the prosecution of Johnson. Requests for copies of Holland's testimony and

Kennedy's order began to flood my telephone and e-mail. But technology made my task easy. A few keystrokes on my computer were all that was required, and the materials were on their way. I could only smile when I thought back to the days of making copies and sending inches' worth of transcripts to Rock Harmon on the next Greyhound bus to Oakland.

CHAPTER SIXTEEN

A Cold-Hit DNA Match Solves an Old Crime

*T*he Daily Planet was a popular night-spot for young couples and singles in September 1993. Located along the ocean on Garnet Avenue in the Pacific Beach area of San Diego, it was typically hopping on a Friday night. September 10 was no different. Except it would forever change the life of a twenty-four-year-old woman. Monica was a server at Moondoggies, another popular beach restaurant. That Friday she ended her shift at 11:00 P.M., then met a few friends at the Daily Planet. She spent a couple of hours talking with them, then went outside for a little fresh air. Monica saw a couple of other friends and started to talk with them. The three decided to walk to a taco shop across Garnet, and Monica spoke with them while they ate a late dinner. After they were finished, Monica returned to the Daily Planet and bypassed the line of people waiting to get in because she had had her hand stamped when she originally entered the bar. Inside, Monica couldn't find her friends from earlier in the evening. They had planned to drive her home, but when she went back outside, she couldn't find their car. Monica decided to walk home.

Although her apartment was in La Jolla and almost five miles away, Monica started walking and thought she would call her roommate when she got closer to home. It was a beautiful evening, people were on the sidewalks, and Monica liked to walk. She walked down Garnet, then turned and went north on La Jolla Boulevard near the ocean shore in the direction of her home. As Monica neared a 7–11 convenience store, she became aware of a man jogging behind her on the sidewalk. Monica became worried because of the lateness of the hour and the fact that the lighting wasn't particularly good on that portion of the street. She decided to cross the street and go inside the open store. When she came out of the store, she had lost sight of the man. Monica felt it was safe to continue on her way home.

Continuing north on La Jolla Boulevard, Monica approached the La Jolla Lutheran Church on her right. As she walked toward the front steps of the church, a man jumped out of some bushes behind her. The man grabbed Monica from behind and covered her mouth with his left hand. He held a small silver handgun to her neck with his right hand. He pushed Monica onto the church steps. Monica began to scream. The man told her he had a gun and would kill her if she continued to make noise. Monica could see traffic driving by on La Jolla Boulevard. The attacker pulled up Monica's skirt and unbuttoned the bottom of her body suit. He unzipped his shorts and pulled out his penis. Kneeling between Monica's legs, he twice tried to rape Monica. He penetrated her slightly each time, but wasn't satisfied.

He stood up and pulled Monica off the stairs. He pointed his gun at Monica and ordered her to move. He forced her to the north side of the church, farther from the street and more secluded. Monica's assailant told her to lie down on the ground. With the gun still in his hand, he knelt down and tried to rape Monica five or six times. Again, he was only partially successful. The man then sat on her chest and forced Monica to orally copulate him. He knelt down between Monica's legs and tried to rape her again. She tried to resist by moving side-to-side. She was crying hysterically. The attacker ejaculated onto Monica's lower stomach, then fled southbound on La Jolla Boulevard.

Monica immediately ran back toward the 7–11 store. Crying, she telephoned her boyfriend. The clerk phoned 911, and police quickly arrived. After describing to patrol officers what had happened to her, Monica was transported to Villa View hospital for a sexual-assault examination. Evidence was collected from Monica's left thigh, and her skirt was kept. Police impounded the evidence. Sperm were determined to be present on both items by the San Diego Police Department crime lab.

But DNA testing was limited in 1993, and only partial information could be obtained from use of the PCR testing process. Like most crime labs at the time, the San Diego Police Department lab was able to type samples at the DQ-Alpha and Polymarker genetic locations only. Even matching results couldn't exclude a large percentage of the population, unlike profiles that were determined using the RFLP technique. Even more problematical was the fact that there was no suspect in Monica's case to compare test results to. Only fledgling DNA databases existed in the early 1990s, and those with PCR-generated profiles were nearly nonexistent. Therefore, DNA testing was not even attempted. The San Diego crime lab's finding that sperm was on the skirt and Monica's thigh was the end of the line, at least until a suspect could be developed. But none was. The crime took place at night and in the dark. Monica could describe almost no features of the man. His clothing was nondescript. Police had almost nothing to go on, and the investigation produced no real suspects. Monica went on with her life. After graduating from college, she taught at an elementary school, married her boyfriend, and started a new chapter in her life.

But California Attorney General Bill Lockyer recognized the power of DNA testing in old cases. In 2000 the state's Office of Criminal Justice Planning set aside fifty million dollars in funding to encourage police and sheriff crime labs in California to take new looks at their unsolved sexual-assault and homicide cases. The goal was to use DNA testing to type evidence samples in suspectless cases and to compare the results with the growing database of convicted offenders both in California and across the nation. The plan was a novel one: to pay law-enforcement agencies to find evidence, screen it for biological material suitable for DNA testing, and use the then-new STR technique of DNA typing to produce profiles that could be compared with databases. For every rape kit that could even be located in their property rooms, police and sheriff's agencies would be paid $50. If the kit was screened for biological evidence, an additional $250 was provided. If DNA testing was done on the evidence, the state would pay the agency $1,750. The method seemed a little mercenary and cold, but the goal was to light a fire under police chiefs and sheriffs to get the evidence off property-room shelves and into the crime laboratory for analysis.

Early on, the San Diego Police Department recognized the potential of the program to solve cold cases. With the promise of state money, the crime lab was able to hire additional analysts and technicians to analyze the hundreds of unsolved rape and murder cases that might be solved by DNA testing. By working in tandem with sex-crime and homicide detectives, the lab prioritized its cases.

In early 2000 the crime lab was working on unsolved cases at every available opportunity. Ian Fitch, a DNA analyst, was given Monica's case. He analyzed the semen evidence from her thigh and skirt and was able to determine the STR profile of the man who had left the evidence in Monica's attack. The information was then uploaded into the California and national DNA databases of unsolved cases. A little over one year later, Fitch received the incredible news. A match had been made by computer between the DNA profile from the evidence in Monica's attack and a crime in Oro Valley, Arizona, a town near Tucson. Sex-crimes Detective David Dolan was assigned the case for further investigation. The information he developed was amazing. Dolan contacted the Arizona Department of Public Safety, the laboratory that had done the testing on the evidence that matched Monica's case.

It turned out that on February 2, 2001, a thirteen-year-old girl had been waiting for her school bus in front of the driveway to her home. She noticed a man standing next to a black truck in the long driveway from the street to her house. The girl returned to her home and told her father what she had seen. The father looked out his front window and saw a truck. Standing next to the truck was a man who was facing the bus stop. The man was masturbating. The father immediately telephoned Oro Valley police. Officers arrived a short time later, although the suspect had already left the scene. The father described the vehicle and also pointed out the location where he saw the man masturbating. Police found what appeared to be semen in the area where the suspect was seen masturbating, and they collected the semen as evidence. During the follow-up investigation, Oro Valley detectives identified a man named Anthony Medina as the suspect, based largely on the license plate observed by the father. Medina, a local resident, was arrested for public sexual indecency. A mouth-swab sample was collected from him.

Bob Blackett, of the Arizona Department of Public Safety Crime Lab, compared the DNA from Medina's mouth-swab sample to DNA he removed from the semen stain taken from the driveway. Medina matched the DNA profile from the stain. The chances that someone else had left the sample: about one in 870 trillion. The DNA profile from the semen stain was entered into the Arizona state and national DNA databases.

Once San Diego Detective Dolan learned of the match, he was worried that the statute of limitations had run on the crimes against Monica. They occurred in 1993; the match to Medina was made in 2001. The statute of limitations for forcible sex crimes at that time was six years. During his follow-up, however, Dolan discovered that Medina moved to Arizona in 1998 and had maintained his residence there since then. He applied for and received an Arizona driver's license, and he had held that license for the preceding three years. Medina told Oro Valley detectives that he had continuously worked for Sprint Communications in Arizona for the prior three years. That sealed it. California law permitted a statute of limitations to be tolled, or suspended, for up to three years if a suspect was living outside California. The six-year limit thus turned into nine years, enough time to allow a prosecution of Medina for the crimes against Monica to go forward.

Dolan brought Monica's case to the district attorney's office for review and the possible filing of charges against Medina. Several other unsolved sexual assaults had taken place in the Pacific Beach and La Jolla areas around the same time in 1993. DNA results, however, did not implicate Medina in any of those other crimes. Jim Pippin had me review each of the cases, including Monica's. It quickly became clear that the only chargeable case against Medina was the attack on Monica at the La Jolla Lutheran Church. Dolan had spoken to Monica, and she was brought to my office for an initial interview. Monica was bright, articulate, and had carried on with her life after her assault. She and her husband were both elementary school teachers and loved their work. But Monica was willing to assist in the prosecution of the man who had assaulted her eight years earlier. She bore the man no malice; she simply felt that no one else should ever suffer the pain that he had forced on her years earlier. I filed formal charges against Medina on August 15, 2001. Medina was arrested in Arizona by San Diego detectives a few days later for the assault on Monica. He waived extradition proceedings and was returned to San Diego by Detective Dolan.

The charges against Medina were three counts of rape, one charge of kidnapping for the movement from the church steps to the side of the building, one count of oral copulation, and an additional charge of sexual penetration. Attached to each of the charges was an allegation that Medina had used a firearm in his commission of the crimes. After he pled not guilty to all the charges, a preliminary hearing was held in December. The judge who presided over the hearing decided that there was enough evidence to hold Medina to answer the charges at a trial. Prior to that trial, however, the kidnapping count was dismissed. The court decided that there simply wasn't enough evidence to support that charge. Additional DNA testing was done on vaginal swabs that had been collected from Monica at the time of her rape exam. Semen recovered from the vaginal swabs also matched Medina. The chance that someone other than Medina had contributed the semen found on Monica's thigh, her skirt, and the vaginal swabs was less than one in a quadrillion—that's a one followed by fifteen zeros.

The case was set for trial, but delays took the case into the middle of 2002. I was occupied with the trial of another defendant, David Westerfield, helping Deputy District Attorney Jeff Dusek. But the public defender representing Medina had cooperated, and her client continued to give up his right to a speedy trial. By mid-summer, Dusek and I were still busy with the Westerfield case, and so the trial of Medina was set for September. I wasn't too concerned. There was no reason Medina wouldn't agree to another continuance until after the Westerfield case was over.

The Westerfield jury was still deliberating when the next trial date for Medina arrived on September 9, 2002. Stephanie Slattery, the attorney representing Medina, called to let me know that Medina was not willing to continue the case again. We would have to start the trial. Not my first choice. Not even my last choice. But there wasn't another alternative. Pippin offered to hand the case over to another prosecutor, but that wasn't the answer. I had developed a rapport with Monica, as is common with victims of sexual assault. Their cases involve private details and emotions that are not encountered in other types of cases. Giving Monica's case to another deputy district attorney wouldn't be fair to her. She had been willing from the start to sacrifice her privacy and reopen old wounds. I didn't want to fail Monica.

It wasn't a difficult case to prepare. There weren't many photographs, particularly because the crimes had occurred so long ago. The facts weren't complex. The incident in Oro Valley made the case a little more complicated, but I still had a few days. I just had to put the Westerfield case out of my mind. But I had learned my lesson from the trial of Paul Vasquez, the first of San Diego's DNA database cases (Chapter 11). Monica's was another "whodunit" case that DNA seemed to resolve. I had to assume that Medina might do exactly what Vasquez had done: turn his defense of the charges into a case of consent instead of an identification case. I wasn't about to get caught flat-footed again.

The trial was assigned to Judge Laura Hammes. We began picking a jury that same day. The next day, we finished selecting the jury, and I began presenting evidence. Monica, like Sandra in the trial of Vasquez, was a compelling witness. Also like Sandra, she was unable to say whether Medina was the man who had committed the vicious attack on her nine years before. She simply did not see enough of his face at that time to describe him in any meaningful way. The rest of the evidence went as I had hoped. Slattery didn't seem to me to make much headway with her cross-examination of Monica. It's difficult to cross-examine the victim of a violent sex attack. But her cross did provide a clue that the defense was going to be consent. Slattery intimated during her questioning that Monica might have falsely reported being raped because of her close relationship with her boyfriend.

The other witnesses and evidence were equally convincing: Monica's friends at the Daily Planet, her boyfriend, the 911 emergency call, the patrol officers, and the rape-exam expert. I was also permitted to call the witnesses from Oro Valley, who described the unusual incident in the driveway that led to Medina's identification in the crimes against Monica. At least this time, unlike in the Vasquez case, the jury would hear the whole story about how Medina came to be identified. The jury also heard from Detective Dolan and from Fitch, the DNA analyst whose results solved the identity of Monica's attacker. The only other witness was Ed Blake of Forensic Science Associates. Blake had performed additional testing on some of the evidence that had already been tested by Fitch.

The case was moving at a lightning pace. On the fourth day my last witness was Blake. I rested my case against Medina that morning. Without hesitation, Slattery called the defendant to the witness stand. Medina started slowly, answering each of his attorney's questions. He said that he had been living in San Diego during the summer and fall of 1993 and described how he had frequented clubs in the Pacific Beach area at that time. He liked watching people, he said. Medina vaguely recalled meeting a woman in one of those clubs around September and walking with that woman to the beach. They began kissing, he thought he may have ejaculated, and then they parted ways. But he didn't directly say that Monica was that woman, even though he had seen her testify in court only a few feet away from him just two days earlier. I was puzzled.

I tried with my cross-exam of Medina to strike at the weak points of his direct examination. I hit Medina at the outset with what I was most curious about. I asked him pointedly if the woman he described meeting and going to the beach with was Monica. Medina agreed that it probably was. "Probably?" I thought to myself. He doesn't even remember? But I felt that Monica had been so convincing that no reasonable juror would believe that she had not been raped. So I turned to the other baggage Medina had to carry: the indecent-exposure crime in Arizona, a previous felony conviction for vehicle theft, and other indecent-exposure crimes. I also asked him about a prior gun-possession conviction.

The evidence was finished, and we turned immediately to closing arguments. I set out the case for the jurors, explaining the law for each of the sex crimes Medina was charged with. Slattery made her argument, attacking Monica's believability and suggesting to the jury that she had made up the sexual assault because she was afraid that her boyfriend would not marry her if he knew that she had had sexual relations with another man. I made my final argument and reiterated much of what I had argued earlier to the jurors. The case was a "whodunit" solved by DNA evidence. I told the twelve jurors that Medina had been unbelievable during his testimony, making up what was obviously a bad lie. I told them that DNA had proved to be a magic tool that solved a case that for years had been unsolvable. I then sat down.

The jurors came back the next day for their final instructions from Judge Hammes. They began their deliberations that morning. I returned to my office and enjoyed one of those rare moments for a trial lawyer, when you feel like a peacock in full plume. Other prosecutors kept coming into my office asking how my jury was doing. They meant the Westerfield jury, which was still deliberating. But I couldn't resist the opportunity. I answered with a question of my own: "Which jury?" I knew my triumphal mood wouldn't last long, but it was devilish fun to make sure other deputy district attorneys knew that I wasn't just a one-trick pony who helped other prosecutors with their DNA evidence.

The Medina jury returned with verdicts at the end of the day. They found Medina guilty of three counts of rape, one of oral copulation, and the sexual-penetration charge. The jury also found that Medina had used a firearm in committing each of the crimes. Two months later Hammes sentenced Medina to prison for forty-eight years.

But several of the jurors waited in the hallway to talk about the case. Discussions with jurors after a trial can be instructive, helpful, discouraging, or downright frustrating. This jury had been relatively quick in reaching verdicts in a serious case, but there had been a bit of a stumbling block during their deliberations. A couple of jurors had thought that Monica might have falsely reported a rape. But one of the few photographs that I had placed in evidence during the trial resolved the problem, they said. I couldn't even imagine which photo would have swayed those jurors. However, one of the Polaroid photos taken by the original patrol officers of the steps at the church showed something that I had never noticed: Monica's shoes lying askew on the steps. The hesitant jurors looked at the photo and had to agree. Monica would not have run down the street to the 7–11 store in her stocking feet if she hadn't been raped. She would have put on her shoes first.

Whew. DNA had again come to the rescue, solving a case that would formerly have stayed cold forever. But in the end the case had come down to jurors' deciding the credibility of witnesses who told different versions of the story. And a photo taken years before to simply record what the scene looked like tipped the scale.

CHAPTER SEVENTEEN

Helena Greenwood Revisited

———

The investigation of the murder of Helena Greenwood in San Diego had continued in 1987, even after David Paul Frediani had been sentenced to prison for his San Francisco Bay Area sexual assault on her. Detective Dave Decker, who originally investigated the killing, interviewed Frediani, who was imprisoned at that time in Vacaville, located near the state capital of Sacramento. Frediani told Decker that he had nothing to do with the killing of Greenwood, and no new leads were developed in the investigation. Although detectives investigating Greenwood's killing strongly suspected Frediani had murdered her, they simply didn't have enough evidence to have him charged and prosecuted. The case became old and cold as the years passed. Frediani was released from prison for his sexual assault on Greenwood after the reversals of his first two convictions and his eventual no contest plea to the charges.

In April 1998 Detective Laura Heilig was assigned to the Sheriff's Homicide Archive Team in San Diego. The group was formed to take a fresh look at unsolved murders and to try to identify the killers in those cases. Although there weren't any active leads or new witnesses in the Greenwood killing, Heilig jumped headfirst into the case file. She knew of the breathtaking progress in DNA testing, particularly with small evidence samples. She scrupulously reviewed the evidence lists in the case and in November instructed the sheriff's laboratory to ship several items of evidence, including Greenwood's fingernail clippings and scrapings, to SERI, the Serological Research Institute, in Richmond, California, in order to determine whether PCR DNA testing could produce any results. Because of the way Greenwood had struggled trying to save her life, her killer's DNA might have been left on her. Killers sometimes leave DNA when the victim scratches or claws the attacker in self-defense. Nearly a year later the news arrived on Heilig's desk. SERI had been successful in testing Greenwood's fingernails and was able to get results using the DQ-Alpha and Polymarker genes. Most important, a DNA profile was developed that could not have come from Greenwood.

The next question was whether that foreign DNA profile might belong to Frediani. There could be no innocent explanation for Frediani's DNA being on the body of Greenwood. The two had no contact whatsoever after the night of the original sexual assault by Frediani on Greenwood in 1984. Heilig contacted the California Department of Justice to see whether they had a known sample of Frediani's DNA. Even though he was convicted and sentenced to prison before DNA testing existed, California prison officials had begun collecting samples from defendants under laws that permitted the taking for ABO- and protein-testing databases. Frediani was one of those inmates whose sample had been taken by the Department of Corrections. The Department of Justice had a card of dried blood provided by Frediani sitting in one of their freezers.

A portion of Frediani's collected blood was sent to Cellmark in Maryland. Heilig decided to send Frediani's known sample to a different laboratory just to avoid any later argument that the sample might have been accidentally mixed or contaminated with the fingernails. Heilig got the word from Cellmark and could only marvel at the power of DNA testing. Frediani's DNA types matched those found on the fingernails at all six of the genetic markers tested by SERI.

She then asked SERI for additional testing. Heilig knew that STR DNA testing had provided a breakthrough in the ability to use PCR on small biological samples. Earlier that year a California appeals court had even specifically approved the use of STR testing. Cellmark had determined Frediani's own STR types at nine additional genes. Heilig asked SERI to go back to the DNA from the nails and test it at those added STR locations. On December 9, 1999, Gary Harmor of SERI telephoned Heilig. The additional testing of the nails led to the same conclusion: Frediani matched the profile found on Greenwood's fingernails. The chances that someone else had left that DNA: less than one in two quadrillion.

Four days later Frediani was charged with the murder of Greenwood, and a warrant was issued for his arrest. Within a week, Heilig arrested Frediani in the San Francisco Bay Area. He had been released from prison years earlier and had begun leading a normal life working for a communications company. When Heilig told Frediani that he was being arrested for the murder of Greenwood, he turned ashen. Frediani was brought to San Diego, was arraigned on the charges in the San Diego Superior Court, and pleaded not guilty. Two special circumstances were alleged that would make Frediani eligible to be sentenced to life in prison without the possibility of parole. The case was assigned to Valerie Summers. Because the murder had happened in the Del Mar area, the case was going to be tried in the Vista branch of the San Diego court. Summers was assigned to that office of the San Diego district attorney's office and was a natural choice.

She immersed herself in the case. She came to know the facts backward and forward. Equally important, she wanted additional testing done on the evidence. To make the right choices in testing, she consulted with Heilig and the Sheriff's Department crime laboratory. Summers also enlisted the help of Rod Englert, the bloodstain-pattern and crime-reconstruction expert from Portland who two years later would help recruit me for the Fox TV show on postconviction DNA testing (Chapter 14). Englert reviewed the photographs and physical evidence from the crime scene. His examination of the evidence led to additional DNA testing by SERI on DNA retrieved from Greenwood's pantyhose, her jacket, and some of her other fingernails. DNA from one of those nails provided results that were consistent with a mixture of the DNA of both Greenwood and Frediani. Duplicate DNA testing performed by Ed Blake of Forensic Science Associates confirmed the results obtained by SERI. Blake's testing revealed that other fingernails contained a mixture of DNA from both Greenwood and Frediani. Blake also determined that a stain on Greenwood's jacket proved to contain a mixture of both of their DNA.

The case made its way toward trial. Frediani was represented by attorney David Bartick. Summers and I began to talk regularly on the telephone. The case was assigned to Judge John Einhorn in the court's Vista branch. Because the new method for STR testing used in the case played such a critical role in the proof against Frediani, it was obvious to both of us that Einhorn would require a hearing on whether the evidence would be heard by the jury. Although the one court of appeal opinion would help, *People v. Allen* from northern California, it involved an earlier and different technique for testing STRs than the one that was used in the typing in the Greenwood case, and Summers wanted my help.

The first step was to decide what evidence would be the most effective in convincing Einhorn that the testing met the California standard of general acceptance in the scientific community. We had a couple of items in our favor. First, we were convinced the testing method was scientifically iron-clad. Second, Einhorn had already heard a similar case and allowed the evidence in. I convinced Summers that a transcript of the testimony of a pair of witnesses in that case, along with live testimony of one or two of the analysts who performed testing in the Frediani case, should be enough. She agreed. I was confident that Summers would grab the bull by the horns. She backed down from nothing.

We scheduled witnesses for the upcoming hearing, which was always no small feat. Robin Cotton from Cellmark was a natural. During the Simpson trial I always liked the fact that several in the media referred to her as "America's scientific sweetheart." Anyone who was described as Ginger Rogers was okay in my book. Summers knew who Cotton was and immediately agreed. The other witness would be SERI's Harmor, who had done most of the testing on the fingernails.

The hearing began in front of Judge Einhorn. Summers handled the questioning of both Cotton and Harmor. I sat next to her like a proud father. She didn't need my help and dove in and didn't look back. A few suggestions here and there, but Cotton and Harmor knew their stuff. Bartick called one witness, Marc Taylor. Taylor was a former serologist who, like many forensic analysts, had transitioned into DNA testing. But Taylor had reservations about the ability of STR testing to accurately separate mixtures of DNA samples. Also, Taylor didn't believe that the technique was generally accepted in the scientific community. For one thing, Taylor complained, the manufacturer of the most widely used kits was unwilling to reveal the exact contents of the chemicals used in its PCR copying process.

Einhorn heard the evidence and made up his mind. The DNA results would be heard by the jury. In his ruling Einhorn made it clear that the scientific community did accept STR testing using the method employed by both SERI and Cellmark. Any complaints about the ability of the technique to provide accurate results would be heard and decided by the jury that would ultimately determine Frediani's fate.

The jury was selected, and Summers began calling witnesses. The events leading to the discovery of Greenwood's body at the front gate to her home on August 22, 1985, were described. Detectives and other members of the San Diego Sheriff's Department testified about the investigation. The medical examiner explained the cause of death and his findings based on the autopsy he conducted on Greenwood's remains. And the jury heard the evidence of Frediani's attack on Greenwood in the San Francisco Bay Area in 1984. Her original testimony from the preliminary hearing in that case in 1985 was read to the San Diego jury. The San Diego jury was also told how Greenwood was unable to identify Frediani as her attacker at that hearing but could at least say that nothing about Frediani's appearance eliminated him as her assailant. Other witnesses called by Summers described the kitchen window as the point of entry and the match made between Frediani and the fingerprint found on the teapot that was next to that window. The jury heard how even after Frediani was arrested for the crimes against Greenwood, he had been released on bail and was free at the time of the killing in San Diego.

Additional testimony hurt Frediani's defense. An acquaintance of his testified that Frediani had spoken to him sometime after the preliminary hearing in the Bay Area and described to the friend that he was a suspect in a nearby break-in. Frediani told the acquaintance that he needed him to testify that the two of them had been looking at the Greenwood house, which had recently been listed for sale, and that Frediani had been peering in one of the windows. His friend told Frediani that he would think about helping him but later refused. Frediani tried to convince his friend to change his mind.

Summers pressed on. She was able to show the jury that only one week before the murder Frediani had been involved in a vehicle accident. The collision was in the Los Angeles area near the Magic Mountain amusement park. Police conducted an investigation of the incident and filed routine reports. Frediani later told a roommate that he had been in Los Angeles on a business matter. Frediani explained to another friend, the one who had previously refused to help with the requested false testimony, that he had been in the Lake Tahoe area, not Los Angeles. The jury was allowed to hear that Frediani had pleaded no contest to the charges involving the sexual attack on Greenwood in 1984. They were also informed that he had served six years in state prison for the assault and was then released before being formally charged with the killing of Helena Greenwood in San Diego.

Summers then turned to the forensic evidence. She had Englert describe his findings, including his opinion that Greenwood had used every means possible to fend off her attacker. Sheriff's Department evidence specialists and analysts testified to their roles in collecting evidence at the crime scene and its initial examination. Harmor and Blake described the DNA results. The jurors were obviously moved when they heard that the blood from underneath Greenwood's fingernails included a DNA profile that exactly matched Frediani. With scalpel-sharp skill Summers had the witnesses describe for the jury the chances that the blood from beneath the fingernails came from someone other than Frediani. The evidence seemed undeniable.

It was then Frediani's turn. Bartick called Taylor, who had testified in the earlier hearing on whether the STR DNA evidence should be admitted.

As at the hearing, Taylor was critical of the testing kits that were used by SERI, Cellmark, and Blake. Taylor specifically attacked the refusal of the manufacturer to provide its underlying research data to the scientific community to enable a complete review of the reliability of the technique. He conceded that the method was appropriate for samples from one donor but maintained that mixtures couldn't be reliably typed. Summers's cross-examination cut to the chase. She got Taylor to concede that a large majority of laboratories use the same technique and kits in actual cases. Taylor also admitted that he had purchased for his own lab, at a substantial cost, the STR typing machine whose use he had just criticized.

The hallmark of Frediani's defense, however, was his own testimony. During his direct examination by Bartick, Frediani completely denied having anything to do with either the 1984 sexual assault or the 1985 murder. He said that he had never been to the area of San Diego where Greenwood lived at the time of her slaying. Frediani testified that on August 22, 1985, the date of Greenwood's killing, he had been at his apartment in the Bay Area playing tennis. Frediani admitted that he had told his friend that he planned on going to Lake Tahoe, but that he had changed his mind and had driven to the Los Angeles area to vacation instead. Summers took over. She confronted Frediani with questions about the earlier sexual assault on Greenwood. They went back and forth, making little progress. Frediani would concede only that he had pleaded no contest to the charge. Finally, Frediani admitted that he had entered Greenwood's residence and had forced her to perform a sex act on him. Turning to the murder, Summers was unrelenting. She asked Frediani bluntly, "How did your DNA get on Helena Greenwood?" Frediani answered, "I have my own theories." He offered no other explanation.

The jury empanelled to determine Frediani's fate eventually decided that he had committed first-degree murder in the slaying of Greenwood. The jury agreed that the special circumstance had been proven that Frediani had committed the murder to prevent Greenwood from testifying in the earlier sexual-assault case and in retaliation for her testimony at the preliminary hearing in the Bay Area. Frediani was sentenced by Judge Einhorn to life imprisonment with no possibility of parole.

But the case didn't end with the jury's verdicts. When she originally arrested Frediani in 1999, Detective Heilig notified the father of Helena Greenwood of the arrest. A British citizen, Greenwood's father lived in London. He explained to Heilig that although he was ill and was not expected to live much longer, he wanted to see his daughter's killer brought to justice. Over a year later the jury returned its guilty verdict. Heilig telephoned

Greenwood's father in England to tell him. The information had to be relayed to him through a nurse. Within twenty-four hours of receiving the news of the conviction of his daughter's killer, Greenwood's father died. Heilig could only marvel at the power of the human spirit.

A murder committed fifteen years earlier had been solved by the remarkable development and progress of DNA testing. The fingernail clippings and other evidence collected by sheriff's detectives and laboratory personnel predated the discovery of DNA testing. But during the time that evidence sat on property-room shelves science moved forward to the point that it allowed Greenwood's killer to be identified from the smallest pieces of biological evidence—evidence left by a man identified by the very material Greenwood had devoted her life to researching: deoxyribonucleic acid.

GLOSSARY

ABO blood grouping   Blood typing system used to determine differences that exist among humans in blood and, in most persons, other body fluids. Most common types are A, B, AB, and O.

adenine (A)   One of the four nucleotides, or bases, that are the building blocks of DNA. Pairs with thymine (T) in DNA in its normal state.

allele   Form, or type, at a single location (locus) of DNA. One allele is inherited from each parent at a single DNA locus.

amplification   The process of copying portions, or segments, of DNA using the polymerase chain reaction.

autoradiograph   Most commonly, X-ray depiction of the relative positions of DNA segments following the use of the RFLP testing process.

base   A nucleotide that together with its complementary nucleotide forms a base pair, which is a basic building block of DNA.

biological evidence   Evidence consisting of body fluid, organ, or other tissue normally containing DNA.

ceiling principle   Mathematical formula suggested in 1992 National Research Council report, *DNA Technology in Forensic Science*. Promulgated to provide an alternative approach to the use of the unmodified product rule for statistical estimates of the rarity of matching DNA profiles.

cell	Smallest unit of an organism that can function on its own. Cells with a nucleus contain DNA that can be tested for DNA profiles.
chain of custody	The description and documentation of the collection, preservation, and movement of evidence.
chromosome	Structure by which DNA is transmitted to each succeeding generation. Contains a single DNA molecule. When all twenty-three chromosomes are present in pairs, they make up the entire human DNA complement.
CODIS	Also known as the Combined DNA Index System. The FBI computerized system software linking national, state, and local DNA database systems.
cold hit	A computer match of the DNA profile of evidence in an unsolved case and the DNA profile either of a convicted offender or of evidence in another case.
contamination	Normally, the inadvertent transfer of DNA to an evidence item or other sample in a case.
control	A sample used to help ensure the accuracy of DNA or serological profiles determined from evidentiary and known samples. Controls may be positive or negative. They help reveal any irregularities in DNA testing procedures.
cytoplasm	The area inside a cell but outside the nucleus. Contains the mitochondria that can be tested for mitochondrial DNA.
cytosine (C)	One of the four nucleotides, or bases, that are the building blocks of DNA. Pairs with guanine (G) in DNA in its normal state.
degradation	The process during which DNA breaks up; it ultimately prevents the determination of DNA profiles.
DNA	Deoxyribonucleic acid. The molecule containing genetic information, which is transmitted through reproduction. Determines the structure and regulates the functioning of humans, animals, and other living organisms.
DQ-Alpha	First genetic marker, or locus, tested following polymerase-chain-reaction amplification of samples to

	detect differences among people and to compare evidence samples in criminal cases.
electrophoresis	Physical process that permits the separation for typing of segments of DNA, as well as of serological proteins and enzymes.
enzyme	A protein that causes biological functions, such as human digestion, to take place. Certain enzymes can be tested using serological techniques to determine differences among people.
epithelial cells	Cells that provide a surface coating on body structures. Commonly found in saliva, vaginal secretions, and other mucous-membrane fluids.
exclusion	The determination by DNA or serological typing that a specific person could not be the donor of a sample of biological evidence.
forensic hit	A computer match of the DNA profile of evidence in an unsolved case and the DNA profile of evidence in another case.
forensic science	The application of science to the legal system.
gene	The basic unit of heredity. A portion of a DNA chromosome that governs a specific function of the body or provides a product for its use. In serological or DNA testing, a location where DNA differences among humans has been determined.
genetic marker	A gene or location (locus) where DNA or serological types can be determined.
genotype	The types (alleles) inherited from a person's mother and father at a specific location or genetic marker.
guanine (G)	One of the four nucleotides, or bases, that are the building blocks of DNA. Pairs with cytosine (C) in DNA in its normal state.
heteroplasmy	A phenomenon in which the mitochondrial DNA sequence for samples from the same person may differ at a specific site.
heterozygote	A person who inherits a different type (allele) from each parent at a specific gene or locus.
homozygote	A person who inherits the same type (allele) from each parent at a specific gene or locus.

inclusion	The determination by DNA or serological typing that a specific person could be the donor of a sample of biological evidence.
inconclusive	A result that does not permit the determination of the serological or DNA profile of a tested sample or a result that does not permit the determination whether a specific person could or could not be the donor of a specific sample.
likelihood ratio	A statistical method for comparing the likelihood of two or more different events. Sometimes used in the interpretation of mixtures of DNA evidence and with other results.
locus	A specific gene (genetic-marker) location where DNA can be typed.
match	The determination that genetic-marker types from an evidence item and a specific person are indistinguishable. Also applies when types from multiple evidence items cannot be differentiated.
mitochondrial DNA	DNA from the mitochondria within cells. Inherited maternally only. Siblings and relatives who share the same maternal lineage have the identical mitochondrial DNA sequence in the absence of any mutation.
negative control	A control used in testing that contains no DNA or serological types. Normally manipulated in the same manner as samples with actual DNA and positive controls. Positive results obtained from negative controls usually indicate a problem in the testing process or with the control.
nuclear DNA	DNA from the nucleus of a cell. Used in RFLP, DQ-Alpha, Polymarker, and STR testing.
nucleotide	A base that together with its complementary nucleotide forms a base pair, which is a basic building block of DNA.
nucleus	Portion of the cell that contains nuclear DNA.
phenotype	The actual appearance or characteristics of an individual as a result of the types (alleles) inherited from the individual's mother and father at a specific location or genetic marker.

Polymarker	A set of five genetic markers (loci) typed simultaneously using a kit following use of the polymerase chain reaction.
polymerase chain reaction (PCR)	Process by which small portions of DNA can be genetically copied and greater amounts obtained for typing. Relies on the use of chemical and other agents, the enzyme *Thermus aquaticus* (Taq), and a thermal cycler instrument to complete the process.
polymorphism	The existence of multiple types (alleles) at a specific genetic marker (locus).
positive control	A control used in testing that contains known DNA or serological types. Normally manipulated in the same manner as samples with actual DNA and negative controls. Negative results obtained from positive controls usually indicate a problem in the testing process or with the control.
probe	A portion of DNA used to detect types by finding its complementary sequence of base pairs.
product rule	A mathematical principle used to estimate the rarity of a DNA profile. Relies on multiplication of statistical estimates at each genetic marker (locus) for a final match probability.
profile	The entire set of results from testing of a particular sample.
protein	Fundamental components of cells that govern the functioning of organisms. Certain proteins can be tested using serological techniques to determine differences among people.
quality assurance	The overall program employed by a laboratory to ensure that valid and reliable results are obtained in its testing.
quality control	The steps taken in a laboratory to ensure that equipment, chemicals, and other necessities for testing and analysis are appropriate.
random match probability	The probability calculated for a DNA profile that another person, selected at random from a given population, would have the same exact types.

restriction fragment length polymorphism (RFLP)	The technique of testing DNA for length differences at specific genetic markers (loci). Also known as variable-number-of-tandem-repeat testing. Forensic DNA method of choice from 1986 to the mid-1990s.
serology	The field of ABO, protein, and enzyme testing employed from the 1970s until the introduction of DNA typing in 1986.
short tandem repeat (STR)	Polymerase chain reaction–based method that types genetic markers that are similar to RFLP loci. Thirteen STR loci are commonly typed in criminal cases and for DNA databases.
substrate control	Also known as an unstained control. A piece of evidence collected from an area immediately adjacent to biological material that was also seized. Used to help determine whether DNA or serological types are present on the material itself in addition to a bloodstain or other tissue found on that material.
thermal cycler	Scientific instrument that facilitates, through timed heating and cooling cycles, genetic amplification of samples by use of the polymerase chain reaction.
Thermus aquaticus (Taq)	Enzyme used in the polymerase-chain-reaction process to catalyze the formation of identical DNA segments.
thymine (T)	One of the four nucleotides, or bases, that are the building blocks of DNA. Pairs with adenine (A) in DNA in its normal state.
unstained control	See "substrate control."

INDEX

About the Author

George "Woody" Clarke is a judge of the San Diego Superior Court, appointed in 2003. Prior to obtaining that position, Clarke had been a deputy district attorney for the County of San Diego for twenty years. During that time he tried numerous felony offenses, including capital crimes. After 1988, he specialized in the introduction and use in court of scientific evidence, particularly forensic DNA testing results. He has published and lectured internationally on forensic DNA evidence.